Janine Leschke

Unemployment Insurance and Non-Standard Employment

Four European Countries in Comparison

VS RESEARCH

Bibliographic information published by the Deutsche Nationalbibliothek
The Deutsche Nationalbibliothek lists this publication in the Deutsche Nationalbibliografie; detailed bibliographic data are available in the Internet at http://dnb.d-nb.de.

Dissertation FU Berlin, 2006

This publication is financially supported by the European Trade Union Institute (ETUI-REHS)

1st Edition 2008

Editorial Office: Christina M. Brian / Anita Wilke

VS Verlag für Sozialwissenschaften is part of the specialist publishing group Springer Science+Business Media.
www.vs-verlag.de

Cover design: KünkelLopka Medienentwicklung, Heidelberg
Printed on acid-free paper
Printed in Germany

ISBN 978-3-531-15992-8

Janine Leschke

Unemployment Insurance and Non-Standard Employment

VS RESEARCH

Table of Contents

Table of Contents **5**

List of Tables and Figures **9**

Acknowledgement **13**

1 Introduction **15**
1.1 Flexibility and security in the public discourse 22
1.2 Literature overview 24

2 Theoretical background **31**
2.1 Risk and uncertainty 31
2.2 Segmented labour markets 35
2.3 Insurance 38
2.3.1 Advantages of institutionalised unemployment insurance 39
2.3.1.1 Public vs. private insurance 40
2.3.1.2 Voluntary vs compulsory insurance 44
2.3.1.3 Insurance vs welfare principle 46
2.3.1.4 Redistribution in unemployment insurance schemes... 48
2.4 Welfare state theory 51
2.4.1 Worlds of welfare capitalism 52
2.4.2 Critical assessment 55
2.5 Assumptions from theory 57

3 Labour market indicators and the occurrence of non-standard employment **63**
3.1 Labour market developments 64
3.2 Part-time employment 71
3.3 Temporary employment 75
3.4 Extent of non-standard employment and implications for empirical analysis 80

4 Regulation of temporary and part-time employment 83
4.1 Framework agreements and directives on non-standard employment... 84
4.2 Part-time employment... 86
4.2.1 Equal treatment clauses... 86
4.2.2 Care obligations as reason for part-time work 89
4.3 Temporary employment.. 93
4.3.1 Employment protection legislation and the extent of temporary employment 94
4.3.2 Specific regulation of temporary contracts in the four countries 98
4.4 Implications for the empirical analysis 101

5 Are unemployment insurance systems adapting to non-standard employment?.. 103
5.1 The male breadwinner model and standard employment.................. 104
5.2 Unemployment insurance.. 108
5.2.1 Active line reforms in Denmark.. 108
5.2.2 From unemployment assistance to basic allowance in Germany 110
5.2.3 Trade unions challenge reforms in Spain............................... 111
5.2.4 Jobseeker's Allowance and the New Deal in the United Kingdom 113
5.3 Unemployment benefits and non-standard employment................... 114
5.3.1 Part-time employment and unemployment insurance 116
5.3.1.1 Hours and earnings thresholds limiting access to benefits 116
5.3.1.2 Minimum contribution period as access barrier 119
5.3.1.3 Are net replacement rates beneficial to former part-time workers?.. 121
5.3.1.4 Specific legislation benefiting former part-time workers 125
5.3.2 Temporary employment and unemployment insurance 127
5.3.2.1 Minimum contribution period as an obstacle to entitlement.. 127
5.3.2.2 Duration of unemployment benefits 129
5.4 Summary and outlook 131

6 Risk of job loss and the insurance situation of non-standard workers ... 137
6.1 The European Community Household Panel ... 138
6.2 Mobility patterns of non-standard workers ... 140
6.2.1 Year-to-year transitions ... 142
6.2.2 Exits from employment ... 146
6.2.2.1 Comparative exit patterns ... 149
6.2.2.2 Multivariate models of transitions from employment ... 154
6.2.3 Summary ... 159
6.3 The insurance situation of non-standard workers ... 161
6.3.1 Entitlement to unemployment benefits ... 164
6.3.1.1 Descriptive results ... 166
6.3.1.2 Multivariate analysis ... 171
6.3.2 Benefit levels and composition of benefits ... 181
6.3.2.1 Descriptive analysis ... 182
6.3.2.2 Multivariate analysis ... 190
6.3.3 Summary ... 194
6.4 Influence of institutions on benefit coverage ... 196
6.4.1 Using institutional information to cluster countries – a literature review ... 196
6.4.1.1 Choice of variables ... 198
6.4.1.2 Cluster analysis ... 202
6.4.1.3 Characteristics of the resulting cluster groups ... 204
6.4.1.4 Empirical validation of cluster results ... 209
6.4.1.5 Limitations and possible solutions ... 211
6.4.2 Multilevel analysis as a solution? ... 212
6.4.3 Restrictions and data problems ... 215

7 Conclusion ... 219

References ... 229
Legislation ... 246

Annex ... 247
Annex 1: Construction of ECHP variables and descriptive statistics ... 247
Annex 2 ... 257

List of Tables and Figures

Table 1:	Forms of flexibility	16
Table 2:	Flexibility and security: trade-offs and complementary situations	21
Table 3:	Unemployment insurance principles	60
Table 4:	Non-standard employment among women in 2007	81
Table 5:	Birth rates and female employment by age of children, 2005*	90
Table 6:	Summary indicators of the strictness of employment protection legislation	96
Table 7:	Development of employment protection legislation*	97
Table 8:	131	
Table 9:	Upward, downward and sideward transitions from and to full-time and part-time employment	144
Table 10:	Upward, downward and sideward transitions from and to permanent and temporary employment	145
Table 11:	Odds of different exit types compared between countries: reference Germany	156
Table 12:	Odds of different exit patterns for part-time workers as compared to full-time workers (reference)	157
Table 13:	Odds of different exits for fixed-term/short-term (casual) workers compared to workers with permanent contracts (reference)	159
Table 14:	Registration at the employment office by former working hours*	165
Table 15:	Registration at employment office by reason for leaving last job	166
Table 16:	Unemployment benefit receipt for low- and high-hours part-time workers: comparison of registered unemployed and all unemployed jobseekers	168
Table 17:	Duration of fixed-term contracts	169
Table 18:	Random effects logistic regression on unemployment benefit receipt	173
Table 19:	Individual predicted probabilities of benefit receipt for ideal types (based on regression results in Table 18)	175
Table 20:	Random effects logit model – access of non-standard workers to unemployment benefits	179

Table 21: Individual predicted probabilities of benefit receipt for typical non-standard and standard workers ... 180
Table 22: Interaction between working part-time and having a temporary job ... 180
Table 23: Random effects linear model on unemployment benefit level for unemployed benefit recipients ... 193
Table 24: Cluster analysis variables as basic statistics ... 201
Table 25: How do the country cluster groups score on the different indicators? ... 208
Table 26: Multilevel analysis with individual-level and country-level variables, 3-level model ... 214
Table 27: Flexibility and security: trade-offs and complementary situations . 224
Table 28: Part-time employment by year and country as share of working population in dependent employment ... 248
Table 29: Employment contract by type in 1995 and 2001 as share of working population in dependent employment ... 249
Table 30: Share of persons that simultaneously work part-time and on a temporary contract ... 250
Table 31: Comparison of retrospective and lagged information, wave 8 ... 252
Table 32: Individual characteristics of part-time and temporary workers ... 253
Table 33: Employment characteristics of part-time workers ... 255
Table 34: Employment characteristics of temporary workers ... 256
Table 35: Individual characteristics of the total sample ... 257
Table 36: Employment characteristics of the total sample ... 257
Table 37: Multinomial logit models for single countries (reference category: remaining in employment) ... 258
Table 38: Cluster Analysis: summary statistics for cluster 1 ... 260
Table 39: Cluster Analysis: summary statistics for cluster 2 ... 260
Table 40: Cluster Analysis: summary statistics for cluster 3 ... 261
Table 41: Cluster Analysis: summary statistics for cluster 4 ... 261

Figure 1: Development of unemployment ... 65
Figure 2: Unemployment rates by qualification level in 2007. ... 66
Figure 3: Duration of unemployment in 2007. ... 67
Figure 4: Development of employment rates. ... 68
Figure 5: Development of employment rates by gender: 1998, 2003 and 2007. ... 69
Figure 6: Development of inactive population by gender: 1998, 2003 and 2007. ... 70
Figure 7: Development of part-time employment ... 72
Figure 8: Share of women's part-time employment by level of education in 2007 ... 73
Figure 9: Part-time employment by gender and age-group in 2007 ... 74
Figure 10: Reasons for women to work part-time in 2004 (25–49 years) ... 75
Figure 11: Development of temporary employment ... 76
Figure 12: Development of temporary employment (absolute numbers in 1000) ... 77
Figure 13: Share of temporary employment by level of education in 2007 ... 78
Figure 14: Reasons for temporary employment in 2006 (25–64 years) ... 79
Figure 15: Duration of the temporary contract, 2007. ... 80
Figure 16: Part-time work among prime-age women (25–54) by presence of children (under 15 years) in 2000 ... 91
Figure 17: Enrolment rates of children in childcare and early education services, 2003/2004 ... 92
Figure 18: Comparison of importance of exit types by country (cumulated failure) ... 150
Figure 19: Exits from employment for full-time and part-time workers ... 151
Figure 20: Exits from employment for workers with permanent and with temporary contracts ... 153
Figure 21: Unemployment benefit receipt of former full-time and part-time workers: comparison of registered unemployed and all unemployed jobseekers ... 167
Figure 22: Unemployment benefit receipt for former permanent and temporary workers: comparison of registered unemployed and all unemployed jobseekers ... 168
Figure 23: Any social benefit receipt at unemployment ... 170
Figure 24: Conditional effect plot on the probability of receiving unemployment benefit conditional on the current household income among the long-term unemployed ... 176
Figure 25: Conditional effects plot on the probability of receiving unemployment benefits conditional on the former wage ... 178

Figure 26: Social benefit receipt as main individual source of income at unemployment in per cent ... 182
Figure 27: Average annual social benefit receipt and composition of benefit receipt ... 184
Figure 28: Comparison of distribution of monthly benefit levels ... 185
Figure 29: Average monthly unemployment benefit level by working time .. 187
Figure 30: Distribution of monthly benefit levels for former full-time and part-time workers ... 188
Figure 31: Average unemployment benefit level by former contract type ... 189
Figure 32: Distribution of monthly benefit levels for former permanent and temporary workers ... 190
Figure 33: Ward cluster analysis of indicators on unemployment insurance systems ... 203
Figure 34: Access to unemployment benefits for non-standard workers ... 204
Figure 35: Net replacement rates at unemployment for couples with 2 children and low earnings (66.7 APW) in 1999 ... 205
Figure 36: Social protection receipt: tax vs contribution financing, 2001 ... 207
Figure 37: Expenditure on passive and active labour market policies, controlled for the unemployment rate, 2001 ... 207
Figure 38: Share of former part-time workers receiving unemployment benefits ... 209
Figure 39: Share of former temporary workers receiving unemployment benefits ... 210
Figure 40: Share of unemployed (registered and all unemployed jobseekers) receiving unemployment benefits ... 262

Acknowledgement

I would like to thank my supervisor Prof. Dr. Günther Schmid for his strong interest in the subject of my dissertation. He provided me with very helpful suggestions on the set-up and conduct of my research and over the years gave many valuable comments on the different chapters of this book. I also want to thank Dr. Miriam Hartlapp, who commented on the chapters that deal with the institutional configurations, and Prof. Dr. Jaap de Koning, who provided good ideas for the empirical analysis. I am grateful also to my current employer, the European Trade Union Institute (ETUI-REHS)*, which supported this publication financially. Last but not least, I owe thanks to my former colleagues in the Labour Market Policy and Employment unit of the Social Science Research Center Berlin (WZB), who over the years provided important ideas and support.

Janine Leschke

* The ETUI-REHS is financially supported by the European Community. The European Community is not responsible for any use made of the information contained in this publication.

1 Introduction

Non-standard employment forms have been gaining in importance in western European countries since the 1980s, with the growing labour market participation of women and continuing mass unemployment. The promotion of more flexible employment in the form of part-time employment, temporary employment and self-employment is seen as a possible solution to persistent unemployment, underemployment and also to the need to better reconcile work and family life.

Flexible employment forms as a remedy for unemployment have in fact been actively promoted through labour market policies. Social insurance systems thus, by installing and preferring certain measures, contribute to the diffusion of insecure employment. In the context of the German Hartz reforms policy instruments that encourage self-employment (Ich-AG), marginal employment (Mini- and Midi-jobs) and temporary work agency employment (PSA), for example, have been introduced or broadened. Flexible employment forms are in many countries also promoted through incentives and subsidies or indirectly through changing the law in relation to employment rights (for country-specific examples see Rubery et al. 1998a: 188 et seqq.).

The increasing importance of non-standard employment forms has brought up the question of the extent to which those affected have access to social security benefits, because benefits are often connected with standard, full-time continuing employment careers (compare, for example, Rubery et al. 1998a). The European Foundation (2003: 2) phrases this dilemma in the following way:

> "For the workers affected by these flexible forms of employment – which themselves are in many cases synonymous with a form of insecurity – this situation is made worse by the inappropriateness of some social protection schemes to their personal situations. Insofar as these schemes assume the existence of 'typical' employment, and make some of their benefits conditional upon it, they do not necessarily offer a sufficient guarantee of security (in terms of replacement income) when social contingencies arise."

If standard employment is defined as full-time, indefinite, dependent employment that is equally spread over the work week and takes place at a single employer, non-standard employment forms encompass part-time work, fixed-term contracts, casual work, temporary work agency employment and selfemployment, as well as shift work, night work and week-end work. The latter three work forms will not be treated here because they usually do not raise social protection problems. Self-employed workers are in most countries excluded from a range of social protection schemes. Due to relatively clear regulations concerning access to unemployment benefits (in most countries self-employed workers are excluded from unemployment insurance systems) and due to the scope of this study self-employment will not be treated here.[2] Hence, this study will concentrate on part-time employment and temporary employment (fixed-term employment, casual employment and temporary agency work[3]). Shares of part-time and temporary employment have increased in many countries during the two preceding decades (Eurostat 2006). Part-time employment has been growing extensively with women's increasing participation in the labour market. Temporary agency work has been significantly deregulated during recent years and has been growing rapidly since the 1990s (Storrie 2002; Michon 1999). Restrictions on the use of fixed-term contracts have in many European Union countries been relaxed, from the early 1980s on (K. Schömann et al. 1998). Table 1 shows the different types of flexibility and their interrelations.

Table 1: Forms of flexibility[4]

	numerical flexibility	**functional flexibility**
internal flexibility	adaptation of working hours: **part-time**, overtime, working time accounts, employment-securing reduction of working hours, week-end working	adaptation of work organisation to new needs: continuing education, on-the-job training, life-long learning, job rotation
external flexibility	hire and fire: **temporary employment**, work on call, **marginal employment**	adaptation of unemployed (preventing mismatch) and productive flexibility: active labour market policies, subcontracting, use of freelance labour

Source: adapted from European Foundation (2003) and Keller et al. (2002).

2 For information on social insurance coverage of solo self-employed workers (non-agricultural employment with no or few employees) see Schulze Buschoff (2006; 2004).

3 Temporary agency employment will be discussed in the institutional part but will not be treated separately in the empirical analysis due to a lack of information in the ECHP data.

4 The different categories are not exclusive; there is often overlapping. Part-time workers may, for example, engage in measures that contribute to the firm's adaptation to new needs (functional flexibility).

Part-time employment can be termed internal-numerical flexibility. On the demand side it is, for example, used due to organisational or economic needs (to meet peaks in service requirements or regular variations of workload). It is especially attractive to employers if it is exempted from contributions (marginal employment) (Smith et al. 2000: 179 et seq.). On the other hand, it often also caters to employees' needs if they want to or have to combine wage employment with other activities, such as child or elderly care.

Temporary employment creates external-numerical flexibility by making it possible to adjust the number of workers according to requirements. It mainly meets the employers' demands for a more flexible workforce that can be hired and fired according to need and at low cost (the legislation concerning regular dismissals usually does not apply).[5] Temporary employment contracts are typically used for specific activities of limited duration and in order to replace workers who are temporarily absent due to maternity leave, education and the like. In a number of countries temporary employment contracts are also used in order to screen workers for their occupational qualifications, abilities and social competences before they are 'permanently' recruited. In countries such as Germany, Denmark and Austria temporary contracts with a probationary function are to a certain degree compensated by the 'dual system' of vocational education and training that already provides the employers with important information about the qualifications of the newly employed.

The above forms of flexibility that relate to the characteristics of the employment relationship (working hours, contract duration or pay) may have important implications for entitlement to social security benefits (Grimshaw et al. 1998, 1997; Eurofound 2003). This assumption is tested here in a comparative way: Denmark, Germany, Spain and the United Kingdom are taken into account. The analysis will be restricted to unemployment benefit systems and will not take into account other social protection schemes, such as pensions or health care, although it can be assumed that people who have problems accessing unemployment benefits will also face problems in other social security branches.[6]

Entitlement to unemployment compensation depends on specific qualifying conditions, namely hours or earnings thresholds and contribution requirements.

---

5 Bielenski et al. (1994: 173–257) support this. Their firm survey covering eight countries shows that in an overwhelming majority of the cases fixed-term contracts were accepted by employees only because they did not have another option.

6 Ginn et al. (1998) looked at the regulations of pension schemes that concern part-time workers in Denmark, Germany and the United Kingdom. They came to the conclusion that flexibility is promoted at a time when pension policies are magnifying the penalties of part-time work. Concerning occupational pensions, O'Connell et al. (2003) show on Irish data that part-time workers are much less likely than full-time workers to have occupation pension entitlements when other relevant variables are controlled for.

Qualifying conditions vary between countries and – as will be shown – are also frequently modified within countries. Hours and earnings thresholds as prerequisites for entitlement to unemployment benefits are problematic for some groups of part-time workers. Minimum contribution requirements can be problematic for temporary workers who frequently switch between jobs of short duration and unemployment; problems for part-time workers arise only if entitlement conditions are not specified in weeks or months but in hours. In some countries, such as Germany and Spain, the duration of benefit payments is scaled according to the former employment period, which can lead to shorter maximum benefit periods among temporary workers with short contract duration.

Another question, predominantly concerning part-time workers, is whether – in case of entitlement to benefits – benefit levels are sufficiently high to make ends meet. Here, differences between countries should also be evident depending on whether the systems are based on insurance principles and calculate benefits subject to former earnings or more strongly based on welfare principles and rather grant needs-based (flat-rate) benefits.

Although, at first sight, part-time work and temporary employment seem to differ substantially, in the context of unemployment insurance coverage simultaneous treatment might prove to be useful. This allows us to assess the influence of eligibility criteria and other design features on benefit coverage and benefit distribution more comprehensively. The combined treatment of both flexible employment forms should thus help us to be more precise about the inclusiveness of different countries' unemployment insurance schemes.

What are the advantages of granting non-standard workers broad access to unemployment benefit systems?

Unemployment benefits fulfil a range of important functions: besides guaranteeing the maintenance of the achieved living standard for a provisional period, they make effective job search possible and prevent transitions to inactivity. Social assistance payments as benefits of last resort, besides their stigmatising image and their heavy reliance on means-testing, are usually much less aimed at labour market re-entry. Inadequate protection in the event of job loss – even more problematic in the case of pensions – hampers employees' incentives to risk taking and further discriminates against those who do not have any choice but to accept sub-standard employment. If broad social protection is granted workers might be more inclined to take up risky or substandard employment (incentive function). This would not only contribute to raising employment levels – as stipulated by the European Employment Strategy – but by supporting active participation among the (long-term) unemployed and the inactive population through non-standard employment liable to social security it could in the long run also add to the viability and sustainability of welfare state financing.

Workers who are ineligible for unemployment benefits or pensions have to be supported in other, often more costly ways (Maier 1992). Furthermore, secure non-standard employment can take on a stepping-stone function into regular employment, for example by granting unemployment benefits as a search subsidy which would make it possible to look for more adequate employment (compare, for example, Booth et al. 2002b). It will be of special interest to explore whether some certain countries' unemployment insurance regulations are potentially more favourable towards non-standard employment situations than others'.

The countries chosen for analysis each correspond to one of the welfare regimes postulated in Esping-Andersen (1990; 1999). Denmark is usually identified as a social democratic welfare regime; the combination of weak employment protection legislation and comprehensive protection in the case of unemployment, coupled with activation measures, makes it an appealing choice for research on non-standard employment forms and benefit coverage. Additionally, there have been comprehensive reforms of the unemployment insurance system over the 1990s. Germany represents the prototype of the corporatist welfare regime. Institutions are family-centred; the unemployment system is less individualised than in Denmark and the insurance principle prevails. Non-standard employment forms – especially part-time employment – were promoted during the 1990s; the recent wide-ranging labour market reforms have in some ways redefined the relationship between flexibility and security. In the EU context the United Kingdom comes closest to representing the liberal welfare regime. Employment protection regulation is weak, part-time employment rates are very high and the unemployment benefit system strongly relies on the welfare principle. Furthermore, wide-ranging unemployment insurance reforms that strengthened activation elements took place during the 1990s. According to modified versions of the welfare regime typology Spain represents the 'Mediterranean' regime (compare, for example, Muffels et al. 2002; Arts et al. 2002; Schulte 1998; Ferrera 1996). A closer look at this country is not only appealing in view of its very strong familialistic tradition, but especially because strict employment protection legislation for permanent jobs has led to enormous increases in the share of temporary employment forms since the mid 1980s. The design of the unemployment benefit system is similar to the German one; there is a strong emphasis on insurance principles.

An in-depth analysis and comparison of social protection regulations pertaining to non-standard workers in four countries should allow us to answer the central question: *'Are unemployment insurance systems in Europe capable of covering the special risks that persons with non-standard employment contracts are facing?'* The following hypotheses, illustrated below and further specified in the theoretical chapter, will be tested in order to answer the above question:

1. Persons with non-standard employment contracts face greater risks in making transitions to unemployment or inactivity than persons with regular contracts.
2. Unemployment insurance systems that strongly incorporate welfare principles instead of insurance principles grant better coverage of non-standard workers.

The first hypothesis seeks to clarify whether non-standard workers are more often faced with downward transitions than standard workers. Especially among temporary workers as compared to permanent workers, due to the short-term nature of contracts, more changes between employment and unemployment are expected. The situation is less clear for part-time workers. The second hypothesis implies that the unemployment protection systems of some countries are modelled less strongly on standard employment and are therefore better suited to cater to the needs of non-standard workers. It is expected that unemployment systems that incorporate welfare principles rather than insurance principles, that are tax-financed rather than contribution-financed and that grant individualised instead of means-tested benefits are comparatively more advantageous to non-standard workers.

The following matrix adapted from Wilthagen et al. (2004) complements the flexibility matrix by adding security components. Security can take on different forms: job security (remaining in a specific employment situation), employment security (employability), income security (income protection) and combination security (combination of work and private responsibilities) (Wilthagen et al. 2003: 4). Table 2 illustrates the different possibilities for combining flexibility and security that can act either as trade-offs or as complementary strategies. External-numerical flexibility – in our case temporary employment – is surely associated with less job security (trade-off). As to combination security, in some instances temporary employment can strengthen it but there will be many situations in which temporary employment is unstable and irregular work forms will run counter to combination security. In order to make external-numerical flexibility more secure employability can be strengthened through training measures, in times of non-employment, for example. Part-time employment as internal-numerical flexibility or in the case of marginal employment as external-numerical flexibility grants combination security by making it possible to combine work with other activities. Job security should usually not be affected by the part-time situation. As concerns employability security, part-time employment can in some instances directly serve to combine work with education or training.

Table 2: Flexibility and security: trade-offs and complementary situations

flexibility/security	job security	employment/ employability security	income security (social security)	combination/ option security
external-numerical				
Internal-numerical				
internal functional				
external functional				

Source: Wilthagen et al. (2004).

The question that will stand at the centre of the analysis concerns how far temporary workers and part-time workers are granted social security at unemployment. The other types of security will also be discussed but the data put clear limits on the possibility of assessing employability security, for example. It should be kept in mind that access to unemployment benefits is in many countries still a prerequisite for access to the whole range of active labour market policies that can contribute to employability in times of non-employment.[7]

This book is organised as follows. The remainder of Chapter 1 discusses the role of flexibility and security in the public discourse and gives an overview of the relevant literature. Chapter 2 frames the institutional and empirical analysis by giving theoretical insight into risk management, labour market segmentation, insurance theory and welfare regime theory. The largest part of this chapter is devoted to insurance theory with a focus on modes of financing and principles of redistribution. Close inspection of theories relating to insurance and welfare principles should allow us to assess the second hypothesis on a theoretical level. Chapter 3 gives some insight into the labour market situation in Denmark, Germany, Spain and the United Kingdom, and focuses especially on the development of part-time and temporary employment. Chapters 4 and 5 are devoted to regulations concerning non-standard employment and unemployment insurance. EU-level regulations, but especially country-level regulations, are reviewed in order to get a better understanding of the general conditions determining the development of non-standard employment in the four countries. The countries' unemployment insurance systems are then examined in detail with a focus on regulations that are discriminatory against or in favour of non-standard workers.

Chapter 6 makes use of the European Community Household Panel (ECHP) data in order to test the hypotheses. Transition patterns, entitlement to unemployment benefits and benefit levels are compared between standard and non-

7 On this issue compare, for example, Rubery et al. (1998a: 183–188) who discuss unemployment benefits as a prerequisite for access to active labour market policies, with a focus on women.

standard workers. In a last step, the influence of institutional features of benefit systems (design, financing) on entitlement is tested on a larger number of countries by means of cluster analysis and multilevel analysis techniques. The concluding Chapter 7 discusses the most important results with a special focus on the recent Hartz reforms in Germany. Some ideas are also put forward concerning how more inclusive benefits for non-standard workers can be financed.

1.1 Flexibility and security in the public discourse

In view of the growing importance of non-standard employment the inadequate social security situation of such employment forms was brought up in the public discourse as early as the mid-1990s. The Dublin European Council (1996) not only stressed that social protection systems should actively encourage preparation for and participation in work but also emphasised that they should be developed in such a way that they are capable of adapting to new work patterns and of providing appropriate social protection to people engaged in such work.

Similarly, the Social Protection Committee (June 2003: 9, 10) emphasised that non-standard employment, besides providing opportunities for new entrants, challenges social security systems and potentially increases the precariousness of jobs. According to the Social Protection Committee, under the current rules social protection systems are ill-prepared to provide non-standard workers with entitlements that are equivalent to those of full-time and permanent workers. It calls for a balance between flexibility features and security rights – among other things – in order to counter the problem that a lack of social protection coverage severely lowers the attractiveness of and therefore the potential labour supply for more flexible jobs.

The Employment Taskforce (2003) that was set up to help identify reform measures that could guide the implementation of the revised European Employment Strategy took up the issue of reconciling flexibility and security. Their report calls for promoting flexibility in its various forms (temporary work agencies are especially stressed) and for fostering new forms of security. It points out the importance of supporting labour market mobility and facilitating transitions through security. The notion of job security is replaced by employability security. Denmark and the Netherlands are put forward as positive examples in this regard. The Danish combination of low employment protection, good access to unemployment benefits and strong emphasis on activation is praised as a suitable mix for reconciling flexibility and security in an adequate way.

The European Employment Strategy (Council of the European Union 6.8.2005) explicitly calls for promoting flexibility (modern forms of work organisation, employment-friendly labour costs) combined with employment security and reduced labour market segmentation. It is stressed that frequent transitions brought about by more diverse and irregular working patterns need to be cushioned. How do the four countries under analysis react to this guideline in their National Reform Programmes? The Danish policy strategy is directly identified with the keyword 'flexicurity': low structural unemployment is accounted for by the flexible rules on hiring and firing, well-developed unemployment benefit systems with strict availability rules and active labour market policies (Danish Government 2005: 35, 48). The German National Reform Programme (Bundesregierung 2005: 47, 48) points out that, in view of increasing labour market flexibility, employees' interests in security are justified and have to be supported. The notion of security remains vague, however: reliable employment rights and co-determination are stressed in this regard but not further specified. Spain's National Reform programme states that a gradual movement to more ample employment stability is necessary that does not run counter to employment creation. In this regard revision of the regulations governing temporary work agencies has, for example, been put forward (Ministerio de la Presidencia. Secretaría General Técnica 2005: 130, 131). The United Kingdom also takes up the flexicurity guideline in their National Reform Programme (UK Government 2005: 1, 29, 39). Security is to be provided for people in need but it is to be coupled with strong incentives to work. Flexibility here is not merely discussed in relation to employers; instead, providing flexibility and choice in balancing work and family commitments in order to enable women to participate fully and equally in the labour market is explicitly stressed. According to the British National Reform Programme, a range of policy measures are being developed to address the various obstacles people face throughout the life-cycle. Skills investment is put forward as a key strategy to increase the flexibility and adaptability of the labour market.

With its reassessment of the Jobs Strategy the OECD has taken stronger account of the potential downfalls of strengthening work incentives through cutting back welfare benefits which has in the past been promoted by their Jobs Strategy. More and better jobs, adequate social protection and the reconciliation of work and family life are stressed in the reassessment. A mutual obligation approach with improvement of employability as counterpart to continued benefit support is favoured.

The trade union perspective on non-standard employment and social security is reflected in Hutsebaut (2002). Current developments in this field and recent achievements in making non-standard employment more equivalent to standard employment are discussed. From the trade unions' position as concerns social protection non-standard workers must have equal rights, at least proportionally to the number of hours worked or to earnings received, and share equal contribution responsibilities. A diversification of the sources of social-protection financing, especially a broadening of tax financing, as well as solidarity measures in favour of atypical workers are asked for. Social protection systems are to react in a more flexible way to non-standard workers. Suggestions include abolishing or significantly reducing hours and earnings thresholds concerning contribution requirements and benefit eligibility, and relaxing reference periods preceding entitlements to social benefits.

1.2 Literature overview

Research results on this topic are relatively sparse; most of the existing studies are descriptive at most. The following studies address the issue of a lack of social insurance coverage among non-standard workers within a broader context, either theoretically (Atkinson et al. 1991; Kvist 1998) or in connection with the analysis of non-standard employment forms (Klammer 2001; Anxo et al. 2000; Keller et al. 2002).

The general information that can be filtered from these studies includes the fact that the proportion of the unemployed entitled to insurance benefits has been declining in many countries. An early study by OECD (1992: 223) explains this mainly in terms of increasing exhaustion of insurance benefits as unemployment spells have increased but also mentions changes in labour force composition (more married women in the labour market, more part-time and short-term contracts) as possible reasons. Similarly, Braun (2001: 614) states that growing non-standard employment forms (temporary employment and, especially, part-time employment) have considerably contributed to increasing risks of repeated unemployment, income poverty and diminished entitlements to social benefits. Concerning part-time workers, Bothfeld et al. (2000) finish their assessment of upward and downward transition patterns with the statement that all kinds of part-time work, but particularly permanent part-time work, have important implications for employees' social security in a long-term perspective. Anxo et al. (2000) support this by emphasising that the development of labour market flexibility, especially as regards the breakdown of standard working time over the life-cycle, raises fundamental challenges for the future of labour regulation an its implications for contributions and entitlement to welfare. An integrated assessment of the effects of employment and social policy regulation are called for and strategies that cushion transitions are put forward as a possible solution.

In their critical assessment of unemployment compensation and labour market transitions Atkinson et al. (1991) stress that the emphasis in empirical as well as in theoretical work tended to be on the effects of changes in benefit levels rather than the different conditions of receipt of unemployment insurance and unemployment assistance. According to them, the analysis is considerably complicated but also enriched by the recognition that coverage of the unemployed is not universal and benefit payments vary considerably, depending on individual characteristics. They point out that it is essential to take account of the diversity of individual receipt of unemployment benefit. Similarly, Kvist (1998: 51) specifies that older, highly paid, permanently employed males may be favoured at the expense of young, low-paid, part-time or temporarily employed women, especially when the access to and the conditions for benefit receipt become stricter and duration of benefits is reduced.

Studies that provide specific analysis of deficient social insurance coverage among non-standard workers can be subdivided into four broad areas: (1) comparative, mostly descriptive studies; (2) country-specific studies focussing on either non-standard employment in general, part-time employment or temporary employment; (3) studies concerned with discrimination against women in social insurance coverage; and (4) studies based on the concept of flexicurity and that take into account recent policy reforms.[8]

(1) Concerning the comparative studies a concise introductory overview on the relationship between flexibility, unemployment and social protection giving consideration to part-time workers, temporary workers and women is given by Bosco (1996).

Eurofound (2003) provides a sound literature review and a comprehensive analysis of flexibility and social protection regulation covering Germany, the Netherlands, Sweden, the United Kingdom, Spain and Greece. The focus is on part-time employment, fixed-term employment and temporary agency work. Regulations concerning unemployment insurance and unemployment assistance, state pensions, health care, parental leave and social assistance are compiled and analysed. In addition, theories relating to this topic are discussed. Among other things, flexicurity, transitional labour market mechanisms and social drawing rights are revised. The study emphasises the need to analyse and monitor flexible employment in a longitudinal way, taking account of the social protection system dimension.

Another noteworthy study is Grimshaw et al. (1997) who stress the need for policy reassessment in line with the heterogeneity of unemployment benefit recipients. Regulations referring to the mid-1990s, potentially restricting access to unemployment benefits such as hours thresholds and contribution time, are reviewed for EU-15 countries. There is a special focus on potential differences

8 The research literature is reviewed only briefly here. Single studies are referred to in more detail in the corresponding sections.

between women's and men's replacement rates. Replacement rates for the initial period of unemployment based on average gross earnings of full-time working men and women are calculated – in about two-third of the countries women are worse off than men based on this calculation. Concerning the countries under observation, according to the calculations, net replacement rates for Denmark and the United Kingdom do not differ by gender, whereas in Spain and Germany men are better off than women, with replacement rates about ten percentage points higher for men.

In a broad assessment of part-time employment in six European countries (Denmark, Belgium, the Netherlands, Great Britain, France and West Germany) Maier (1992) not only presents descriptive results on the extent and structure of part-time employment based on the European Labour Force Survey, but also discusses social security regulations, labour law and policy initiatives aimed at part-time workers. Health insurance, maternity benefits, state and supplementary pension, unemployment insurance and dismissal regulations are treated, and based on analysis of the regulations in place in the early 1990s it is concluded that part-time workers are especially badly off in supplementary pension systems and in unemployment insurance systems.

Similarly, Delsen (1995: 111–129) discusses labour and social security legislation for part-time workers pertaining to the late 1980s in his wide-ranging study on atypical employment that covers EU-15 countries, Japan and the United States. A whole range of social benefits is treated: health insurance, unemployment insurance, pension entitlements, maternity leave, disability benefits and holiday entitlements. The author concludes that social security systems are mainly oriented towards full-time workers and that discrimination against part-time workers is especially pertinent as regards unemployment allowance.

Fringe benefits of temporary workers are discussed by the OECD (2002c: 144–150). It is acknowledged that temporary workers may fail to gain access to some or all benefits when entitlement conditions include earnings thresholds, a minimum duration of employment or a minimum contribution period. General conditions of entitlement to fringe benefits such as paid holidays, sick leave, unemployment insurance, pension and paid maternity/parental leave are illustrated for OECD countries in a comparative table, but the discussion remains general due to the complexity and specificity of the rules.

(2) A range of country-specific studies on non-standard employment and social security regulation is presented in Tálos (1999). Eleven EU-15 countries are treated, including Denmark, Germany, Spain and the United Kingdom. There are also studies on Slovenia and the United States. The development of various non-standard employment forms, as well as labour and social security regulations pertaining to non-standard employment, are described and assessed. Draw-

ing on the country-specific studies the final chapter gives a comprehensive overview of the extent of and motives for non-standard employment, as well as the social security regulations governing non-standard employment in Europe and beyond.

Klammer et al. (2001a) is the most comprehensive study on flexibility and social security in Germany.[9] Income problems and unemployment risks as a consequence of non-standard employment and discontinuous careers are discussed at length. In a further part, recent developments in a range of social security systems (social assistance, active labour market policy and pension insurance) and possibilities for reforms are assessed. The final part draws on experiences in a range of European countries: the Netherlands (regulations concerning part-time and temporary employment), the United Kingdom (especially New Deal policies), Denmark (recent reforms, especially active labour market policies) and Switzerland (pension insurance) are looked at.

A further noteworthy country-specific study is Micklewright (1990), who assesses the reasons for deficient insurance benefit coverage in the United Kingdom in the 1980s. He criticises the fact that studies that examine the adverse effects of unemployment benefit coverage on incentives, for example, often assume full benefit coverage. According to him, new entrants, part-time workers on low earnings, married women, entrepreneurs and temporary workers with short contract duration may well not receive unemployment insurance benefits. The author points out that there has been a decline in coverage with non-means-tested unemployment insurance benefits since the 1960s and assesses the reasons for this trend.

(3) There are a number of studies that directly focus on deficient coverage of women in social security systems. A lack of entitlement in social insurance systems among women can come about either due to their overrepresentation in forms of non-standard employment, especially part-time employment, or due to means-testing, which they are more likely to experience. Luckhaus (2000: 175) summarises the dilemma in the following way: 'Women's dependency on men during periods of unpaid work activity and their peripheral connection with the labour market give rise to income insecurities which then tend to be incorporated into and reproduced by social protection systems.' Income insecurity in social protection systems, according to Luckhaus, is rooted in unpaid care work and in either non-employment or employment in forms of work that are not full-time, not highly paid and not continuous over a working life. Social protection is discussed here in a wider framework also taking account of non-coverage of unpaid

9 This was commissioned by the Ministry of Labour, Social Affairs and Qualifications of North Rhine-Westphalia.

care work, financial dependence of women and social protection regulations as disincentives for women's paid work.

Rubery et al. (1998a) point out the negative side-effects for women of both social security systems that are founded on insurance principles and those that are needs-based. They scrutinise the characteristics of social security systems of EU-12 countries that may have an impact on the relative position of women as compared to men. Eligibility conditions, duration of benefits, replacement rates, access of women to active labour market policies but also contribution requirements are treated.

Jepsen et al. (2002) focus on the individualisation of rights in social protection systems. According to the authors, the non-individualisation of social rights, combined with further gender inequalities in the labour market, not only leads to women's dependence in terms of social protection but furthermore may encourage them to leave the labour market or not to enter it in the first place. The authors examine pension systems as well as unemployment compensation schemes in EU-15 countries and examine derived rights the effects of which are illustrated by showing country-specific replacement rates for different household compositions. The authors conclude that, despite the various reforms of social security schemes undertaken in EU countries, the issue of the individualisation of social rights has rarely been addressed.

Jepsen et al. (1997) point out that non-standard employment and especially part-time employment tend to limit access to unemployment insurance benefits. Hours thresholds, replacement rates of former part-time and full-time employees and the consequences of non-individualised social benefits are discussed for EU-15 countries.

WSI-FrauenDatenReport, which was last published in 2005, discusses a range of social security benefits in Germany (unemployment insurance, health insurance, pension insurance, care insurance, social assistance and family policies), with a focus on women. Concerning unemployment insurance, the access of women to unemployment insurance and assistance benefits as well as to active measures is treated. The 2005 edition also addresses the effects of the Hartz reforms on the benefit entitlements of unemployed women (compare Klammer 2005, 2000).

Bennet (2005), on behalf of the British Equal Opportunities Commission, presents wide-ranging information on the situation of women in the British social security system. Historical analysis, as well as discussion of recent policy developments concerning benefits and tax credit systems, are provided. The reflection of gender-related labour market inequalities in benefit entitlement and the male breadwinner as the anticipated norm for welfare provision are presented as key findings.

Sainsbury (1996) discusses gender and welfare issues in a theoretical and applied perspective. Four countries are compared: the Netherlands, the United Kingdom, the United States and Sweden. Among other things, the male breadwinner model and its effects on women's entitlement are critically assessed. Furthermore, access of women to a range of benefits, as well as benefit inequalities and redistribution, are analysed.

(4) Last but not least, the studies that focus on flexicurity and use this concept in order to analyse recent labour market policies in European countries are briefly reviewed. The term 'flexicurity' depicts the ideal situation of a flexible and thus more adaptable workforce whose increased risks are at the same time cushioned through security provisions ranging from social security to employability measures. Wilthagen (2004; 1998), Tangian (2004) and Muffels (2005) contribute to the theoretical development of the concept and support their results with evidence from both the Netherlands and the European context. The concept of transitional labour markets (Schmid 2006; Schmid et al. 2002) that will be briefly reviewed in the theoretical chapter is closely related to flexicurity but focuses more strongly on the life-course perspective. As to the countries of interest here, a range of studies treat recent social and labour market reform policies in Germany under the flexibility–security nexus (compare, for example, Klammer 2004; Klammer et al. 2001a; Keller et al. 2004, 2002; Leschke et al. 2006). The life-course perspective and also functional flexibility are stressed in the German context. There is also a range of studies that focus on flexicurity in the Danish labour market that predominantly treat the Danish labour market reforms since the mid-1990s (compare, for example, Madsen 2002a; Larsen 2004).

2 Theoretical background

In the following theoretical section, the concept of risk – a central notion of this paper – moves to the centre of analysis. It is assumed that non-standard employment situations are connected with a higher degree of risk concerning employment stability and security of unemployment. In this context, the achievement of 'flexicurity' would imply creating supply side incentives to take up non-standard employment by absorbing the additional risks through a range of inclusive security measures. Additionally, a condensed insight into segmentation theories is given. The standard prerequisites of secondary sector employment – high labour turn-over, low upward mobility and general insecurity – are at least partly fulfilled by non-standard employment. Especially the recent supply-side focussed advances of the theory seem useful for shedding light on risky employment situations. A large part of the theoretical section is concerned with insurance theory. First, the general rationale of installing institutions such as unemployment insurance is assessed. The discussion will then turn to the advantages and downsides of publicly organized unemployment insurance. Furthermore, voluntary and compulsory insurance, contributory financing and tax financing and the resulting predominance of either the equivalence or the welfare principle will be contrasted. Under the assumption that adequate unemployment insurance benefits for non-standard employed require redistribution efforts the possible trade-offs between efficiency and equity are addressed. In the final part of the theoretical section, welfare state theory is revised, enabling a better understanding of the underlying systems of the countries under analysis.

2.1 Risk and uncertainty

The welfare state can not only make careers safer but can also induce and increase risk taking (Sinn 1997). Risk taking incentives within the welfare state are set through the public tax and transfer system, for example in the form of unemployment insurance benefits. The risk taking effect brought about by the welfare state might be its most important function insofar as it can liberate productive forces and thus increase aggregate income (compare Sinn 1997: 507ff). Following Rowe (1977), risk implies something unwanted that is associated with consequences involving losses to the risk taker. The uncertainty in the occurrence of a specific consequence – a probability – is an important component of risk. Renn (1992) develops a similar definition of risk: the term 'risk' denotes the possibility that an undesirable state of affairs may occur as a result of natural events or human activity. The causal relationship between actions or events and their effects is emphasised; the risk concept carries the implicit message that undesirable effects should be reduced through modification of the cause or, less desirable, through mitigation of the consequences. As regards risks inherent in non-standard employment – a possibly higher unemployment probability, especially for temporary contract holders and deficient coverage in the event of unemployment – modification of the cause could take the following forms: the state could implement more effective barriers against dismissal or support workplace maintenance through training. Mitigating strategies, on the other hand, could consist of comprehensive entitlement to unemployment benefits, equivalent benefit levels, and comprehensive, accessible and possibly obligatory activation policies. Mainly in reference to developing countries Holzmann et al. (2001) broaden the above-quoted categorization by introducing a third risk management strategy – besides prevention and mitigation, coping is suggested. It can take place through reliance on public or private transfers, borrowing or enhancing labour supply within the family. Coping strategies, although usually the least preferable approach, can relieve the impact of a risk once it has occurred.

Renn (1992) emphasises a number of special features of the social science perspective on responsive risk management; the following aspects are especially important in the context of this paper: (1) identifying the context of risk-taking situations, as well as the cultural meanings and associations linked with special risk arenas, and (2) articulating objectives of risk policies that exceed the general economic aim of minimizing risks, such as enhancing fairness and institutional trust or reducing inequities and vulnerability.[10] The context of risk taking situations will be discussed in the institutional part that assesses the country-specific regulations on non-standard employment and unemployment insurance. Enhancing fairness and reducing inequities are central points if one calls for broad benefit entitlement as a solution to the risks inherent in flexible employment. Institutional trust – in our context, dependable social insurance – is a prerequisite for risk-taking.

10 The other social science perspectives on risk mentioned are: identifying and explaining public concerns associated with the risk source; designing procedures to incorporate these cultural values into the decision-making process; designing participative programmes aiming at joint decision making; designing programmes for evaluating risk management performance and organisation structures for identifying, monitoring and controlling risks.

Rowe (1977) suggests a five-step process of risk estimation consisting of causative events, outcomes (probability of occurrence), exposure (controllability, recipients and pathway of risk exposure), consequences and value of the consequences to the people affected. A transfer of the five steps to the subject treated here is straightforward. The causative events can be dismissal, resignation or expiration of the contract. Possible outcomes are unemployment, an immediate new job, inactivity or alternative activities such as child care or further education. Concerning exposure, the recipient is the affected individual and indirectly also his or her family, the pathway of risk exposure is non-standard employment situations and controllability could, for example, be achieved through the acquisition of firm-specific qualifications, greater job effort or intensive search for a new job (prevention of unemployment). Controllability seems to be limited, however; economic downturns and firm specific decline in demand, as well as the utilisation of temporary contracts can hardly be influenced by the employee. Typical consequences are income loss and, especially in the event of prolonged unemployment, a loss of human capital, decreasing self-esteem and, connected with this, decreasing reemployment possibilities. An innovative point of Rowe's process model is that the value of the consequences is considered important. The risk estimation process does not stop with the incidence of the specific consequence but the impact and significance of this consequence strongly depend on one's own attitude towards the situation and on possible mitigation measures. Persons with comparatively good reemployment probabilities due to high and/or specific qualifications might judge unemployment differently than persons with low and/or outdated qualifications. Furthermore, own savings or reliable earnings of a spouse might attenuate the negative consequences of unemployment. Last but not least, the accessibility of unemployment benefits, benefit level and duration, as well as active job search or job preparation measures might bring about a more positive assessment of the risk situation.

Recent theoretical studies on risk and insurance frequently refer to the risk management concept. Holzmann et al. (2001), for example, describe social risk management as an expanded and newly defined version of social protection.[11] Social protection in this context consists of public interventions to assist individuals, households and communities to better manage risks; at the same time, support for the critically poor is to be provided. Within this framework the protection of a basic livelihood is enhanced by the promotion of risk taking. The

11 The authors take their examples mainly from developing countries and focus on poverty reduction strategies that can potentially be advanced through social risk management. Not all of their arguments can thus be transferred to the context of EU countries. In particular, informal risk management strategies are probably more adequate for developing countries than for industrialised ones.

new strategy extends beyond the public provision of risk management instruments by additionally covering public actions to improve market-based and non-market-based (informal) instruments of risk management. Besides provision of unemployment insurance, possibly with greater involvement and responsibility of employers (experience rating), risk management could take place through employability strategies and the like that set in while people are still in employment. As a possible alternative to public or marked-based risk management strategies the authors also discuss risk management within the family. This is seen as problematic insofar as effectiveness and efficiency of social risk management may not be gender neutral (compare Holzmann et al. 2001: 548–549).

Schmid (2002; 2006) states that social policy in terms of risk management calls for institutional arrangements that not only empower individuals through a set of options but also enhance their mobility, employability and flexibility. Not only the traditional external risks, such as cyclical and seasonal fluctuations or technical innovations, are to be covered, but a broadened 'employment insurance' would also have to incorporate internal labour market risks caused by parental leave, life-long learning activities or working-time changes. As a result of more frequent transitions employment trajectories become more discontinuous. In order to cushion transitions and cast a positive light on enhanced flexibility, appropriate institutional arrangements have to be established through so-called transitional labour markets.

Transitional labour markets are organisational bridges that facilitate transitions between different employment forms, working-time arrangements and private activities, such as child care or education, in a way that avoids enduring sub-standard employment or social exclusion. Transitional labour markets are thus for the purpose of enhancing flexibility and ameliorating employment outcomes by allowing socially insured transitions (Schmid 2002: 175-204). Five different types of transitions (working in both directions) are identified that should be promoted through institutional bridges: transitions between education/ training and employment; transitions between part-time and full-time employment or dependent employment and self-employment; transitions between private or family activities and paid work; transitions between unemployment and employment; and transitions between work, disability and retirement (compare, for example, Schmid 2002). Transitional labour markets are characterised by a combination of employment and other useful social activities and by a combination of income sources (wages, transfer payments and alternative sources). They are legally, collectively or privately contracted entitlements, and they finance employment instead of unemployment. Discontinuous employment trajectories resulting not only from labour market failures but also from private decisions stand at the centre of this approach; activating labour market policies and encouraging employability are important components of the concept. By acknowledging increasing flexibility in employment forms, as well as more differentiated employment trajectories, and aiming at cushioning the resulting breaks and shortcomings through a range of security measures, this concept constitutes a good framework for analysing flexibility and security systematically.

Inspired by social choice theory and new public management theory, Schmid (2002) suggests that good transitions should fulfil the following criteria: enhancing individual freedom through empowering strategies, promoting solidarity, strengthening effectiveness (through local networks) and supporting efficiency (risk sharing elements). Empowering strategies call not only for comprehensive access to benefits and activation but also for active participation in employment and training decisions. In turn, employees should be more willing to accept risks and obligations. The second criterion, solidarity, can, for example, be achieved through the generalisation of regulations and the extension of social protection to new risks – here, redistribution comes into play. The solidarity criterion not only calls for a broader financing basis for insurance benefits (for example, through the inclusion of self-employed, civil servants, and the like) but also for a reconsideration of earnings-related benefit payments. In order to guarantee the functioning and financial viability of social risk management strategies a good balance between efficiency and effectiveness has to be found. All in all, risk management strategies that fulfil the above-mentioned criteria could enhance the perception of non-standard employment.

2.2 Segmented labour markets

The dual labour market theory was developed in the 1960s with an initial focus on racial labour market segregation. The aim was to explain urban poverty and underemployment, especially in the context of local labour markets (Gordon 1972). A theory on the dichotomisation of the labour market into a 'primary' and a 'secondary' segment characterised by diverging features emerged. While the primary labour market segment is characterised by high wages, good working conditions, employment stability, advancement possibilities and greater equity, the secondary segment is characterised by low wages, low fringe benefits, poor working conditions, high labour turn-over, low upward mobility and generally unstable employment (Doeringer et al. 1971: 165 et seqq). Most empirical studies reviewed in Dickens et al. (1984) and Huguet Roig (1999: 296, 297) affirm that distinct labour market segments exist. According to dual labour market theorists, access to the primary segment is especially restricted for women, ethnic minorities, migrant workers, the disabled and young persons. Labour market segmentation results not only from employer's discriminatory practices but also from union-imposed constraints on labour supply, information shortages and the working of feedback mechanisms (Peck 1996). The existence of a secondary labour market segment is of advantage to employers and the economy due to its relative flexibility, which can be exploited by way of adapting supply and demand through this channel.

The segmentation approach initially focused on job characteristics, not the special features of individuals. It thus predominantly pointed to the demand side of the labour market. More recent developments pursue a more multidimensional approach and, amongst other things, also take into account labour supply as well as state actions and institutional features. Peck (1996), for example, emphasises the labour market segmentation imposed by the household division of labour between the male 'breadwinner' and the female care-taker with a marginal labour market role at the most. The 'gendered division of labour' not only applies to women in this specific household constellation but by way of employer's discrimination or anticipation to all potential mothers. In this context, part-time employment and especially marginal part-time work can be seen as a component of the secondary labour market segment. Empirical accounts on the wage and insurance discrimination of part-time workers seem to affirm this estimation (compare, for example, O'Connell et al. 2003; Fagan et al. 1998). By reporting that the real causes for sub-standard wages and labour conditions do not lie in part-time work itself but in its disproportional concentration in low wage sectors and low qualified positions, Fagan et al. (1998) implicitly support the demand-side inflicted labour market segmentation hypothesis. The association of non-standard employment forms with the secondary segment is also supported by Atkinson's 'flexible firm' model. Pressures for flexibility and market adaptation are met through functional flexibility within the relatively secure core sector of the firm (full-time permanent career employees with firm-specific skills) and, on the other hand, through numerical flexibility (sometimes also serving functional flexibility) in the form of peripheral employer–employee relations by way of using part-time, temporary and self-employed workers with more general skills (Atkinson 1984). The peripheral group of workers helps to maximise flexibility by minimising firms' commitment to workers' job security and career development.

The application of dual labour market theory to non-standard employment is straightforward. Early theoretical studies already recognised that primary sector work is sometimes shifted to the secondary sector by making use of subcontracting or temporary contracts (Gordon 1972). Spain in particular is associated with segmented labour markets that consist of protected permanent jobs on the one side, and unemployment and insecure temporary employment with relatively low wages on the other side (OECD 2003b). Similarly, Esping-Andersen (1995) points out that evidence, for Spain as well as for France, indicates that temporary contracts nourish dualisms while they hardly generate additional net employment growth. Flexibilisation may not only deepen the cleavage between the core and peripheral workforces, but the wage and job-security privileges of permanent workers or 'insiders' might be strengthened precisely because firms can regulate their labour force needs at the margin through temporary workers who can be easily dismissed (compare Esping-Andersen (1995)). A similar estimation is given by Bentolila et al. (1994) who point out that flexibility at the margin has been created in Spain, leading to a duality within firms that again strengthens the position of insiders.

According to Polavieja (2003), existing studies on segmentation for the most part disregard the important role of institutional regulations regarding labour market stratification. From the author's viewpoint most studies focus too strongly on macro-level factors of segmentation and thus do not take account of the influence of economically rational behaviour on the part of individual workers and firms. To counter these shortcomings an explanatory model that focuses more strongly on the regulatory context and, at the same time, links the macro-outcomes of deregulation to micro-level behaviour is suggested. With reference to the Spanish labour market context Polavieja (2003) argues that deregulation through temporary contracts within an institutional context that is characterised by high dismissal costs for permanent workers will lead to intensified segmentation – workers with temporary contracts will have to work harder than permanent workers in order to avoid unemployment.[12]

If we acknowledge the role of the state in producing, enforcing or weakening segmentation through its institutional settings, it can be hypothesised that through its regulation of employment (stability) and unemployment (security) it influences not only the extent but also the composition of labour market segmentation. It is thus an important function of the state to level out possible job creation incentives brought about by weak employment regulation and resulting polarisation between different employment forms.

12 Polavieja (2003) tests this assumption empirically and concludes that the increasing segment of temporary workers in the Spanish labour market was becoming more and more instable, while the decreasing core of permanent workers was growing ever more secure and impenetrable.

2.3 Insurance

The extent and distribution of social welfare benefits are strongly determined by the structure of society (age distribution, family structure, job structure), its financial resources and the prevailing societal values and norms that are decisive for the design of benefits (H.-G. Petersen 1989: 29). Welfare production is distributed between state, market and family – the importance attached to the respective welfare producer depends on a country's affiliation to a specific welfare regime (Esping-Andersen 1999: 73). In liberal welfare regimes – here represented by the United Kingdom – the welfare state is subordinated to the market and thus plays a marginal role. Rather due to prevailing norms than to financial constraints passive benefits are relatively low, often means-tested and stigmatising. In continental welfare regimes – here Germany – the state is accorded more importance but the subsidiarity principle prevails: ideal-typically, the state will step in only if self-help within the family is exhausted. Benefit entitlements are strongly centred on wage labour. Since status maintenance is accorded high importance, at least theoretically, benefit redistribution is limited. The Mediterranean welfare regimes, here represented by Spain, are characterised by a general shortage of resources to subsidise social policy (Trifiletti 1999: 50). State intervention is low; instead, the family and other informal networks constitute important welfare providers; the subsidiarity principle is even more pronounced than in continental regimes. In social democratic welfare regimes (Denmark) the state, equipped with comprehensive financial resources due to high taxation, plays a dominant role. Broad and often universal social security is granted; achieving a high degree of equity is a central aim.

Although in the countries under analysis the role of the state apparently varies widely, in the case of unemployment insurance the state takes the dominant role in all countries. This section, after providing a rationale for why institutions such as unemployment insurance are important and what functions they fulfil, analyses why the state is usually seen as the most suitable provider of unemployment insurance. In addition, the advantages and drawbacks of voluntary and compulsory insurance, as well as contribution and tax financing are discussed. This section is rounded off by an examination of the redistributional function of unemployment insurance, which is assumed to be influenced by the above principles. In this context, possible trade-offs between efficiency and redistribution (equity) will be discussed.

2.3.1 Advantages of institutionalised unemployment insurance

Institutions such as unemployment insurance that internalise costs sometimes are more adequate than market mechanisms. They are socially defined rules whose enforcement can be expected – the binding character of institutions is of prime importance (Esser 2000: 5).[13] North (1990) additionally stresses the significance of institutions for human interactions by stating that they are humanly devised conditions that structure political, economic and social interactions. Institutions consist of informal constraints such as sanctions, customs, traditions and codes of conduct, as well as of formal rules, including political and judicial rules, economic rules and contracts. Unemployment insurance, being a politically initiated formal rule in the form of a contract, falls into the last category.

The functions of institutions are to facilitate exchange and to reduce uncertainty by establishing a stable structure to human interaction (North 1990: 6, 47). Consistent with transaction cost theory, institutions may decrease information, monitoring and enforcement costs (North 1990). Within secure institutional settings reliability is comparatively high, while costs can be kept relatively low through standardised contracts and through implementing average premiums and thus avoiding information costs. In times of uncertainty, institutions can direct actions and help individuals to leave their usual path and break new ground (engage in risky transitions) (Esser 2000: 17). People are more likely to accept changes if security is granted (compare also Sinn 1997).

Unemployment insurance thus can take over important functions besides income compensation. If insurance is comprehensive and reliable, it can facilitate the take-up of unstable or risky employment, and it can even act as an incentive to voluntary acceptance of non-standard employment.

According to Frey (1992: 194) institutions may serve to weaken deficient individual behaviour at the aggregate level. First of all, preventive functions of institutions guide people so that they behave in a rational way; secondly, institutions serve to mitigate the consequent costs for people; and thirdly, they redistribute costs of irrational behaviour among people and/or between time periods (Frey 1992: 190–192). These three purposes illustrate the tasks of unemployment insurance very well. Preventive functions of unemployment insurance include, for example, sanction regulations (especially in the form of initial retention periods) that might prevent risk adverse people from becoming voluntarily unemployed. Cost mitigation takes place through the allocation of insurance benefits to the unemployed. On the insurer's side, costs may be reduced through implementing stricter requirements for benefit receipt or through using alternative

13 The following paragraphs on institutions are based to a considerable extent on Esser (2000: 1–49).

schemes in close cooperation with firms, such as the German short-time working allowance and the bad weather allowance. Inter-temporal redistribution of costs takes place through prior premium payments and later disbursements; inter-personal redistribution takes place by imposing the same premium level on good and bad risks or – especially in the British system – by paying out universal flat-rate benefits while basing premiums on income. We shall now discuss publicly provided insurance, its assets, drawbacks and leading principles.

2.3.1.1 Public vs. private insurance

Unemployment insurance is generally organized on a public basis; the programmes are administered either by the state itself at the central or a lower level or by state-appointed bodies. In some countries – for example, Denmark and Sweden – trade unions are responsible for unemployment insurance delivery. They are closely monitored by the state, which lays down general binding rules and acts as last resort deliverer of welfare benefits for those who do not qualify for insurance benefits. While there is some discussion about privatising health care or retirement insurance, unemployment is usually regarded as uninsurable, and unemployment benefit delivery is therefore for the most part excluded from privatisation proposals (compare, for example, Berthold 1988). Exceptions include privatisation processes of certain subtasks, such as employment and placement services, that have lately taken place in a number of countries.[14]

Both economic and non-economic arguments are brought forward to justify publicly-provided cash transfers. The non-economic arguments are as follows: within the framework of private insurance the poor cannot afford adequate coverage; it is immoral for insurance companies to profit from people's misfortunes; and the weaker members of society have to be protected (Barr 1998: 185). Barr (1998) questions the validity of these points and instead accords the efficiency criterion high importance if it comes to judging public vs private insurance delivery. Where private insurance is more efficient, equity aims – such as those stated above – should be achieved through income transfers and not through insurance.

What are the reasons for the predominance of publicly provided unemployment insurance if the non-economic arguments cannot hold? Sometimes cost issues are brought forward as arguments against private insurance. Administrative costs arise from marketing, processing (matching premiums and individual risks) and reimbursement. If these costs are taken into consideration, social insurance has an advantage over private insurance insofar as it usually has no marketing costs (no competition), low processing and reimbursement costs due to

14 Well-known examples in this context are Australia and the Netherlands. Compare, for example, OECD (2001b) and Riggs (2000).

standardisation as well as, owing to its size, economies of scale (Barr 1998a). Regarding cost aspects public insurance might be more efficient than private insurance.

When it comes to judging the adequacy of public administration of unemployment insurance, cost arguments are not predominant, however. Wagner et al. (1997) attribute the failure of private unemployment insurance to supply side issues. The predominance of publicly administrated and in most cases obligatory insurance is ascribed to the existence of asymmetric information on the type of risk (adverse selection through hidden knowledge), the employment opportunities of beneficiaries and their job search willingness (moral hazard). While transaction costs arising from enforcing and monitoring contracts are too high for private insurers the state can counter adverse selection through requiring membership or eliminating competition. In this constellation, information about the distribution of good and bad risks and their respective proportions are sufficient for calculating a universal cost covering premium. In a competitive system, good risks can opt for alternative insurance with lower premiums – leaving the bad risks behind, which would eventually lead to the collapse of the insurance market. Public insurance can generally not counter moral hazard problems more efficiently than private insurance. Nevertheless, due to its legislative competences, state-led insurance might be in a better position than private insurance to adjust or strengthen control measures. The following strategies can be applied in order to ameliorate moral hazard effects and thus prevent prolonged benefit entitlement that can pose a threat to the insurance's financial means: enforcement of reemployment through the threat of sanctions, obligatory activation measures or benefit levels that decline with time. Barr (1998a) additionally suggests cost-sharing strategies between the unemployed and the insurer, where the insured person pays a certain percentage of any claim or higher premiums for frequent claims. A number of studies on the moral hazard issue have been published. On activation compare, for example, Atkinson et al. (1993), Barbier (2004), Hvinden (1999) and Kosonen (1999); on incentives and sanctions compare, for example, Card (2000), Holmlund (1998), Hunt (1995), Pearson et al. (2000) and Røed et al. (2002).

In his excellent theoretical article on the role of the state in risk insurance Schönbäck (1988) specifies the following points that might hinder the determination of adequate premiums and therefore might restrict private insurance. Private insurance delivery proves difficult if the probability or the amount of loss is unknown, if risk aversion is low relative to transaction costs and gains of the insurance, or if the required premium amounts to an excessively high share of the insured person's income. Furthermore, private insurance is restricted if moral hazard occurs among part of the prime risk takers, if risks are unequally spread and good risks opt out or, in the case of comprehensive information, the insurance provider refrains from covering bad risks. Last but not least, private insurance delivery is restricted if risks are interdependent and occur abundantly, or if the long-term continuity of the insurance is uncertain.

What does this imply in respect of the possibility of providing private unemployment insurance? The probability of individual unemployment and the corresponding length are relatively uncertain – the calculation of adequate premiums is therefore impossible or at least very costly for the insurer. Economic crises are frequent and usually affect a large area due to complex economic interweavements. Individual work and job search motivation can decline as a consequence of insurance (moral hazard is difficult to detect). At least to a certain degree, selection of good risks would be possible for the insurer because employees exhibit certain easily observable features, such as qualification level, occupational affiliation and gender. This could lead to non-insurance or deficient insurance of assumed bad risks. Risk aversion entails certain upper limits that individuals are willing to pay for premiums; if premiums were set with respect to risk, especially individuals with high risks and/or low income would have to refrain from unemployment insurance. Schönbäck (1988: 56–59) concludes that if a collective insurance scheme is called for, market mechanisms have to be replaced by state regulation.

But in what ways does public unemployment insurance prove more efficient than private insurance when faced with the abovementioned problems? Obligatory public insurance removes the possibility that persons with low unemployment risks opt out of the system. Relative poverty and selection of good risks are corrected through the obligation to pay premiums to a given insurance company that covers all types of risks. This is especially important for assuring adequate insurance of part-time employment (relative poverty due to comparatively low income) and temporary employment (bad risks due to potentially higher unemployment probability). Inter-personal income redistribution might be necessary to ensure adequate coverage of these groups. Universal state insurance, owing to its large and diverse insurance pool, makes it possible to cope better with unexpectedly large sectoral or regional labour market instabilities. Additionally, the possibility to fix premiums centrally make it possible to compensate for the potential accumulation of dependent risks. Last but not least, a large public insurance company is probably more transparent and stable, and thus more reliable for its clients than numerous private ones would be.

Nevertheless, most actors favour public administration of unemployment insurance, though there are some noteworthy exceptions. Hayek (1991), for example, argues against a state-led unemployment insurance that, according to him, merely functions as a device for redistributing income. While a uniform organisation is useful if one wants to guarantee immediate protection for a large number of individuals, as time elapses this organisation can become inefficient. Hayek therefore opts for a clear distinction between benefits to which individuals have a moral and legal entitlement as a consequence of premium payments and needs-based minimum benefits. In his view, public unemployment insurance hinders the reduction of unemployment by hampering more flexible wages and more mobility. He recommends a system that guarantees a means-tested minimum benefit that is topped up by a competitive and voluntary insurance that allows the maintenance of accustomed living standards. Hayek's proposal remains at a general level: no suggestions as how to implement private unemployment insurance are made.

Glismann et al. (2001, 2003), on the other hand, make a specific proposal for private unemployment insurance in the German context. They suggest a system in which employees alone are responsible for covering their unemployment risk.[15] Experience-rated employer premiums are paid into a special fund that is used for recruitment subsidies and unpredictable system crises. Glismann et al. (2003) propose assessing unemployment risk and matching premium structures based on the following individual characteristics: qualification level, occupational sector, employment region, age, gender, unemployment experience and participation in qualification measures. Employees can reduce their premiums if they agree to regional or occupational mobility in the case of unemployment or if they renounce a part of their future replacement income. The system aims to increase efficiency by setting incentives on both the employers' and the employees' side. As a consequence of experience rating and recruitment subsidies, employers could be less inclined to dismiss workers and more willing to create additional jobs. Employees, on the other hand, could be willing to improve their qualifications while they are still employed or change their occupational sector or region in order to pay lower premiums. The state's role would be significantly reduced: it would merely create the legal and institutional prerequisites for a competitive market of private unemployment insurance.

A problematic outcome of this system, hardly acknowledged by the authors, is that especially persons with low income and high risks would have to pay unaffordable high shares of their income as premiums in order to be entitled to adequate benefits. In contrast, persons with high earnings – even if they are bad risks – would attain adequate insurance coverage while paying a much smaller

15 Similarly, Feldstein and Altman (1998) suggest privatising unemployment insurance by replacing the present American system by individual savings accounts. From their scenario calculations, based on data from the panel study of income dynamics (PSID), they conclude that this modified system would result in a substantial improvement of incentive effects for most unemployed.

percentage of their earnings as a premium (compare Table 8 in Glismann et al. 2003: 31, 32). Especially the groups of interest to the present paper – part-time employees with relatively low earnings and temporary workers with more frequent unemployment spells and often lower qualification levels – would suffer serious losses in such a system. Average benefit levels and duration would require prohibitively high social security contributions. Without serious wage income losses, bad risks would be able to afford only very short-term unemployment insurance. Although the idea brought forward by the authors seems innovative at first sight, at closer inspection it proves to be highly unjust, especially for disadvantaged labour market groups.

If equity, justice and fairness are seen as important insurance aims, affordable public insurance has to be provided to cushion unemployment risks. This is partly confirmed by Beenstock et al. (1986: 83) who themselves make a proposal for privatising unemployment insurance. They conclude that privatisation of unemployment insurance might have undesirable redistributive side effects and therefore has to be countered by appropriate fiscal measures.

2.3.1.2 Voluntary vs compulsory insurance

In most countries unemployment insurance is compulsory for the bulk of employees. Usually, all dependent employees are required to pay social insurance contributions; the self-employed and civil servants are often excluded from the general unemployment insurance schemes.

The ability to enforce compulsory membership is one of the arguments in favour of public unemployment insurance. Obligatory participation allows for a pooling solution and thereby reduces the efficiency problem caused by breaking the link between premium and individual risk. Within a pooling solution, universal coverage, independent of risk probability, is possible (Barr 1992: 791).

Why, then, do some countries abstain from compulsory unemployment insurance, notably Denmark, Finland and Sweden? Interestingly, these systems not only differ from other unemployment insurance systems in that they are voluntary but they are all administered by trade unions and are open to the self-employed (European Commission 2003d). How do voluntary systems counter adverse selection and free-riding problems and do they entail potential advantages as compared to obligatory insurance?

Although a standard pooling solution is not possible in a voluntary system, premiums are usually uniform and thus independent of individual risk. In order to avoid excessively high premiums – brought about by the potential opting out of good risks – voluntary unemployment insurance is usually heavily subsidised out of general revenues.[16] This helps to counter adverse selection losses.

Another argument brought forward in favour of compulsory insurance is that society has to be protected from a free-riding mentality in the form of recourse to alternative tax funded welfare benefits. This concern is expressed by, for example, Parsons et al. (2003) in their empirical account of Danish voluntary unemployment insurance. Self-selection can take place either through rational free-riding consumers with risk aversion of varying intensity, or through myopic consumers who poorly calculate their risk probability. The researchers find substantial evidence for rationality in individual decisions for or against insurance. The non-insured are over-proportionally those individuals who have low unemployment probabilities or who have access to alternative forms of public income support (Parsons et al. 2003: 7). Free-riding within voluntary unemployment insurance can be reduced either through strong means-testing of alternative benefits or through introducing compulsory basic insurance (comparable in size to social assistance) while maintaining a voluntary up-grading component that provides earnings-related benefits.[17] Membership of voluntary systems can be encouraged through certain features such as additional benefits only indirectly related to unemployment, solidarity, social pressure or insurance requirements for union members. While, at least for Denmark, the last three points probably play a minor role, early retirement benefits (*efterløn*) granted to long-term unemployment fund members seem to substantially influence membership decisions.[18] Parsons et al. (2003) found empirical evidence of increasing fund membership as a result of the extension of eligibility requirements to this benefit in the early 1990s.[19]

From their empirical analysis of voluntary unemployment insurance in Denmark, Parsons et al. (2003) conclude that high voluntary participation, as well as substantial adverse selection, argue for a compulsory public system or alternatively – but more difficult and more costly to implement – premiums based on risk rating. Their answer as to why Scandinavian unemployment insur-

---

16 Between the mid-1970s and the mid-1990s fund membership fees in Denmark covered approximately one-third of costs, on average (Parsons et al. 2003). In Sweden individual contributions to unemployment insurance funds are even smaller; approximately 95 per cent of insurance costs are met from government funds that are for the most part funded from employers' contributions (Eurofound 2004).

17 In 1997, the voluntary unemployment insurance system in Sweden was modified by introducing a compulsory basic insurance (*grundförsäkring*).

18 Voluntary unemployment insurance coverage in Denmark and Sweden is approximately 80 per cent of the labour force. Obligatory unemployment insurance was introduced in Sweden in the early 1990s but was abolished after only one year.

19 Obligatory membership to qualify for fund-linked early retirement supplements was increased from 10 to 20 years.

ance systems nevertheless remain for the most part voluntary is that revenue gains would be modest and, more importantly, a high share of increased revenue would come from low skilled workers.

What results can we draw for our group of interest? Does voluntary unemployment insurance carry possible advantages for non-standard workers? From the theoretical literature on this issue and the limited empirical evidence, we can conclude that potential bad risks such as temporary workers would be disadvantaged in a voluntary system only if it operated with a risk-rated premium structure – and this is usually not the case. Generally – in order to avoid unbearably high premiums and opting out of good risks – voluntary systems are highly subsidised by the state. This implies a predominantly tax-financed system. The fact that the existing voluntary unemployment insurance schemes coincide with comparatively comprehensive universal safety nets allows persons with high unemployment risks but simultaneously high probability of access to alternative benefits to opt out of the system. This calls for a closer look at the importance and level of potential complementary benefits.

2.3.1.3 Insurance vs welfare principle

Although unemployment insurance is usually financed through a mix of taxes and contributions, in most countries there is a clear tendency towards either contribution or tax financing. Contributions to unemployment insurance are typically based on gross wages and are financed by employers and employees. In many systems lower and upper contribution and benefit ceilings are defined that considerably influence the redistributive power of the specific system. By definition, tax financing is based on a broader group than contribution financing. Additionally, the connection between taxes paid and subsequent benefits is much less clear than the relationship between contributions and benefits.

According to Schmid et al. (1996: 238), the countries looked at here belong to three different unemployment insurance financing systems: Spain and especially Germany are good representatives of the insurance principle; contributions as opposed to taxes are very important and Germany additionally operates with high earnings ceilings. The British scheme deviates from the insurance principle insofar as income-based national insurance contributions are levied in total and contributions to unemployment insurance cannot clearly be distinguished from the remaining public dues. Furthermore, benefits are granted on a flat-rate basis. Due to these features, the insurance principle is very weak in the British system (Schmid et al. 1996; Hills 2004). The Danish system takes a middle position. The insurance principle is not as strong as in Germany but stronger than in the United Kingdom. In addition to income-based contributions, employees pay flat-rate contributions to unemployment insurance funds that are to a considerable degree co-financed out of general taxes. Although benefit payments depend on former earnings the system is relatively redistributive because maximum benefits are comparatively low.

In unemployment insurance systems with close links between contributions and benefits, the equivalence principle predominates. This is the case if contribution financing is more important than tax financing and contributions as well as benefits are strongly earnings related. The welfare principle prevails in schemes with no clear linkage between benefits and contributions (systems with flat-rate contributions and/or benefits or a high degree of tax financing). Accordingly, insurance benefits can pursue two fundamentally different allocative aims: either protecting accustomed living standards and therefore ensuring contributory justice or preventing and mitigating poverty (Rolf 1988: 525). The first aim is more pronounced in insurance schemes based on the equivalence principle; the second function is more evident in schemes in close accordance with the welfare principle. Although the practical implications of the predominance of one of the two principles should not be underestimated, the validity of the term equivalence in connection with unemployment insurance is restricted. This is due to the predominant use of risk independent premiums and, in some countries, the consideration of family composition in benefit allocation.

What are the pros and cons of the insurance and the welfare principle, and how do these principles fare when it comes to the insurance situation of the non-standard employed?

The insurance principle incorporates a strong reciprocity between contributions and benefits, insurance benefits are thus perceived as a right, and cutbacks in times of economic downturns are more difficult to justify than in schemes based on the welfare principle. In schemes that are more strongly based on welfare principles there is theoretically a higher chance that benefit levels will be challenged arbitrarily.

Due to the close connection between former wages and benefit levels, schemes in which insurance principles predominate are usually advantageous for persons with higher wages. Our group of interest – especially part-time workers – is comparatively disadvantaged. Petersen (1989) confirms this by stating that schemes which focus too strongly on equivalence exclude persons with below average incomes from a satisfactory insurance situation. Although flat-rate welfare principle systems grant equal benefits to all the insured – levels only vary subject to family composition – possible advantages for non-standard employed are attenuated because benefit levels usually are lower than in equivalence schemes. High or no ceilings on contributions in combination with low benefit ceilings serve the needs of workers with lower wages without incorporating the drawbacks of flat-rate benefit systems. This is the case in Denmark where replacement rates decrease with income.

There is no clear preference for either the insurance principle or the welfare principle in the scientific literature. Krupp (1988), for example, accords the insurance principle at least as much adaptability as the welfare principle. Basing his assessments on the German system, he even calls for contribution-financed minimum insurance (replacing social assistance) for those left out of general insurance due to discontinuous employment careers. Spahn et al. (1988) cannot find allocative advantages of contribution financing as compared to tax financing that, according to them, better serves minorities in the system. They vote for an effective mix of both instruments. Rolf (1988: 527–531) also argues for a flexible design of social insurance that should allow for better management of long-term demographic, economic and societal changes.

It seems that the financing of unemployment insurance schemes is not clear-cut but some schemes tend more towards protecting accustomed living standards, while others grant benefits that are more strongly based on equity principles. We assume that schemes that are more in line with welfare principles are more favourable towards non-standard workers than schemes that are strongly characterised by insurance principles. Schmid et al. (1996) confirm this by stating that insurance principle based schemes are biased towards protecting core workers as opposed to marginal workers (women, young, casual), while welfare schemes usually generate more equal outcomes. However, it has to be tested how systems perform that are at first sight more inclusive and equitable regarding non-standard workers when it comes to benefit levels and duration of benefit payments.

2.3.1.4 Redistribution in unemployment insurance schemes

Redistribution can be defined as the allocation of money across persons or households; it refers to interventions that reallocate market outputs or inputs in a way believed to be closer to collective goals (Shanahan et al. 1994). Social insurance always incorporates a certain degree of income redistribution between persons or generations or over time. According to Eisen (1988: 125 et seq.), redistribution from good to bad risks has to take place in order to increase efficiency of market outcomes in the presence of asymmetric information. Redistribution occurs not only by way of omnium insurance with average premiums but also through other channels: application of low maximum benefits, flat-rate benefits and family complements constitute possibilities for redistributing insurance benefits. These regulations vary between countries and thus make certain benefit systems more redistributive than others.

The extent of redistribution that social insurance schemes generate is a consequence of the underlying intentions. Redistribution will probably be stronger if poverty relief or solidarity considerations are central aims of the scheme, whereas if great importance is attached to protection of living standard or income smoothing benefits will at least be partly earnings-related and therefore at first sight less redistributive.

The financing principles which underlie benefit systems reveal a lot about the importance accorded to redistribution within a certain scheme. According to Barr (1992: 776 et seq.), the most redistributive unemployment insurance schemes comprise income-tested benefits financed out of progressive contributions (Australia); flat-rate benefits financed out of general taxation are the second most redistributive; the least redistributive are earnings-related benefits financed out of regressive proportional social insurance contributions. This ranking order, although very broad, gives us a general idea of the redistributive effects of different insurance schemes. At least from a theoretical viewpoint – based on knowledge about benefit financing – Germany and Spain can be ranked in the least redistributive group. The schemes of the United Kingdom and Denmark diverge in certain aspects from the examples given here but they probably conform closest to the second group. Denmark operates with comparatively low maximum benefits. The United Kingdom pays out flat-rate benefits that are financed out of earnings-related, though unspecific contributions. Due to this design the British scheme seems to be somewhat more redistributive than the Danish one.

While this classification looks appealing at first sight, two points have to be stressed that in some ways question the above categorisation of the countries under analysis. First, according to Barr (1992: 778), a programme with a highly redistributive formula has little redistributive effect if expenditure is small. This is confirmed by Korpi et al. (1998) who criticise the fact that the debate on the redistributive outcomes of welfare state programmes has focused almost exclusively on how to distribute the money available for transfers while it has largely ignored variations in the size of the redistributive budget. According to them, the degree of redistribution that is finally achieved depends on both the size of the budget and the degree of low-income targeting. Based on their empirical analysis, which focuses on pensions in a range of OECD countries, they put forward a second point that questions the above classification. They show that comprehensive social insurance institutions, by providing high-income earners with earnings-related benefits and thereby crowding out private pensions and other sources of income that tend to be even more unequal than public pensions, can reduce gross income inequality and poverty more efficiently than can flat-rate or targeted benefits.

Although the results cannot be generalised and they relate to pension insurance and not to unemployment insurance they nevertheless remind us that redistribution should be regarded in a broader sense and should not be judged solely on the basis of the working of a specific social insurance system. Individual welfare actually does not primarily derive from state institutions but from at least four sources: labour market, private provision, voluntary welfare (family) and the state. This issue will be considered more closely in the next section, on welfare production between family, market and state.

Redistribution is frequently discussed in terms of equity and efficiency and is often described as conflicting with efficiency goals.[20] The question is whether a certain programme can simultaneously satisfy the inherently conflicting goals of reducing poverty or redistributing income from rich to poor and, at the same time, correcting existing market failures in the provision of unemployment insurance. Barr (1992: 745 et seqq.) specifies efficiency and equity objectives of social institutions in the following way: in order to achieve efficiency benefits should be constructed so as to minimise adverse effects on labour supply, employment and savings. Important dimensions of the equity objective are vertical equity (redistribution to individuals or families with lower income), horizontal equity (differences in benefits should account for age, family size, and so on) and social solidarity. While poverty relief as a possible insurance aim mainly fulfils equity objectives, efficiency and equity objectives form the basis of the alternative aims of protecting accustomed living standards and income smoothing.

Economic literature often treats equity and efficiency as trade-offs (compare Okun 1975). Snower (1995: 629–632), for example, favours efficiency objectives within unemployment insurance in order to tackle market failures, such as moral hazard and adverse selection. Equity, according to him, should not be an objective of unemployment insurance but should rather be achieved through negative income tax schemes and related measures. In the case of unemployment insurance, equity if achieved through redistribution to individuals with low income or a specific household composition can thus evoke incentive problems. This popular argumentation can stand in the way of redistributing benefits. Possible solutions to incentive problems are obligatory activation measures, sanctions if job offers are rejected or reemployment incentives. Snower (1995) emphasises that unemployment benefit systems in practice are far from being optimally designed to achieve either equity or efficiency objectives.

Equity and efficiency do not have to be treated as trade-offs, however. In fact, Headey et al. (1999), based on an empirical assessment of the economic and social performance of the three prototypes of welfare regimes, come to the con-

20 For a thorough literature review of theory and empirical research on distribution and redistribution see Shanahan and Tuma (1994).

clusion that there is no sharp trade-off between equity and efficiency.[21] On the basis of Rawls' 'Theory of Justice' Schmid (2003) asserts that equity and efficiency are compatible if the rules of the game are regarded as fair because people will then participate in a dedicated way in competitive or cooperative actions and will thereby achieve efficient outcomes. Four rules that can support allocative justice are put forward: fairness or distributive justice, solidarity or redistributive justice, equal opportunities that do not necessarily lead to equal outcomes, and equality of outcome.

2.4 Welfare state theory

What concepts and definitions underlie the welfare state and what are its impacts? The origin of the welfare state idea is contested. Depending on one's perspective, it was inspired either by the Beveridge report that initiated social reform in Great Britain (Beveridge 1942) or by the Bismarckian social legislation of the 1880s (Schulte 1998). A third group traces it back to the Swedish social democracy of the late 1920s (Esping-Andersen 1994: 713–714, 727).[22] While Bismarck's welfare conception was characterised by authoritarian, étatist and corporatist views, the Beveridge reforms and the Scandinavian social democratic model favoured universal and egalitarian ideals (Esping-Andersen 1995), as summed up in the following statement from the Beveridge report: 'The insurance scheme is one for all citizens irrespective of their means' (Beveridge 1942: 121, 122). Among the principles of social insurance as laid out in the Beveridge report are flat-rate benefits and contributions as well as adequate and comprehensive benefits. Spain's modern welfare state is comparatively new, dating back to the Socialist Party's period of office after the end of the dictatorship of General Franco in 1975. Traditionally, the Catholic Church had played an important role in welfare provision in Spain. Welfare was to a high degree occupationally segregated and designed to support patriarchal family structures and the authoritarian state (Almeda et al. 1996). According to Galluppi (2004) Spain's present-day welfare state is a mix of the 'Bismarck' and the 'Beveridge' models and still lags behind as regards scope and level of welfare policies.

---

21 According to a study by Headey et al. (1999) the Netherlands, which they define as a prototype of the social democratic welfare regime, not only performs very well in reducing poverty and inequality but equals the other two countries (Germany and the United States) on their favoured welfare goals – household income stability and economic growth, coupled with efficiency.

22 In the 1928 electoral programme of the Swedish social democrats Gustav Möller, the architect of the Swedish welfare state and long-time Minister of Social Affairs, defined a 'welfare state' as a state that is indisputably obliged to grant its citizens welfare in all important areas.

Despite the various ambiguities the term 'welfare' implies an active role of the state in governing economic and societal structures with the aim of achieving more comprehensive equality of prospects. The concept incorporates a broad state policy designed to accomplish the extension of social civil rights, such as securing consumption, encouraging economic growth and employment, as well as reducing unequal participation in society and politics (Alber et al. 1996). An important function of the welfare state is the protection of its citizens in critical circumstances and risky situations within the life cycle. In this respect work ability and opportunity, as well as possible restrictions (insufficient or mismatching work offers, health constraints or care obligations) have to be taken into account. Kohlberg et al. (1992) ascribe the following principles to the advanced welfare state: it should optimise the abilities of unemployed and inactive persons to find and take up work, strengthen their capabilities to execute work and facilitate the combination of family life and employment, as well as of productive activities and leisure. The welfare state is therefore accorded an important securing and activating function; the significance of linking social policy and labour market institutions is stressed. Giddens (2000), in his account of dynamic and responsive welfare states, notes that the current design of the welfare state is not in accordance with new risks emerging from technological change, social exclusion and increasing numbers of lone parent households. Consequently, the risks that are insured no longer comply with real needs, and the groups benefiting from insurance are no longer the needy. In relation to the continental welfare state, Esping-Andersen (1995) notes that it is based on the social, economic and demographic circumstances of the 'Fordist' era that was characterised by stable full employment among men and the residual position of women in the household. Recent demographic and social changes and labour market modifications have led to a situation in which much more emphasis has to be placed on the active phase of life and on more varying employment situations. More comprehensive and activating security for non-standard workers and persons with discontinuous employment thus requires at least a partial redefinition of welfare state concepts and activities. The degree to which modifications are necessary seems to depend heavily on the underlying welfare regime type.

2.4.1 Worlds of welfare capitalism

The basic idea of welfare state typologies is to find groups of countries that are similar as regards the characteristics under analysis and to contrast them with country groups that, preferably, diverge strongly. This is to allow more general statements about the efficiency of specific institutional settings and the transferability of successful policies. The most influential study in this regard is *The Three Worlds of Welfare Capitalism* by Esping-Andersen (1990). It not only initiated a whole range of studies on classifying welfare states (Ferrera 1996; Lessenich et al. 1998; Aspalter 2001; Goodin et al. 1999) but also provoked a critical discourse on the general usefulness of typologies, the dimensions that should be included and suitable methodological approaches (Powell et al. 2004; Arts et al. 2002; Hicks et al. 2003; Bonoli 1997; Rehm et al. 2001).

Esping-Andersen's welfare regimes are based on historical developments and political, societal and economic conditions. He explicitly delimits his typology from earlier conceptualisations (compare, for example, Titmuss 1974) by stating that welfare state results and not merely social expenditure should form the centre of the typology. The basis of his construction is welfare regimes and not individual welfare state programmes; the term 'regime' denotes how welfare production is allocated between state, market and households (Esping-Andersen 1999: 73 et seq.). The criteria used to classify welfare states are decommodification potential and the welfare state as a system of stratification. 'Decommodification occurs when a service is rendered as a matter of right, and when a person can maintain a livelihood without reliance on the market' (Esping-Andersen 1990: 21 et seq.). Accordingly, the concept captures the guarantee of social rights that strengthens the position of the individual vis-à-vis the market. The minimal definition indicates that citizens can self-determinedly opt out of the market without potential loss of job, income or general welfare (compare ibid: 23). The stratification criterion captures how far social policy is able to achieve more equality by making social classes permeable.

The decommodification potential is an index of rules and standards that apply to a range of welfare programmes. It is composed of eligibility and entitlement criteria, duration of benefits and income replacement levels. Stratification is measured first by status segregation (number of occupationally distinct pension schemes) and the degree of 'étatism' (expenditure on civil servants' pensions); secondly, by means-testing and share of private-sector welfare; and thirdly, by universalism (share of the population eligible for benefits) and equality in the benefit structure. The criteria chosen reflect attributes accorded to the anticipated three welfare regimes: conservative, liberal and social-democratic (Esping-Andersen 1990: 69–78). On the basis of the different variables, summary indicators are formed that capture decommodification and stratification. Somewhat intuitively, indices are developed based on the distribution of countries around the overall mean of the specific variables; the standard deviations are used in order to quantify the distance. Some adjustment for outliers takes place and some variables are accorded more weight than others. Based on this choice and treatment of variables, the countries clearly cluster around the three welfare regimes: Italy, Germany, Austria, France and Belgium correspond closely to the conservative regime; Australia, Canada, Japan, Switzerland, the United States and, to a lesser degree, the United Kingdom are characterised by strong liberalism; Sweden, Denmark, Norway, Finland and the Netherlands comply closest with the social-democratic cluster.[23] The extent of decommodification and stratification is mirrored in the specific design of social policy.

In the liberal model, the welfare state takes a marginal role subordinate to the market. The scope of social reforms is limited through traditional norms of a liberal work ethic; financial welfare benefits are usually low, often means-tested and therefore stigmatising; additionally, social services are generally deficient. In conservative welfare regimes, subsidiarity prevails; the state mainly steps in if the self-help capacity within the family fails. Social drawing rights are more important than in the liberal regimes but they are centred on wage labour. The emphasis on status upholding results in low redistribution within conservative regimes. By granting comprehensive security to mostly male labour market insiders with standard contracts and, on the other hand, according derived rights to non-working women and giving low priority to social care services this welfare regime supports the male breadwinner model. The social democratic regime type, in contrast, is characterised by comprehensive and relatively egalitarian universal social security granted as a civil right. In addition to highly decommodified social programmes, social services are extensive. By taking over care responsibilities the state, that plays a pre-eminent role in this welfare regime type, supports women's active participation in the labour market. In order to be able to finance these comprehensive benefits and services the social and labour market policies of the countries belonging to the social democratic regime are geared to high labour market participation.

As to the universalism of benefits (priority of the welfare principle over the insurance principle) in the post-war years, similarities between the social democratic and the Anglo-Saxon liberal welfare states were strong. The United Kingdom's social insurance system inspired by Beveridge was based on principles of equality and universalism. Similarly, the social democratic welfare regimes granted basic social benefits with high coverage rates but well into the 1950s quality and level of benefits remained low.[24] Only in the following decades did the two systems drift apart. The British system stagnated: the Labour Party was too weak to counter the gradual privatising of social insurance. On the other hand, the social-democratic governments in the Scandinavian countries pursued

23 Spain was not among the countries that were used to identify the three welfare regimes.

24 Esping-Andersen (1990: 53, 54) points out that the high degree of decommodification in Scandinavia did not exist before the 1950s, while Great Britain in the 1950s belonged to the countries with the highest degree of decommodification.

a highly decommodifying strategy. As regards the principles of unemployment insurance, social democratic and liberal regimes still converge more closely than the conservative regimes with either of them, but in terms of welfare outcomes conservative regimes increasingly take a middle position.[25]

2.4.2 *Critical assessment*

Despite their analytic and conceptual advantages, typologies are static structures that reflect a specific point in time but do not easily display changes. 'The three worlds of welfare capitalism' are, for example, based on the political, ideological and socio-economic conditions of the 1970s and 1980s. At that time, non-standard employment situations were still rare or just emerging, and society was dominated by male wage earners with relatively stable employment contracts. Accordingly, as Esping-Andersen (1999: 73) himself points out, from a contemporary perspective the typology is too strongly based on programmes that focus on a retention of work income and it refers too much to state–market connections and to the standard industrial worker.

Some critical contributions point to the idea that three welfare regimes might not suffice to categorise welfare states correctly (Ferrera 1996; Arts et al. 2002; Schulte 1998). Usually, a fourth regime is proposed that encompasses the southern Mediterranean countries ('southern model', 'Mediterranean regime', 'latin rim' or 'catch-up welfare state'), and in some cases singles out Japan, Australia and New Zealand. For the purpose of this paper the consideration of a fourth welfare regime could be important because Spain is usually assigned to this group.

In their study of labour market transitions Muffels et al. (2002: 10, 20), for example, use a welfare typology that includes a fourth southern regime consisting of Spain, Portugal, Greece and Italy. Not only do the specific constellation of flexibility and work security point to the existence of a fourth regime whose outcomes differ strongly from those of the other regimes, but an empirical test of the reliability of this classification also proves its relevance. By looking at welfare institutions and rules in Italy, Spain, Portugal and Greece, Ferrera (1996) identifies the following main components of the southern model: fragmented income maintenance systems, dualistic social protection schemes with relatively generous protection for the core sector and very weak protection of 'outsiders', low state penetration of the welfare sphere and persistent clientelism.

25 Ziegelmayer (2001: 72) stresses that the German model is to be placed between the social democratic and the liberal market model, or between solidarity and subsidiarity.

Castles et al. (1993), based on data from the Luxembourg Income Study and on information on partisan politics and trade union density, propose splitting the group of liberal welfare states into a liberal and a 'radical' welfare regime. While both are characterised by low social expenditure, the distinctive feature is benefit equality through redistribution: the liberal welfare regime disposes of low levels of benefit equality; the 'radical' welfare regime consisting of the United Kingdom, New Zealand and Australia generates high levels of benefit equality.[26]

Since women form a considerable part of non-standard workers, especially among part-time workers, the feminist critics of Esping-Andersen's typology will be assessed shortly. Langan et al. (1991: 130 et seqq.) and Ostner (1998) criticise the fact that, although welfare regime institutions considerably influence women's labour market participation, neither women nor the family are systematically theorised in welfare regime typologies. From a feminist point of view, Esping-Andersen's typology incorporates at least three shortcomings: the family and its maintenance potential are not given a weight comparable to that of the economy and the state, therefore the distinctiveness of welfare production within families is neglected (Ostner 1998: 228 et seqq.). Secondly, and this critical point is especially noteworthy within the framework of this study, continuous full-time employment and the corresponding social rights are at the centre of analysis. This is not adequate as concerns the position of non-working women but also of non-standard workers in the labour market. Thirdly, especially for women, decommodification as central criterion for the quality of the welfare state is problematic insofar as in many cases the precondition of exiting the labour market – regular employment – is not given in the first place.[27] How are welfare regimes re-conceptualised from a gender perspective? In particular, Esping-Andersen's partisanship towards the social-democratic welfare regime is called into question. At first sight, in this regime high consideration is given to the situation of women in the labour market. Social insurance and tax policies that are focused on the individual are beneficial to women's employment. Additionally, double-wage-earner families are supported through comprehensive social services. But it is often ignored that women's employment mainly takes place in the public sector, while men's employment is focussed on the private economy. Formerly unpaid care responsibilities are primarily taken over by women, leading to a high degree of gendered labour market segmentation. The conservative or 'Bismarck-

26 Possible members of a Mediterranean regime were not considered in this study, except for Italy.

27 Sainsbury (1996: 129–147) offers a critical contribution to the stratification concept by looking at women's and men's social benefit entitlements. She especially criticises the fact that Esping-Andersen's typology excludes consideration of the interplay between different eligibility principles (instead he associated one dominant principle with each welfare regime type) and the complete neglect of derived entitlements and the principle of care.

ian' welfare regime is characterised as a 'gendered status maintenance model'. Traditional allocation of wage and household work between men and women is still supported; due to their dependent position women not only face high risks but also lack bargaining power. In contrast to Esping-Andersen (1996: 68) and Schönig (2001: 412), who accord the conservative welfare regime a very low adaptability as regards higher labour market flexibility and economic independence of women, with regard to Germany Ostner (1998: 246 et seqq.) points out a variety of starting points for identity upholding reforms. The researcher, however, remains critical of women's social security gains resulting from an expansion of part-time work or other flexible employment forms between market and family. Feminist analysis of the Anglo-Saxon welfare regime also reveals deficient outcomes. Equality outcomes are an important aim but while they might be achieved if the market alone is regarded, equality does not hold for the private sphere. The accentuation of the market in combination with only residual benefits strengthens the role of women as workers, but at the same time women are treated as if they did not have any special care obligations. This does not take account of their real situation. The Mediterranean regime is referred to as a 'mixed women's family support economy'. Labour market participation of women in this regime often takes place in labour market segments which generate neither acceptable work conditions nor sufficient security. Women thus remain dependent on family welfare; the existing social programmes support a passive status for women rather than working mothers (Langan et al. 1991: 141). Esping-Andersen (1999) reacted to feminist critics by publishing a comprehensive contribution on this issue. Although welfare regimes are enriched by information on women's position in the labour market and in the household, this information is not used systematically to review and possibly modify the existing welfare regime typology.

2.5 Assumptions from theory

The risk-taking and -absorbing function of the welfare state and its social insurance programmes should not be underestimated. Risks in the labour market can take on multiple forms. Here, risks associated with non-standard employment situations (unemployment or inactivity, and insufficient social insurance coverage) are at the centre of the analysis. If the positive functions of risk taking – increased job possibilities, higher aggregate income and possibly also higher productivity – are to get the upper hand, the risks associated with non-standard employment have to be tackled and mitigated. Institutional trust has to be built up.

Labour market segmentation exists not only between standard and non-standard workers but also between different groups of non-standard workers. It can be assumed that type and significance of risk varies considerably, depending on specific characteristics. Highly qualified individuals who are engaged in fixed-term project work probably do not face the same unemployment risks as low qualified temporary workers. Additionally, the level of personal income but also the household context plays an important role. Voluntary part-time workers who can rely on the income of a full-time working spouse are to be judged differently from persons who undertake part-time work involuntarily because of a particular family situation or insufficient child care. Accordingly, socio-demographic, qualification and employment characteristics as well as the household context of non-standard workers have to be taken into account in further analysis. Compensation of individual entitlement to insurance benefits by household income is contestable, however, because risk management within the family is often not gender neutral.

We assume that through its regulatory function the state considerably influences the extent and composition of labour market segmentation; this will be regarded more closely in Chapter 4.

Welfare regime theory showed that the question as to which institutions are meant to manage risks is answered differently from welfare regime to welfare regime. In corporatist and even more so in Mediterranean welfare regimes the family is still accorded an important role in risk management; the state usually steps in when risk management through the family fails or is insufficient. In social-democratic welfare regimes, on the other hand, the state is much more central for risk management, which can, for example, be observed in the importance accorded to the public provision of services such as child care. In the liberal welfare regimes risk management through the market is attributed prime importance. We thus assume that the context of risk-taking situations, their cultural meanings and associations vary between countries. Usually, more comprehensive social insurance is expected in countries with a strong state. In contrast, in countries that place high importance on risk management through the family or the market a more deficient or asymmetrical distribution of public insurance is expected. The viability of these assumptions in the case of unemployment insurance will be tested.

What hypothesis for further analysis can we derive from insurance theory? The theoretical part showed that public organisation of unemployment insurance is very important for non-standard workers because it makes a pooling solution possible. Publicly organised unemployment insurance in most cases eliminates competition and thus prevents good risks from opting for more profitable alternative insurance. The state, as opposed to private contractors, clearly has a higher interest in achieving comprehensive insurance because insurance deficits would have to be compensated through social assistance or the like. Since all established unemployment insurance systems are organised publicly this criterion is not adequate for deriving hypotheses.

Voluntary as opposed to compulsory organisation of unemployment insurance is a better discriminator. Among the countries examined here, only the Danish unemployment insurance system is voluntary. At first sight, compulsory insurance seems more adequate for covering special risks. But since voluntary unemployment insurance systems in Europe operate with uniform premiums and level out deficiencies through high tax financing they are assumed to cover the risks of the non-standard employed at least as well as obligatory systems.

As regards financing principles, the first hypothesis that can be drawn is that tax financing, which by definition is based on a broader group, probably generates a more inclusive system than contribution financing. The assumption that contribution financing more likely results in a perceived entitlement right further complicating redistribution adds to this hypothesis. Hypotheses can also be drawn from the perceived aims of the respective unemployment insurance systems. Schemes that more strongly promote the maintenance of accustomed living standards (insurance principle) by, for example, making use of high earnings ceilings are probably less adequate for non-standard workers than those that aim to prevent and mitigate poverty (welfare principle) through either flat-rate benefits or the application of low maximum benefits. The part on redistribution has shown, however, that redistributive effects tend to be limited if expenditure is small – resulting, for example, in very low flat-rate benefits. We can therefore assume that tax financing, coupled with relatively low maximum benefits and high expenditure, generates the highest degree of inclusiveness and equality. Until now, assumptions have remained at a rather general level. Table 3 presents the dominant principles in the countries under observation. It makes it possible to deduce more solid hypotheses on the insurance situation of non-standard workers in the different countries.

Denmark is the only country in this sample that operates with voluntary unemployment insurance. One point that indicates higher inclusiveness of voluntary systems is that, in contrast to most other systems, they are open to self-employed people. On the other hand, the voluntary character could possibly lead to the deliberate recourse of non-standard workers to alternative benefits. Questions relating to this issue cannot be answered with the data at hand. The voluntary organisation of unemployment insurance in Denmark should be kept in mind when interpreting analytical results, but no great distortions of the comparability of results are expected because most people are members of an unemployment

Table 3: Unemployment insurance principles

	Denmark	Germany	Spain	United Kingdom
welfare regime affiliation	Social democratic	Conservative	Mediterranean (controversial)	Liberal (not very strong)
public vs private	public, but administration through trade unions	public	public	public
voluntary vs compulsory	voluntary	compulsory	compulsory	compulsory
contributory vs tax financing	contributory financing (partly flat-rate) global contributions to the Labour Market Fund	contributory financing of unemployment insurance, tax financing of unemployment assistance and deficit financing	global contributions to systems of social security, the state covers the costs of unemployment benefits that are not covered by contributions	mix of contribution financing (contribution-based JSA*) and tax financing (income-based JSA) per capita national insurance fund contribution dependent on income
equivalence vs welfare principle	mix of equivalence and welfare principles – strong welfare component due to low benefit ceilings	equivalence principle – high ceilings, family components	equivalence principle	welfare principle (global contribution to general national insurance and flat-rate benefits)
general redistribution (theoretical)	+	–	–	? (welfare principle, weak contributory system, relatively low spending)
family-related redistribution	– (strongly individualised system)	+	+	– (contribution-based JSA) + (income-based JSA)
means for redistribution**	high (2.68)	relatively high (2.31)	medium (1.50)	low (0.37)

Note: * JSA: Job Seekers' Allowance; ** public expenditure on passive benefits as percentage of GDP in 2003, OECD (2005).

insurance fund. Contributions are paid globally and are partly earnings related and partly flat-rate (weak equivalence principle), which might favour redistribution. Benefit payments are earnings related but redistribution takes place via low benefit ceilings, which is assumed to be favourable for non-standard workers with low earnings (especially part-time employees).

In the United Kingdom the equivalence principle is rather weak because no specific unemployment insurance contribution is levied, but only a general National Insurance contribution. Therefore there is no clear connection between premium payments and subsequent benefits, which is further supported by the flat-rate nature of benefit payments. All this speaks for a potentially high degree of redistribution. A reason why this system may nevertheless not be as favourable to non-standard workers as the Danish one might be the fact that overall expenditure on unemployment benefits is comparatively low.

In the unemployment insurance systems of Germany and Spain there is a strong link between contributions and benefits (equivalence principle). Both schemes aim at maintaining accustomed living standards and therefore are presumably less redistributive than their British and Danish counterparts. This should be especially true for Germany which operates with high benefit ceilings and thereby provokes status maintenance. On the other hand, financial means that can be used for redistribution are high in Germany, which could counteract this effect.

Chapter 5 will look more closely at country-specific design features of unemployment insurance that might either benefit or stand in the way of comprehensive coverage of non-standard workers. In the following two chapters the labour market situation in the four countries, with a special focus on non-standard employment, moves to the centre of analysis – we discuss the extent of non-standard employment, as well as its regulation.

3 Labour market indicators and the occurrence of non-standard employment

This section provides information on the development of non-standard employment. It is important to take into account the wider labour market situation. People might be more inclined to take up temporary employment in labour markets that are characterised by high unemployment. Another assumption is that part-time employment is more relevant in countries with high employment and low inactivity rates for women. The following sections do not attempt to confirm or reject these assumptions, but the discussion of the extent and development of non-standard employment within the broader labour market framework may allow us to discover certain country-specific patterns. In some instances the indicators are broken down by gender, age and qualification levels; furthermore, reasons for taking up part-time or temporary employment are looked at. This will not only allow us to outline country differences in the extent and composition of non-standard employment and unemployment, but will also help us to condense information on which control variables to include in the empirical models.

The following figures are derived from the European Union Labour Force Survey which provides comparable quarterly data on EU, EFTA and candidate countries. The sample survey is representative for the population. The design of the Labour Force Survey is highly suitable for cross-sectional comparison of the development of labour market indicators.

Annual comparative Labour Force Surveys comprising all EU countries have been taking place since 1983. Persons living in private households aged 15 and over are targeted. The results of the survey refer to the labour force characteristics of the interviewed person in a particular week. The country surveys are based on rotating random samples, comprising at least two waves; they are not harmonised. The sampled individuals are interviewed face to face; follow-up interviews are conducted via telephone in some countries. Some of the data can be supplied by way of equivalent information from sources such as population registers; this frequently takes place in the Scandinavian countries.

Comparability of nationally conducted Labour Force Surveys is ensured through the common application of ILO definitions, close links between a common EU list of questions and national questionnaires, application of classifications such as NACE or ISCED[28] and central processing by Eurostat.[29] The content of the Labour Force Survey has remained very stable, ensuring high comparability of results between successive surveys. Potential factors reducing comparability are time-varying reference periods, possible modification of the sample design and varying political and social circumstances that might influence response behaviour (European Commission 2003a: 11).

An essential advantage of Labour Force Survey data as compared to enterprise surveys or administrative records is that they include information about persons outside the labour force and therefore give a more realistic picture of a country. The Labour Force Survey questions refer to three mutually exclusive groups: (i) persons in employment, (ii) unemployment and (iii) inactivity. The following figures display the second calendar quarter data of every survey year available for all countries.[30] The German data include information on the former GDR from 1991 onwards. If not stated otherwise, the figures refer to persons aged 15 (16 in the United Kingdom and Spain) to 64. The ECHP that will be used for the micro-analysis in Section 6 only covers eight years from the mid-1990s to 2001. In order to better frame the later analysis this chapter takes a broader perspective: data in the Labour Force Survey are available from 1983 up to 2004. A range of general indicators will depict labour market developments of the last 20 years. Although labour market indicators often vary strongly between different regions of one country (for example, East and West Germany) the focus here will be on the country average. This is feasible because country comparisons stand in the foreground, and the design of benefit schemes – which is the main concern here – does not vary within the countries (European Commission 2003a: 11–90).

3.1 Labour market developments

Figure 1 compares the development of unemployment in the four countries from 1987 to 2004. The unemployed are persons aged 15 (16) to 64 who were without work during the reference week, were currently available for work and were

28 NACE: Classification of Economic Activities in the European Communities; ISCED: International Standard Classification of Education. For more information, see http://europa.eu.int/comm/eurostat/ramon/

29 Information on the main characteristics of the national surveys can be found in European Commission (2005).

30 Of the countries under observation only the United Kingdom uses seasonal quarters; the reference period for the United Kingdom is therefore not April to June, but March to May.

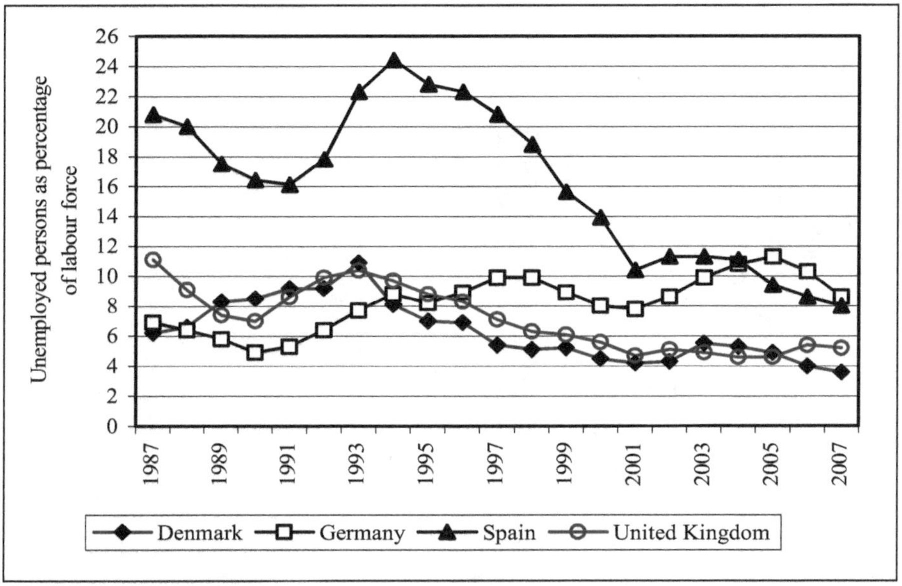

Figure 1: Development of unemployment.
Source: Eurostat LFS data.

either actively seeking work in the past four weeks or had already found a job, starting within the next three months.[31]

Both Denmark and the United Kingdom have experienced declining unemployment rates since the mid-1990s and presently are performing comparatively well, with unemployment rates of 3.6 and 5.2 per cent, respectively. Unemployment in Germany increased strongly after reunification, decreased somewhat at the end of the 1990s, before reaching an all-time high of 10.8 per cent in 2004; it currently lies at 8.6 per cent. Spain's 2007 unemployment performance is similar to Germany's, although in Spain the development has gone in the opposite direction; unemployment affected almost 25 per cent of the labour force in 1994 and since then has been decreasing significantly.

In Denmark, the United Kingdom and Germany differences between men's and women's unemployment are relatively small, while in Spain they are considerable. In spite of huge improvements as compared to the late 1990s, 10.5 per cent of Spanish women as compared to 6.1 per cent of men were unemployed in

31 All the following definitions will be based on the European Commission (2003a: 11–90). On definitions used in the labour force survey data (LFS), compare also Romans and Hardarson (2005: 11).

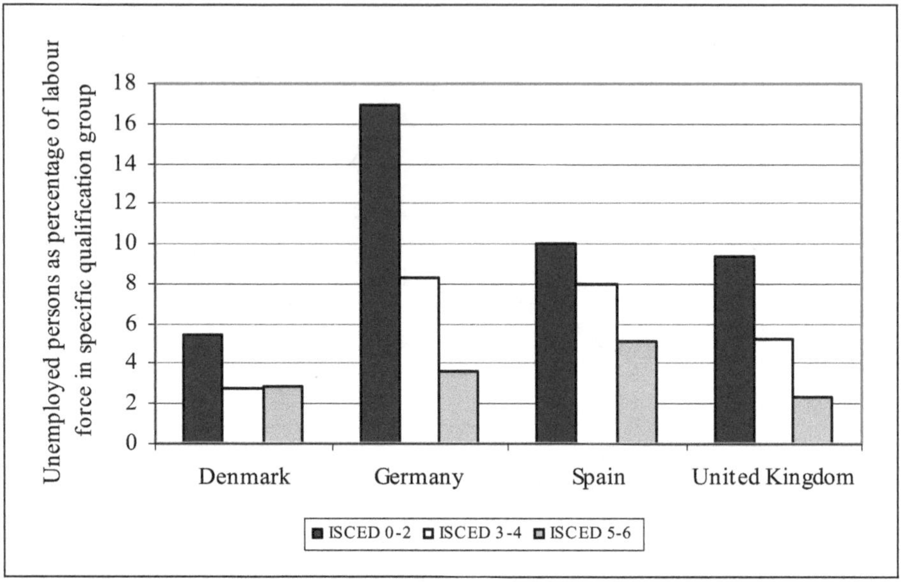

Figure 2: Unemployment rates by qualification level in 2007.
Source: Eurostat LFS data.

2007. Young persons aged 15 to 24 are more strongly affected by unemployment than other age groups in all countries. Differences are smallest in Germany, followed by Denmark, while youth unemployment is more than twice as high as adult unemployment in the United Kingdom and Spain. Unemployment rates also vary with qualification levels; the lower qualified are more affected by unemployment. Dispersion is closest in Denmark and Spain, while differences between qualification groups are very pronounced in Germany, where workers with less than upper secondary education (ISCED 1 or 2)[32] face unemployment rates of about 17 per cent and those with tertiary education (ISCED 5 or 6) rates of only 3.6 per cent (compare Figure 2).

The focus should not only be on the unemployment rate and composition at a given time point; if one is interested in the receipt of benefit the duration of unemployment is of central importance. Figure 3 shows that in Denmark the unemployment spell is five months or shorter for around 70 per cent of the unemployed; in Spain and the United Kingdom this applies to around 60 per cent; whereas in Germany it is true for only around 30 per cent. With less than 20 per

32 For a definition of the different ISCED levels, see European Commission (2003a: 89, 90).

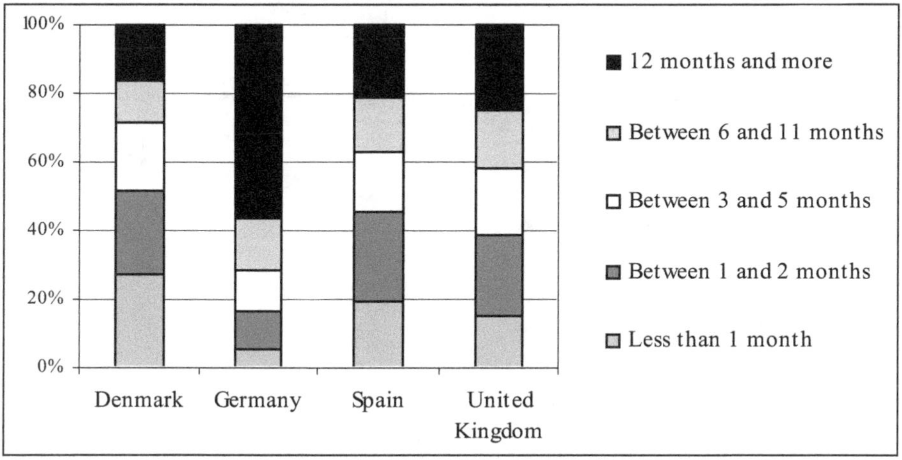

Figure 3: Duration of unemployment in 2007.
Source: Eurostat LFS data.

cent in Denmark and slightly above 20 per cent in the United Kingdom and Spain, comparatively fewer people are affected by long-term unemployment (twelve months or longer). In contrast, in Germany the share is about 55 per cent.[33]

Downward trends in long-term unemployment could be observed since the late 1990s in Denmark, the United Kingdom and Spain, while in Germany there has been an upward trend since 2002. The recent German trend to use labour market policies in a more preventive way in order to avoid long-term unemployment in the first place is not yet observable in the data. The extent of long-term unemployment can be influenced in different ways. A country that makes strong use of active labour market policy measures at an early stage of unemployment – Denmark, for example – is likely to have relatively low long-term unemployment rates. Additionally, the incentives to remain registered as unemployed 'long-term' vary between countries. Comprehensive information on the problems of comparing long-term unemployment is given in OECD (2002b). The picture might become somewhat clearer if we look at employment rates and the inactive population.

33 Shorter unemployment duration does not necessarily mean that people return to employment faster. Shorter durations can also be brought about by more and faster transitions into inactivity or labour market measures. For the United Kingdom of the early 1990s, Cebulla (2001: 611), for example, states that only two-thirds of those who left unemployment within 14 weeks took up employment. Later, transition analysis will help us to solve some of the uncertainty of this indicator.

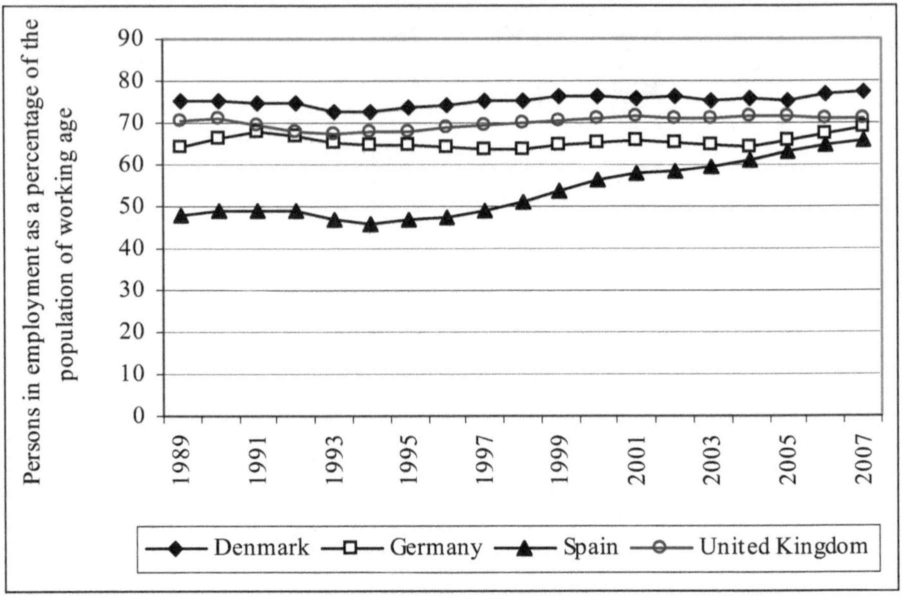

Figure 4: Development of employment rates .
Source: Eurostat LFS data.

In the Labour Force Survey all interviewed persons who work at least one hour for pay or profit during the reference week or who are temporarily absent from a job are considered employed (Romans et al. 2005: 11). Based on this broad definition the employment rate is and has long been highest in Denmark (77 per cent). In Spain, despite strong increases over the last 10 years it is still comparatively low at 66 per cent. Due to the recent increases, at 69 per cent the German employment rate is only slightly lower than the UK employment rate (71 per cent) (compare Figure 4).

Spain has experienced the biggest upward trend over the last 20 years, starting from a very low level; the increase of almost 20 percentage points is mainly due to constantly rising employment rates of women. Nevertheless, the employment rate of women still is lower than 55 per cent of the working age population and therefore clearly lies below the European Employment Strategy's 2010 target of 60 per cent (compare Figure 5). Similarly, in Germany increases in overall employment rates have in large part been due to increases among women. Within ten years the female employment rate increased by 8 percentage points to the current level of about 64 per cent and thus very close to the UK female employ-

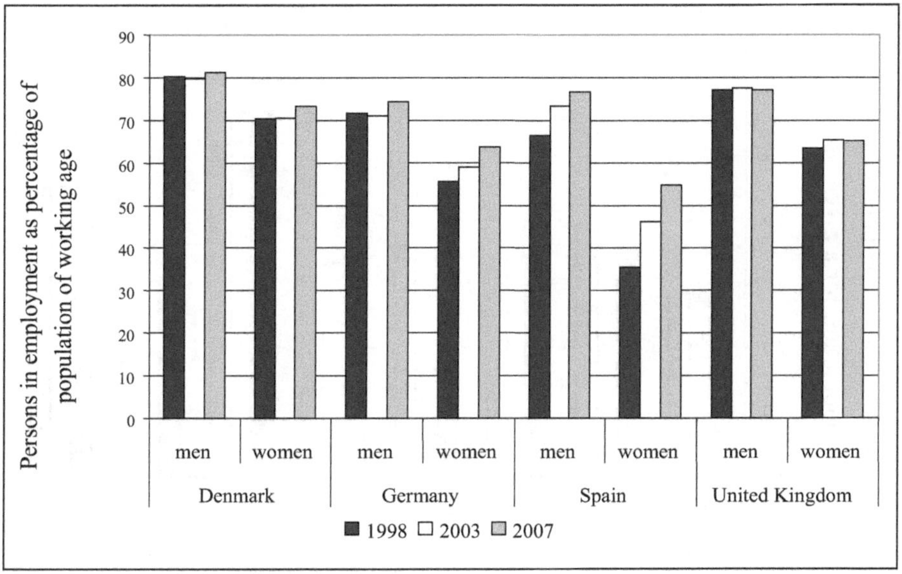

Figure 5: Development of employment rates by gender: 1998, 2003 and 2007.
Source: Eurostat LFS data.

ment rate (65 per cent). In Denmark, differences between men and women are clearly smallest and the last few years have seen some significant increases in female employment rates (73 per cent), up from an already high level.

High unemployment rates among the low qualified are in all countries accompanied by much lower employment rates as compared to the highest qualified. The average employment rate differences between persons with the lowest and persons with the highest qualification levels account for more than 40 percentage points in Germany, more than 25 in the United Kingdom and Spain and close to 20 in Denmark.

Another important labour market indicator is inactivity (compare Figure 6). It is very stable over time for Denmark and, especially for women, comparatively low (39 per cent). Inactivity among women remains considerably higher in the other three countries, but all of them have shown clear improvements in this regard. Germany and Spain show some recent improvements, with inactivity rates of 47 and 52 per cent respectively, while improvements in the UK mainly took place in the late 1980s and in the 1990s. In the UK the inactivity rate of women is currently 45 per cent.

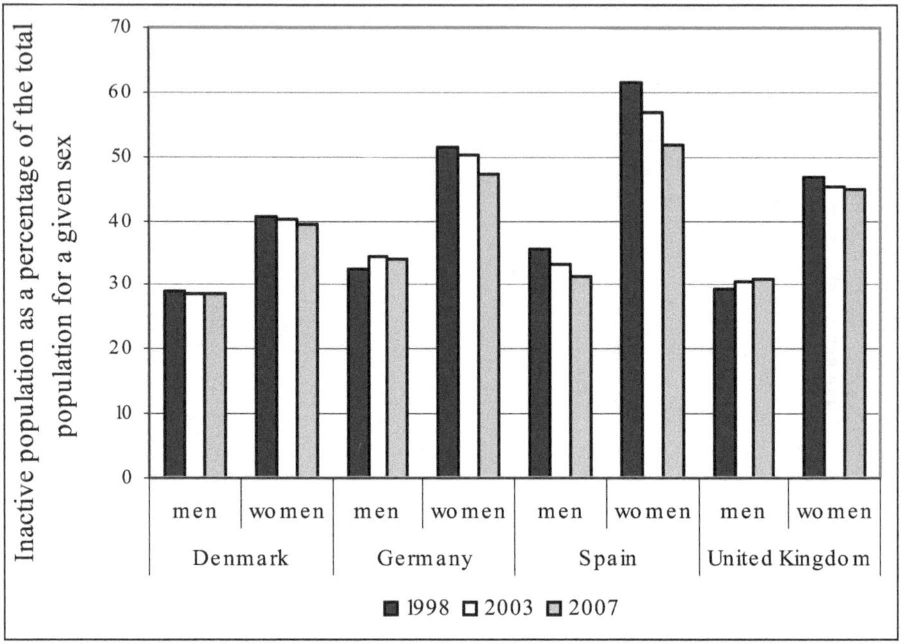

Figure 6: Development of inactive population by gender: 1998, 2003 and 2007.
Source: Eurostat LFS data.

To resume, labour market performance is most favourable and most stable in Denmark, which combines low unemployment rates and low inactivity rates for both men and women with high employment rates. Equality between men and women and between different qualification groups is also highest in Denmark in the four-country comparison. The United Kingdom also performs comparatively well on the above indicators. Germany has lately seen some improvements in its unemployment rates, and employment-wise its outcomes now are close to the UK ones. Nevertheless, large differences in outcomes remain between low and high qualified, and long-term unemployment is by far the highest in Germany. Spain has also considerably improved its performance in relation to employment and unemployment, but gender differences in unemployment rates remain large and inactivity rates of women are still considerably higher than in the other three countries.

Sections 3.2 assess the share and characteristics of the active population in non-standard employment. How pronounced are non-standard employment forms in the four countries? Have there been upward or downward trends? Do high part-time employment rates go along with high temporary employment rates? Does the extent of part-time employment go hand in hand with women's employment rates?

3.2 Part-time employment

The distinction between full-time and part-time employment in the Labour Force Survey data is based on self-assessment of the interviewed persons and thus depends on whether a person perceives his or her employment contract as part-time or full-time.[34] Already in the early 1990s, part-time employment rates had been above 20 per cent in the United Kingdom and Denmark (compare Figure 7). Part-time employment in the United Kingdom increased steadily to its present level of 25 per cent, whereas part-time employment rates in Denmark have been decreasing from a high level for many years and only recently picked up again. In contrast to the other countries, women's employment in Denmark had already been high in the late 1980s and has remained relatively stable over the last 20 years. Germany and, especially, Spain started at moderate part-time levels of 15 and 5 per cent, respectively. Strongly increasing employment rates of women were accompanied by increasing part-time employment rates in both countries, but growth was much greater in Germany, where part-time employment has now surpassed the Danish and British levels. Part-time employment in Spain, as in the other Southern countries, remains comparatively low, at 12 per cent in 2007.

Part-time employment is the domain of women. In the United Kingdom and Germany more than 40 per cent of total employment of women takes place as part-time employment. In Denmark this share is somewhat lower, at about 35 per cent, and in Spain it is only 23 per cent. In Germany the share has been strongly increasing over the last 20 years, while it has decreased by ten percentage points in Denmark – possible reasons for this development will be discussed in Chapter 4. Participation of men in part-time employment increased slightly in all countries under observation but remains marginal, with shares of 4 (Spain), 9 (Germany and the United Kingdom) and 12 per cent (Denmark) of total male employment.

34 The part-time indicator in the European Community Household Panel, which will be used in Section 6, is mainly based on working hours. People who state that they usually work fewer than 30 hours a week are automatically classified as part-time workers.

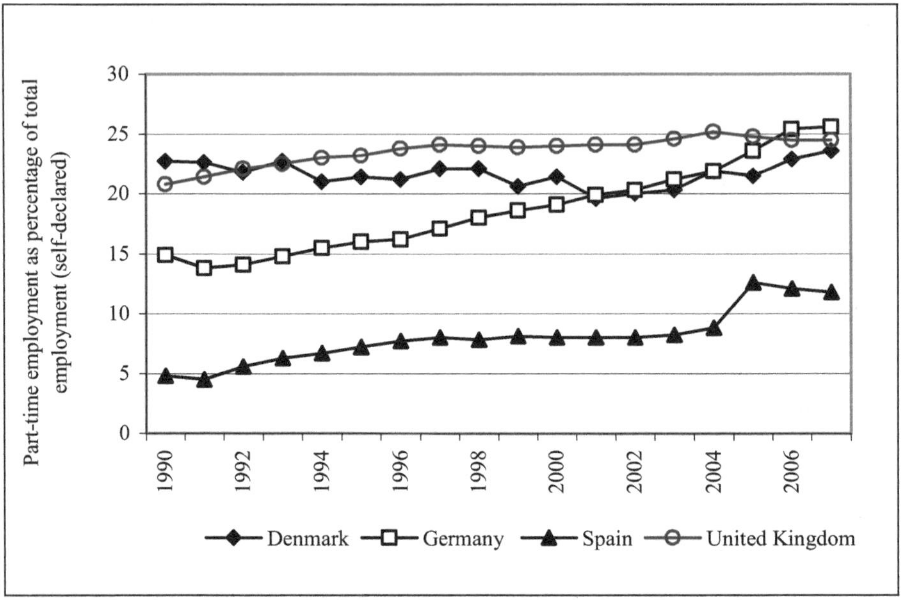

Figure 7: Development of part-time employment.
Source: Eurostat LFS data.

The level of education is inversely related to women's part-time employment rate; the higher the qualification level the lower the share of part-time work in the total employment of a given education group (compare Figure 8). People with the lowest qualification levels have part-time employment shares of around 50 per cent in Germany and the United Kingdom, around 45 per cent in Denmark and 30 per cent in Spain.[35] In contrast, among people with the highest qualification level the part-time shares range from 16 per cent in Spain to 36 per cent in Germany. The concentration of low qualified people in part-time employment is especially problematic because the coupling of low hours and low hourly wages leaves them with marginal incomes that in many welfare states are carried forward into the benefit schemes – if they are eligible at all.

35 The Danish results are driven by the fact that part-time employment is often used by students who have not yet reached their highest education level.

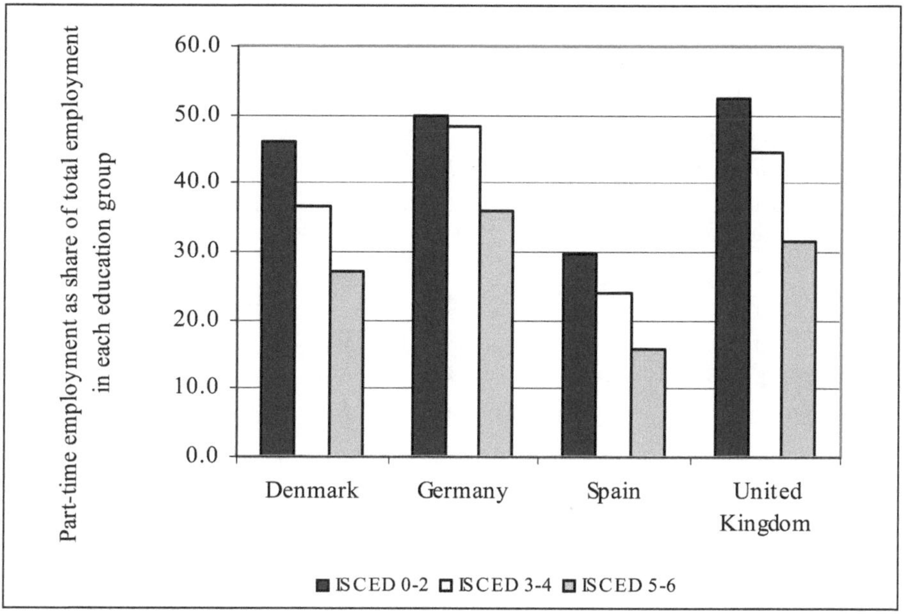

Figure 8: Share of women's part-time employment by level of education in 2007.
Source: Eurostat LFS data.

If we look at part-time employment for different age groups we are faced with high country variation (compare Figure 9). In Denmark and, to a lesser degree, Spain, young people work part-time to a much higher degree than other age groups. Especially in Denmark this is due to a combination of work and studies (compare Hoffmann et al. 2003: 37–42). In Germany, among women part-time employment increases with age; the part-time employment rate of middle aged and elderly women is more than 20 percentage points higher than that of young employees. In the United Kingdom age differences are less pronounced than in the other countries. In all countries part-time employment is used as a transitional route into retirement, especially among women.

In order to illustrate why part-time employment is used in the countries under observation, we shall now explore motives for working part-time more comprehensively. The central question is whether part-time employment is exercised voluntarily, or workers – mostly women – have no other choice; in the latter case it might be even more essential to compensate the need to work part-time by adequate insurance coverage. We expect that middle-aged women, at least in

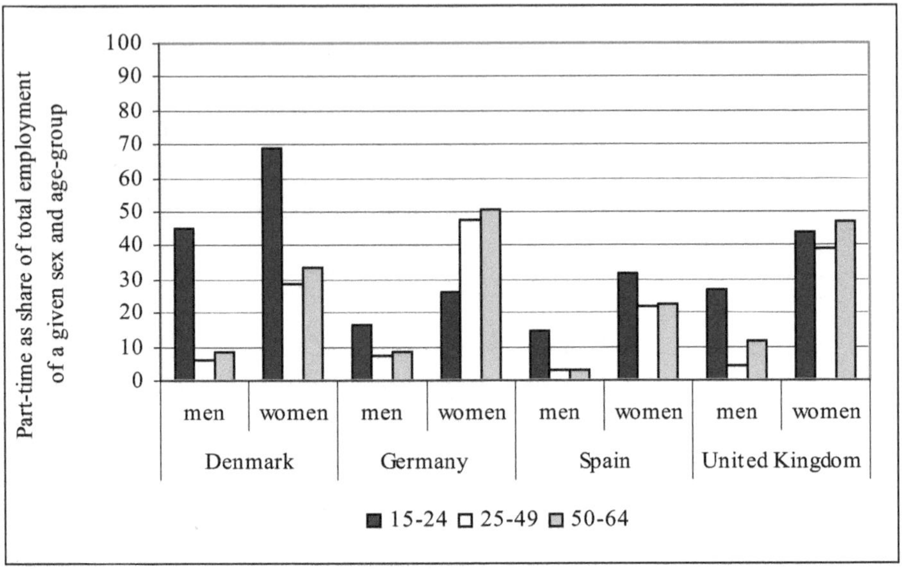

Figure 9: Part-time employment by gender and age-group in 2007.
Source: Eurostat LFS data.

countries that still adhere to the male breadwinner model, often indicate family reasons. But is this the case for all the countries under consideration? This assumption seems to be true only for Germany and the United Kingdom, where about 70 per cent of part-time employed women between 25 and 49 declare that they chose part-time employment due to family responsibilities (see Figure 10). In Denmark this share stands lies at only 5 per cent, and in Spain at 15 per cent.[36] It can be assumed that the underlying reasons for these low shares vary strongly between the two countries. In Denmark this result can be traced back to high coverage with child-care facilities, especially for very young children; we shall examine this in the following section (Eichhorst et al. 2001: 414). In Spain, on the other hand, permanent withdrawal from the labour market after marriage or childbirth is still common (OECD 2002d: 70–73). In Denmark, in contrast to the other countries, voluntary part-time employment is high: over 50 per cent of part-time workers state that they do not want a full-time job. This share stands at only around 10 per cent in the other three countries. A combination of education or training and part-time employment plays a substantial role only in Denmark.

36 Assessing the results for Spain is difficult since 50 per cent of the sample state "other reasons", on whose contents we have no information.

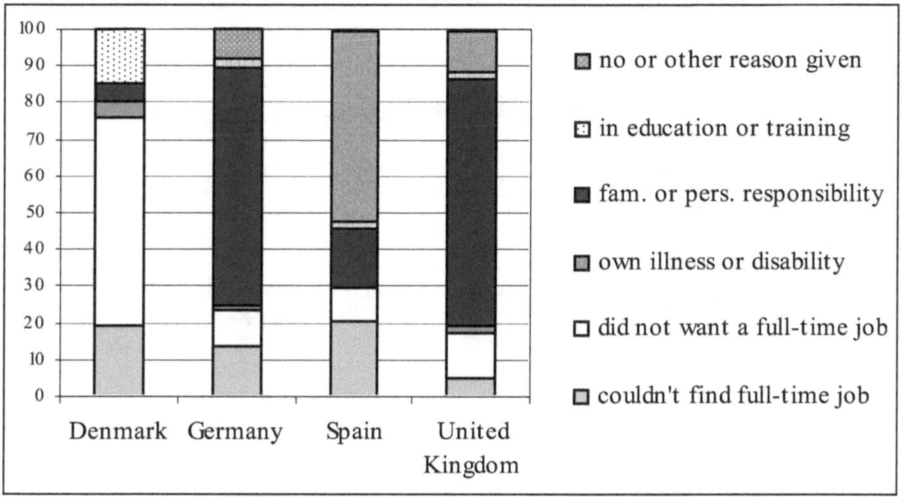

Figure 10: Reasons for women to work part-time in 2004 (25–49 years).
Source: Eurostat LFS data. In more recent data releases the response category that depicts voluntary part-time employment "did not want a full-time job" has been dropped. We therefore report 2004 data.

If we look at the reasons why young people work part-time, our assumption for Denmark that high part-time employment in this group results from a combination of education and employment proves true. In Denmark 80 per cent of young workers (15–24 years) state as the reason for part-time employment education or training; in the United Kingdom this share is 72 per cent, in Germany 45 per cent and in Spain only 20 per cent (not shown). In the latter two countries the share of workers who could not find full-time employment in this age group is comparatively high, at around 25 per cent.

3.3 Temporary employment

According to the OECD (2002c) temporary jobs are less stable, tend to pay less than permanent ones – the differences are especially high in Spain – and sometimes restrict access to training measures, sick leave, unemployment benefits and other fringe benefits.

According to the Labour Force Survey definition a job may be considered temporary if employer and employee agree that the end of the job is determined

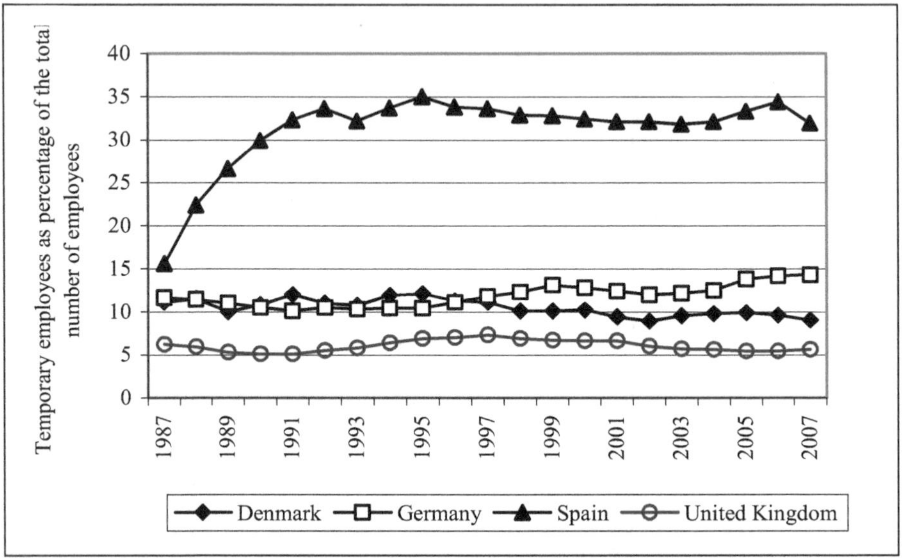

Figure 11: Development of temporary employment.
Source: Eurostat LFS data.

by objective conditions, such as a specific date, the completion of a task or the return of an employee who has been temporarily replaced.[37]

Temporary employment in Spain increased drastically between the late 1980s and the mid-1990s (Figure 11). It reached its peak in 1995 and at present lies at 32 per cent of total employment. Among the EU countries, Spain is way ahead on this indicator. In Germany, gradual increases can be observed since the late 1980s, and temporary employment has now reached 14 per cent. For the other two countries, on the aggregate level not much has happened; temporary employment shares are 5.6 per cent in the United Kingdom and 9 per cent in Denmark. Except for Germany, where no difference is observed, women are more likely to be affected by temporary employment than men.

To capture real changes it is useful to look at absolute numbers instead of relative numbers (compare Figure 12). The size of the absolute level, of course, depends on the size of the labour force and can therefore not be compared be-

37 Furthermore, the following categories are termed temporary in the Labour Force Survey: persons with seasonal employment, persons engaged by an agency or employment exchange and hired to a third party (unless there is a written work contract of unlimited duration with the agency), and persons with specific training contracts (Eurostat 2007).

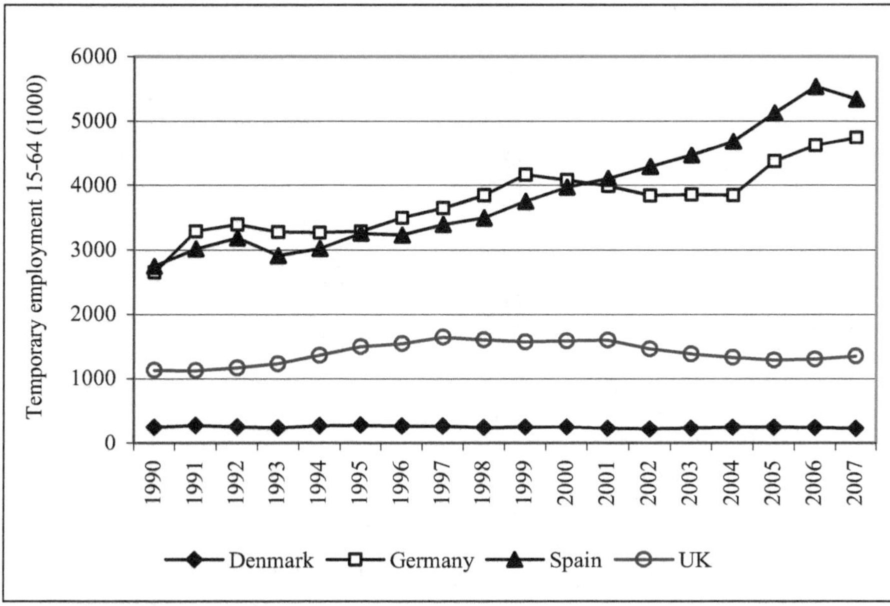

Figure 12: Development of temporary employment (absolute numbers in 1000).
Source: Eurostat LFS data.

tween countries; but if we look at developments over the years the increase in Germany is much greater (even if we do not take into account the natural jump after reunification) than the relative numbers suggest. The comparison between relative and absolute numbers for Spain shows that the increasing employment rate has been achieved through a further extension of temporary contracts during the last ten years.

Although at least in the United Kingdom, Denmark and Germany only a small part of all employees have a temporary contract, if we look at specific labour market sub-groups the outcome is different. In Germany and Spain, for example, 56 and 63 per cent of young employees (<25 years), respectively, have fixed-term contracts. In Denmark this share lies at 22 per cent, and in the United Kingdom at only 13 per cent. If temporary employment is assessed separately for different qualification groups the following picture emerges: in all countries except for the United Kingdom people with the lowest qualification level are affected by temporary employment to a higher degree – this pattern is especially evident in Germany, which may be explained by the fact that the training contracts of young employees who have not yet finished their education are often

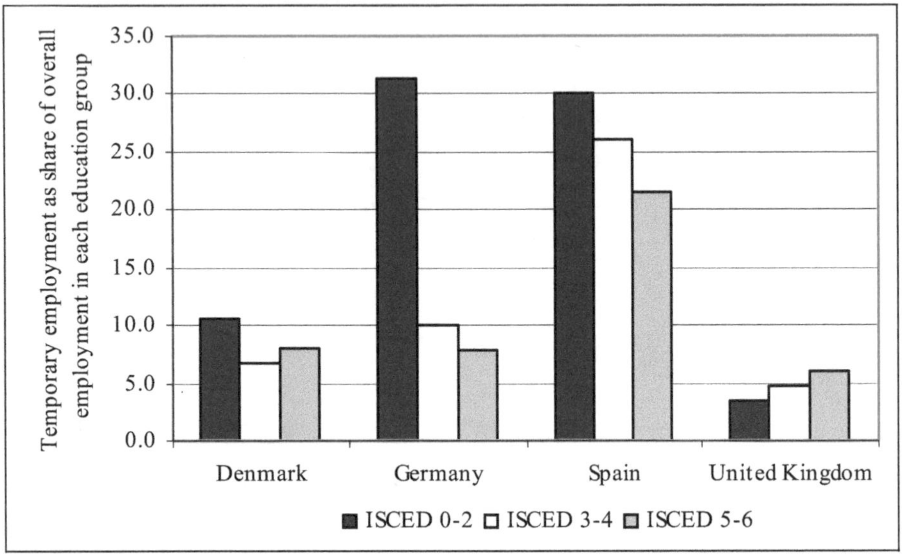

Figure 13: Share of temporary employment by level of education in 2007*. *Note*: * Due to some non-responses this figure is not entirely comparable to Figure 12.
Source: Eurostat LFS data.

temporary (see Figure 13). In the United Kingdom, the share of temporary employment in overall employment increases somewhat with the qualification level, which points to a different function for temporary employment in the United Kingdom (on this issue compare Slater 2003).

What are the reasons for taking up temporary employment? Once again, the country profiles differ strongly. In Spain, more than 90 per cent of all adult respondents (25–64 years) hold temporary jobs involuntarily, because they could not find a permanent job (compare Figure 14). In Denmark and in Germany, this is also true for the majority of respondents, whereas in the United Kingdom the share stands at only 47 per cent. In Denmark and Germany, about 16 and 19 per cent of adults have a temporary contract due to education or training. Among young workers in Germany and Denmark, 85 and 50 per cent, respectively, state as the reason for temporary employment that they are in training or education – this can be explained by the dual education systems that prevail in these countries (not shown). In the other two countries these shares are marginal. In the United Kingdom, about one third of young respondents could not find a permanent job, whereas about half of all respondents stated that they did not want a

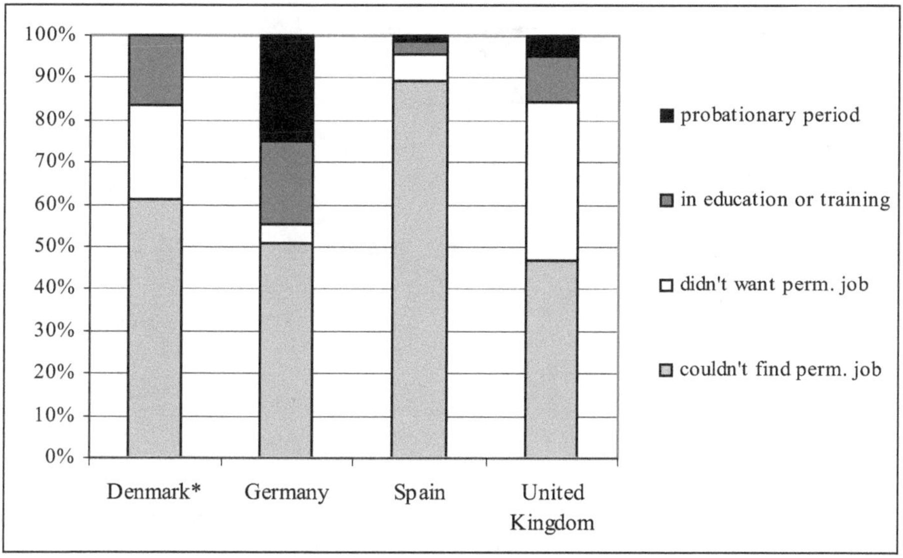

Figure 14: Reasons for temporary employment in 2006 (25–64 years).
Note: *Data missing for "probationary period".
Source: Eurostat LFS data.

permanent job. The situation looks very different in Spain, where three quarters of young people engage in temporary employment involuntarily.

Another important question is the average duration of temporary contracts. The longer the duration of the contract the more likely people are to gain entitlement to unemployment insurance benefits. In this regard we see large country differences. Contract duration is on average shortest in Spain, where more than 60 per cent of respondents have contracts of less than 6 months and about 80 per cent contracts of less than 12 months (compare Figure 15). The situation in Denmark looks somewhat better, but the majority of respondents nevertheless have contracts of less than one year; the share in Germany is about 45 per cent. The results for the United Kingdom cannot be easily interpreted because about half of all respondents did not answer the question.[38] The high non-response rate may be due to the fact that in the United Kingdom the share of casual contracts in overall temporary employment is comparatively high and contract duration is often not specified for casual contracts.

38 Evidence for the mid-1990s from the ECHP data indicates that about 50 per cent of temporary contracts in the United Kingdom are shorter than one year.

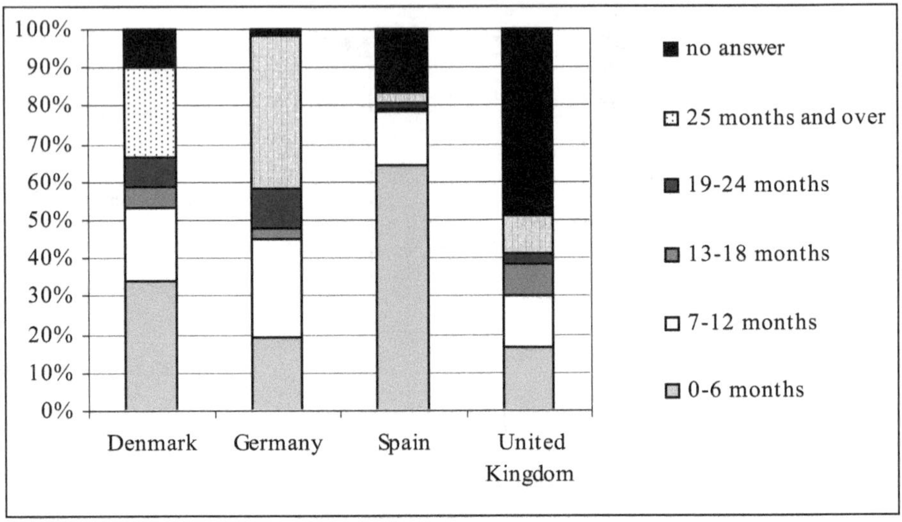

Figure 15: Duration of the temporary contract, 2007.
Source: Eurostat LFS data.

3.4 Extent of non-standard employment and implications for empirical analysis

As the above analysis has shown for some groups of workers – particularly women, but also the low qualified – non-standard or atypical employment has already become 'typical' (compare also Hutsebaut 2002: 3, 4). Table 4 presents the share of women who are either part-time or temporary workers or both in 2007.[39] At least in the countries looked at here, there is no clear pattern as to the use of non-standard employment forms. While Germany and Denmark combine high part-time employment rates with average temporary employment rates, the United Kingdom combines high part-time employment with low temporary employment. As in the other Southern European countries part-time employment is engaged in reluctantly in Spain, while the share of temporary employment is much higher than anywhere else.[40] Part-time employment in Spain seems to per-

39 Simultaneous part-time and temporary employment will be treated in Chapter 6.

40 Self-employment, especially solo self-employment – as another form of non-standard employment – is not taken into account here. Non-standard employment is therefore even more pronounced than stated above.

Table 4: Non-standard employment among women in 2007

%	Denmark	Germany	Spain	United Kingdom
Part-time	36	46	23	42
Temporary	10	14	33	6

Source: Eurostat LFS data.

form another function than in the other three countries – possible reasons for the relatively low use, such as discrimination or culture, will be looked at in Chapter 4.

The above analysis calls for carefully constructed empirical models. Especially for the mobility analysis that is to capture the downward (unemployment and inactivity) and upward (standard employment) mobility of part-time and temporary workers, the following characteristics should be controlled for: gender and presence of children to capture a possible need to take up part-time employment in the absence of sufficient child-care; human capital and job characteristics in order to take into account varying non-standard employment rates depending on qualification level and occupational sector; and age, which captures different propensities to exposure to part-time or temporary employment during the life cycle.

4 Regulation of temporary and part-time employment and reasons for using them

This chapter assembles information on the regulation of non-standard employment in the countries under analysis and provides some insights into possible reasons for taking up or making use of temporary contracts or part-time employment. Among young women and men, part-time work allows a combination of studies and work; for dual employment couples or for lone parents it constitutes a possibility to combine employment and care work; for the elderly, it is often used as a phased alternative to early retirement. Important determining factors for the labour market participation of parents – especially mothers – and their decision to take either full-time or part-time employment are availability and cost of child-care facilities, parental leave arrangements and, in the case of married couples, tax policies. The extent of part-time employment is also likely to be influenced by its regulation in national, as well as in international law. Booth et al. (2002a: 182) describe three important functions of temporary employment: expanded screening of young employees without sufficient work records (probation periods), replacement of permanent workers on leave and cost reduction through a firm's possibility to adapt to changes more easily. The pre-eminence of one or the other form of temporary contracts and the extent of temporary employment depends on the degree of regulation in the different countries. Regulation of temporary contracts is heavily influenced by the strictness of employment protection legislation.

A discussion of the above aspects is necessary in order to help us better judge the situation in the different countries. Furthermore, it will enable better informed decisions about which independent individual, household, and institutional variables to include in the empirical analysis. Section 4.1 will first give some insight into the regulation of both non-standard employment forms via a condensed account of the relevant EU directives. Subsequently, part-time employment regulations in the different countries will be described before the focus shifts to child-care availability and cost in order to capture an important factor potentially influencing the extent of part-time employment. In the case of temporary employment the influence on its extent of employment protection legislation is explored.

4.1 Framework agreements and directives on non-standard employment

After more than 15 years of unsuccessful European legislative initiatives on non-standard employment – UK Conservative governments had, for example, blocked proposals at Community level to adopt directives on part-time work – in 1997 and 1999 framework agreements were reached at EU level on the employment conditions of part-time and fixed-term workers (The Council of the European Union 1999, 1997).[41] They not only set out the general principles and minimum standards relating to part-time work and fixed-term contracts, but also aim to improve the quality of non-standard employment via removal of discrimination and prevention of abuse. The implementation via directives leaves the choice of form and methods to the member states – only the results are binding.[42]

The framework agreements remain very general in their requirements. This is due to the very different starting positions among the EU social partners that led to framework agreements that are heavily built on compromises (on this issue compare Falkner 2000). Most formulations are vague ("should", "shall"), and some categories of workers (initial vocational training, apprenticeship schemes, retraining, as well as part-time workers on a casual basis) are excluded. The Part-time Directive that emerged from the framework agreement on part-time work, for example, lays down only one compulsory minimum standard: part-time workers may not be treated less favourably than comparable full-time employees unless such unequal treatment is objectively justified. Employers are, for example, required to offer benefits such as pay, holidays and occupational pensions to part-time workers that are at least equivalent to the proportion of hours that they work in relation to a comparable full-time worker. Besides this compulsory part, 11 non-binding soft-law provisions are included in the Directive (Falkner et al. 2005: 159–161).

41 Signatory parties to these agreements are the European-level social partners (European Trade Union Confederation (ETUC), l'Union des Industries de la Communauté Européenne (UNICE) and the Centre Européen des Entreprises à Participation Publique et des Entreprises d'Intérêt Èconomique Général (CEEP).

42 Condensed information on the implementation process and problems, as well as on the legal impact of this directive in the single member states, is given in Clauwaert (2002) and European Commission (21/01/2003). A very good overview of the implementation of the Part-time Work Directive is given in Falkner (2005: 159–177).

There are no supranational competences on matters relating to statutory social security, but the preambles of both framework agreements recall the Employment Declaration of the Dublin European Council of December 1996 that emphasises the need to develop social protection systems capable of adapting to new work patterns and that provide protection to people engaged in such work. In its comments on the legislative text of the part-time framework agreement the European Trade Union Confederation (ETUC) calls for more pressure on governments to make social protection less dependent on continuous, full-time working patterns as a prerequisite of more flexible labour markets (Clauwaert 2002: 99). Similarly, the European Parliament criticised the exclusion of all questions of social security and the possibility to make exceptions to the principle of non-discrimination (Clauwaert 2002: 6). In the framework agreement on fixed-term work the necessity to adapt occupational social protection schemes to current conditions is explicitly mentioned. In this context ETUC emphasises the great importance of establishing more secure pension rights for people with non-standard contracts and embraces the employers' recognition of this fact, which should open up the floor for European and national level discussion (I. Schömann et al. 2003: 76).

In contrast to the EU part-time work directive, the ILO part-time work convention concluded in 1994 explicitly calls for the social protection of part-time workers: "Statutory social security schemes which are based on occupational activity shall be adapted so that part-time workers enjoy conditions equivalent to those of comparable full-time employees (ILO 1994a: article 6)." An extra clause excludes those workers whose working hours or earnings are below a specified threshold that is to be sufficiently low so as not to exclude "an unduly large percentage of part-time workers" and which is to be reviewed periodically (article 8). The impact of this convention can be considered as severely limited; only ten of the current 178 member countries have ratified it, among them five EU-15 countries but none of the countries treated here.[43] A part-time work recommendation adopted by the ILO's general conference further specified how social security schemes should be adapted. Especially interesting are the recommendations for a progressive reduction of earnings or hours thresholds and better access to private occupational schemes (ILO 1994b: 6(a), 7(1)).

43 The EU-15 countries that ratified this convention are Finland, Italy, Luxembourg, the Netherlands and Sweden.

4.2 Part-time employment

Part-time employment is usually defined in reference to full-time employment, where the normal number of working hours depends on the statutory provisions in force and on working hours specified in collective agreements that vary between industries and occupations. In all four countries, part-time work is defined rather vaguely as consisting of less than full-time hours (in the same enterprise, a comparable collective agreement or a comparable trade), which complies closely with the ILO definition.

National statistics on part-time employment are based on either self-declaration or an hours cut-off. In Germany, Spain and the United Kingdom a combination of both definitions is usually applied. Self-declared part-time jobs are reclassified as full-time if working time exceeds 36, 35 or 40 hours, respectively (Lemaître et al. 1997: 7, 8). In Denmark there is no official legal definition of part-time work; in the Labour Force Survey it is based on the respondent's own assessment (Bishop 2004, March: 115).

4.2.1 Equal treatment clauses

In the 1980s and 1990s part-time employment was in all four countries put on a par with full-time employment as concerns specific rights, such as employment protection legislation, rights to maternity leave, and so on.

The EU Directive on part-time work was implemented in **Denmark** in June 2001 through a new dual method.[44] In an important step concerning the rights of marginal part-time workers, the Act on Salaried Employees (*Funktionærloven*) – which governs aspects of the employment conditions of white-collar workers such as holidays, seniority, dismissal regulation and redundancy payments, and salary during sickness – was amended. Now part-time workers who work more than eight hours a week are covered by this legislation, while previously at least 15 hours of work were required (Jørgensen 2001). For information on the situation of marginal workers prior to this amendment see Fink (1999a: 94 et seq.).

In **Germany**, the 1985 Employment Promotion Act (*Beschäftigungsförderungsgesetz*) was intended to strengthen incentives to offer and take up part-time

44 Traditionally, directives had been implemented exclusively through collective agreement. As a result of European Commission intervention, the Parliament extended the provisions of the agreement between the trade union confederation and the central employers' confederation to those areas without their own collective agreements on this issue (Jørgensen 2001). This step was criticised for undermining the Danish collective bargaining model (compare Leiber 2005: 133–136).

employment; among other things it established non-discrimination clauses following a decision of the Federal Labour Court. In January 2001 the Act on part-time work and fixed-term contracts (*Gesetz über Teilzeitarbeit und befristete Arbeitsverträge*) came into force that transposed the EU directives on part-time and fixed-term employment into national law. Almost all non-binding recommendations were taken up. The Act aims, for example, at facilitating transitions between full-time and part-time employment and vice versa, and seeks to grant access to part-time work at all levels of the firm. The most innovative part of the law is the provision that introduces a legal right for workers in companies with more than 15 employees to reduce their working time. The right cannot be enforced if the employer can prove that this would be detrimental to the functioning of the firm, however.[45]

Policies on the regulation of part-time work in **Spain** have usually targeted employers (adaptation of working time to the changing needs of business organisation), employees (the fulfilment of personal interests) and the public authorities (instrument of employment policy) (Valdés Dal-Ré 2004). In 1984, restrictions on access to part-time employment were removed and application of the princeple of equality and proportionality between part-time and full-time employees was called for (Cebrián et al. 2000: 211). But according to Valdés dal-Ré (2004), the "normalisation" of part-time work that was brought about by Law 32/1984 consisted of the installation of a non-permanent and precarious type of contract that mainly served employers' flexibility needs. Part-time employment in Spain is predominantly of a temporary nature. Laws 18/1993 and 11/1994 further elevated the function of part-time employment as an instrument of enterprise flexibility by, for example, widening the scope for using flexible working hours that vary from day to day. In 1998, following the Part-time Directive and against fierce opposition from employers' representatives, the government and the trade unions reached a new agreement on promoting stable part-time contracts. The possibility temporarily to increase working hours of part-time workers was restricted to part-time workers with permanent contracts; employees' rights in this regard were strengthened by requiring early notification. Besides improving social security rights – which will be discussed in Chapter 5 – the 1998 law (Royal Decree 489/1998) suppresses the differences between part-time workers and marginal part-time workers (less than 12 hours a week or less than 48 hours a month). Furthermore, the voluntary nature of part-time work is strengthened by asserting that conversion of full-time to part-time employment and vice versa will happen at the will of the employee and not of the employer (Miguélez

45 For more information on the regulation of part-time work in Germany and for detailed information on the contents of the 2001 legislation, see Fuchs (2004). For information on the implementation of the framework agreement in Germany, see Leiber (2005).

1998). Many of the non-binding standards from the Directive were transposed into national law in order to promote voluntary part-time employment (Hartlapp 2005: 106-109). As a concession to employers' interests, Law 5/2001 removed many of the aspects providing a framework of legal security for part-timers that had been installed with the 1998 legislation; working hours, for example, can be used more flexibly again.[46]

Between 1975 and 1995 **UK** legislation required persons working between 8 and 16 hours per week to have been continuously employed for five years – a much stronger requirement than among 'standard workers' – in order to qualify for a large number of statutory rights, such as protection from unfair dismissal, the right to maternity pay and the right to return to a specific work place after childbirth. People working less than eight hours were excluded from all of these rights (Kilpatrick et al. 2004: 308–313). Only in 1995, after a judgment by the House of Lords, was equal treatment concerning employment protection, severance pay and maternity leave accorded to part-time workers with low hours (Fink 1999a: 174). The regulations repealed the hours thresholds throughout UK employment law, not only with regard to working times between 8 and 16 hours but also with regard to working times of less than 8 hours per week. In the 1990s the United Kingdom had excluded itself from the EU-level social policy law-making mechanism and only signed up to the Social Chapter after the Labour Party came to office in 1997. The Part-time Directive was then extended to the United Kingdom and implemented into national law via the Part-time Workers (Prevention of Less Favourable Treatment) Regulations that came into force in July 2000. This regulation introduced new statutory rights for part-time workers, such as hourly pay rates, overtime pay, access to training and access to pension schemes comparable to that of full-time workers. As concerns non-discrimination, the British government made use of all possible restrictions in the definition of the comparator (same type of contract) and restricted the comparison to the company level; this led to a situation in which the vast majority of part-time workers effectively could not benefit from the non-discrimination principle (Falkner et al. 2005: 168).[47] Kilpatrick et al. (2004: 335) assess the 2000 legislation very critically and accord it at best the achievement of modest progress with regard to the amelioration of the inferior terms and conditions of part-time work. In 2002,

46 For in-depth information on the content of these laws, see Selenkewitsch (2004); for the circumstances of their implementation, see Valdés dal-Ré (2004: 233–239).

47 Six different subcategories of contract types, such as fixed-term and apprenticeship contracts, are specified in the regulation; comparison between different subcategories is not allowed. In line with the implementation of the Fixed-term Work Directive the subcategory "fixed-term employment" was abolished in 2002; part-time workers with a fixed-term contract can now compare themselves to full-time workers with a permanent contract. On this issue, see also Treib (2004).

proposals from a Work and Parents Taskforce that had been set up in 2001 and was made up of employers, trade unions and parents' representatives were introduced into the Employment Bill. Among them is a right for parents of young or disabled children to request in writing a different working pattern and have it considered seriously by the employer (Kilpatrick et al. 2004: 337–342).

4.2.2 Care obligations as reason for part-time work

Part-time employment is often associated with care obligations. Chapter 3 showed that the importance of using part-time employment in order to combine work with family obligations differs strongly between the countries looked at here. This section will provide more insight into this topic.

The focus on prime-age female part-time workers in this section makes sense insofar as part-time employment among the elderly is usually used as phased early retirement and therefore should no longer conflict with (a lack of) rights to unemployment benefits. Similarly, young people who combine work and studies via part-time work are usually protected through other channels. If part-time employment is used to reconcile work and family life, incentives should be set to take up part-time employment – possible incentives could be non-discriminatory access to unemployment benefits, as well as reliable and adequate public and occupational pension insurance. Only in Germany and the United Kingdom do a majority of prime-age women state that they work part-time for family reasons. In Denmark, on the other hand, part-time employment is mostly exercised voluntarily. In Spain, part-time employment takes place involuntarily, but in the majority of cases this is not due to family responsibilities; instead of combining child-care with part-time employment mothers tend to withdraw from the labour market altogether.

Table 5 relates women's employment rates to the presence of children. The general patterns are similar in Spain, the United Kingdom and Germany. The employment rates of women with young children are considerably lower than overall female employment rates and they tend to increase with the age of the youngest child. In Denmark, on the other hand, female employment rates are not only by far the highest, but they also remain above 70 per cent for women with very young children. Employment rates of mothers with children older than 3 surpass those of all women. The difference between overall employment rates and employment rates of mothers with very young children is by far the most pronounced in Germany, where only 36 per cent of mothers with very young

Table 5: Birth rates and female employment by age of children, 2005*

		Employment / population ratio			
		Women	**Mothers**		
	Children per woman	**All**	**Youngest child <2**	**Youngest child 3–5 years**	**Youngest child 6–16 years**
Denmark	1.80	73.2	71.4	77.8	77.5
Germany	1.34	61.5	36.1	54.8	62.7
Spain	1.34	54.0	45.1	47.9	50.9
UK	1.80	66.8	52.6	58.3	67.7

Note: * Overall employment rates refer to 2006; fertility rates and mother's employment rates refer to 2005, except for Denmark, where mothers' employment rates refer to 1999. *Source*: OECD (2007).

children work.[48] The smaller difference between mothers and all women in Spain has to be seen in light of a system in which women are still relatively likely to leave the labour market when they get married and/or have children. Fertility rates are higher in Denmark and the UK than in Germany and Spain, but as in all EU countries they remain below replacement rates.[49]

Figure 16 reports the shares of working mothers who combine work and family life by means of part-time employment. The part-time employment profile of mothers is very similar in the United Kingdom and Germany: children significantly increase part-time employment among women but further reduce already low part-time employment rates among men. Part-time employment among women with at least two children surpasses 60 per cent, whereas the part-time employment rates of women without children stand at about 20 per cent. The results for Spain confirm that part-time employment fulfils a different function there – part-time employment rates do not vary strongly between women without and women with children. The results for Denmark once again are surprising; the part-time employment share even somewhat decreases among women with children as compared to women without children.

48 The maximum duration of maternity and parental leave varies strongly between the countries looked at here. The maximum duration in Germany used to be three years and has been 14 months since 2007. It is about 3 years in Spain, about one and a half years in Denmark and less than a year in the United Kingdom (OECD 2001a: 144). The above data may not record maternal employment entirely accurately because, according to OECD (2005), while Labour Force Surveys generally regard those on maternity and parental leave as employed, people who use child-related leaves that last until a child is about three years of age, as in Austria, Finland, France, Germany and Spain, are by convention not counted as employed.

49 In Europe there is today a positive correlation between fertility and women's paid employment – the higher the rate of female employment, the greater the level of fertility. For more information, see Esping-Andersen (1999b: 67–70).

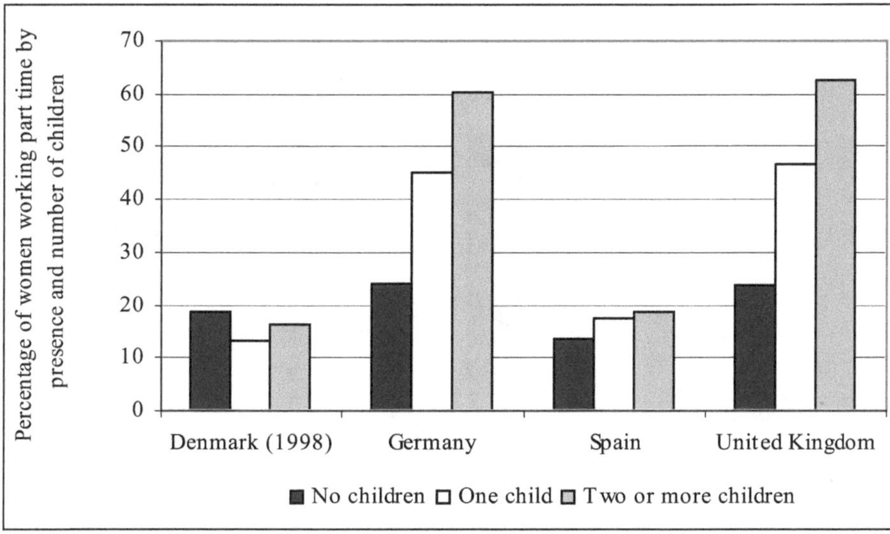

Figure 16: Part-time work among prime-age women (25–54) by presence of children (under 15 years) in 2000.
Note: To our knowledge, these are the most recent comparative data on this indicator.
Source: data from OECD (2002d: 78).

Why are Danish mothers able to work full-time? OECD (2001a) demonstrates that there is a positive relationship across countries between policies designed to improve the reconciliation of work and family life (formal child-care coverage and paid maternity leave policies) and women's employment rates. Similarly, Lind et al. (1999: 223–226) argue that declining part-time employment rates in Denmark are due not only to reduced access to unemployment benefits since about 1980, but also to the strong expansion of public child-care facilities that allow women to opt for full-time employment. For the United Kingdom, on the other hand, they argue that many women work part-time in order to fit in care for children in the absence of sufficient state-provided child-care.

In this sense child-care facilities could act as functional equivalents of more accessible social insurance benefits. If mothers or, in the long run, parents were free to choose full-time employment, benefit coverage would be less of a problem. Enrolment rates of children in child-care and early education services are presented below (see Figure 17). Generally, enrolment in and provision of child-

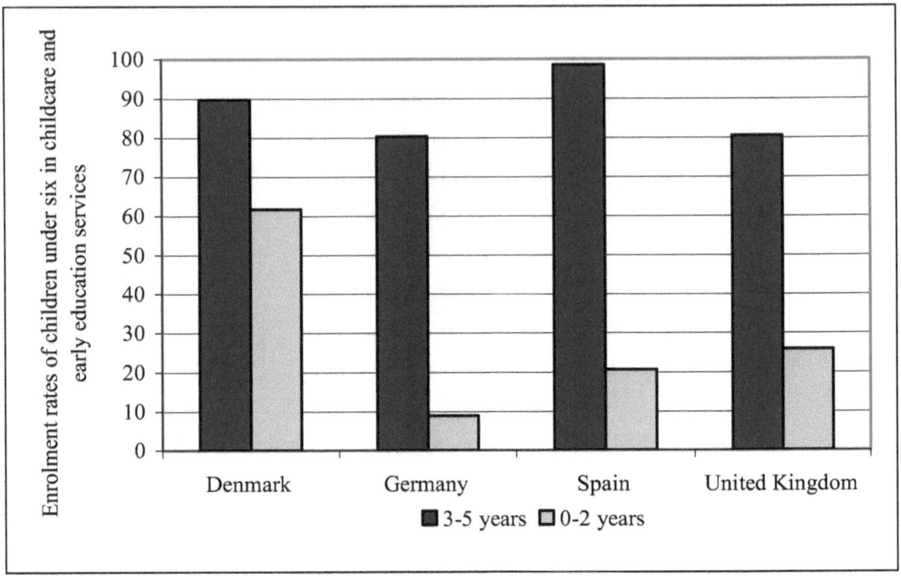

Figure 17: Enrolment rates of children in childcare and early education services, 2003/2004.
Source: data from OECD (2008).

care facilities are much higher for children older than 3 than for very young children, and enrolment rates for older children are also more uniform over the four countries. Nevertheless, also in the age group 3 to 5 years problems can arise for parents, for example in the case that child-care places are offered only on a part-time basis, which is often the case in Germany. In line with expectations drawn from the high employment rates of mothers in Denmark, child-care enrolment rates are exceptionally high in this country, especially for very young children.[50] The other three countries – and especially Germany – display very low enrolment rates for children up to 2 years, which is for the most part due to a lack of public, affordable child-care services for this age group.

Although the general availability of child-care facilities should have the strongest influence on parents' work decisions, their price also matters. According to OECD (2004b: 39–45) in Denmark child-care fees for day care institutions are heavily subsidised for all households; for low-income families up to 100 per

50 According to OECD (2003a) child-care capacity in Denmark was not developed prior to the high level of women's labour force participation; on the contrary, it was a response to the expectations of women who already had a job.

cent of the fees are covered. In Germany, there is a tax allowance for child-care costs; in Spain most children aged 3 to 5 are in subsidised public child-care or in school, and all communities provide free child-care for families with serious socio-economic difficulties. In the United Kingdom the Working Tax Credit, formerly the Working Families Tax Credit, allows parents to claim up to 70 per cent of child-care costs, up to a maximum that depends on the number of children. Additionally, free part-time care is provided for children from 4 to 5 years in nursery and reception classes.

The Danish example shows that in the presence of encompassing child-care facilities part-time employment seems to be less important for combining work and family obligations. In fact, in Denmark female part-time employment has been decreasing since the late 1980s, while female employment rates have further increased (see Hoffmann et al. 2003: 37–42).

4.3 Temporary employment

According to van Peijpe (1998: 42), fixed-term contracts and temporary work agencies can act as compensating mechanisms for strict employment protection legislation because they create numerical flexibility for employers. Do empirical results confirm that temporary contracts are used to circumvent strict employment protection legislation (EPL), and to what extent does employment protection legislation create labour market segmentation between insiders and outsiders?

Potential benefits and costs of EPL for workers, employers and society are discussed in OECD (2004d: 80; 1999a: 76 et seq.) and Wagner (1997: 195), for example. On the workers' side, strict EPL enhances job and income security and, by way of the longer-lasting employment relationship, workers as well as employers might be inclined to invest in skills that might increase promotion prospects and, in case of layoffs, re-employment possibilities. Stable employment relationships can enhance firms' productivity by generating higher motivation and cooperation among the employees; similarly, firms benefit from the accumulation of firm-specific knowledge that can increase internal flexibility (see, for example, Jahn et al. 2003). What are the potential costs for workers? Strict EPL for permanent workers can enhance the dualism between protected workers (insiders) and, on the other hand, jobseekers as well as temporary workers (outsiders) and thereby create segmented labour markets. Strict employment protection legislation may restrict overall hiring and may impede transitions between jobs and upward mobility. By imposing an implicit tax, strict EPL could also raise firms' labour costs.

All in all, society might benefit from strict EPL if it potentially enhances productivity, living standards and growth, and internalises the social costs of dismissals. On the other hand, EPL can also generate costs, such as long-term unemployment, sclerotic labour markets, cycling between unemployment and temporary jobs, and increased problems of labour market inequality or segmentation. These assumptions cannot be tested here; instead, the next section focuses on the relationship between the incidence of temporary employment and the strictness of EPL.

4.3.1 Employment protection legislation and the extent of temporary employment

Based on comparative data collected by Grubb et al. (1993) the OECD has developed indicators for the strictness of employment protection legislation that are regularly updated (OECD 2004d, 1999a). There are 18 basic items that make up three main areas: protection of permanent workers against individual dismissal, requirements for collective dismissal and regulation of temporary employment. Based on these indicators the countries are accorded summary scores for the different areas – the higher the scores, the stricter the legislation (for further information, see OECD 1999a: annex 2.B; 2004d: annex 2.A). The EPL indicators show that there has been a trend towards convergence across OECD countries, mainly through liberalising temporary employment – temporary work agencies in particular have been legalised in many countries; legislation on permanent employment, on the other hand, has remained more or less unchanged (OECD 2004d: 63). Spain belongs to the four OECD countries that have undertaken comprehensive reforms concerning both permanent and temporary employment (OECD 2004d: 76).

Since temporary workers can be laid off more easily (see Booth et al. 2002b: 189) one would expect a positive relationship between the incidence of temporary employment and the strictness of EPL for permanent jobs (circumvention strategy), and a negative relationship between the incidence of temporary employment and the strictness of EPL for temporary jobs.

Using the 1999 OECD indicators Booth et al. (2002a: 184–186) validate the first assumption, namely that temporary employment seems to provide flexibility in labour markets with strict EPL for permanent contracts; the second assumption, however, does not hold. Similarly, Grubb et al. (1993: 25–27), based on graphic results making use of EPL indicators for the late 1980s, conclude that the incidence of fixed-term employment increases strongly with regulation of the dismissal of permanent workers. OECD (1999a: 50, 79, 80), which uses the updated EPL indicators, does not support the earlier findings. One explanation is that in some countries too little time might have passed since the changes were made to EPL regulations. In contrast, OECD (2004d: 86–89), based on the most recent EPL indicators, observes that over the 1990s the incidence of temporary employment grew faster in countries where EPL for temporary contracts had been significantly relaxed compared with regulation of permanent contracts. Furthermore, based on regression analysis on a range of labour market groups (men, women, young people, low skilled, elderly), it concluded that the larger the relative difference in employment protection between regular and temporary contracts, the higher the incidence of temporary work for young people and low skilled workers. The results are not significant for prime-age men and women, and for older workers. Facilitating the use of temporary work without changing EPL for permanent employment could thus aggravate labour market segmentation and further impair the situation of specific disadvantaged labour market groups.

Büchtemann et al. (1996: 668) question the usefulness of comparative studies concerning the labour market impacts of dismissal protection because they have to operate with gross generalisation and simplification and lack sufficient data on implementation. Further advancements of the OECD indicators may have weakened this argument, at least in part. Zachert (2004: 135) argues against mono-causal correlations and notes that the high incidence of temporary employment in Spain and Portugal results not only from strict EPL, but also from industry structure, business size and widespread seasonal employment. OECD (2002c: 137) notes a number of other factors that appear to be important for explaining the share of temporary employment: prolonged recession, a high share of agricultural workers and large-scale public employment programmes. Ignoring for the time being these other possible reasons for temporary employment, how do the countries under analysis fare when it comes to employment protection legislation?

The indicator for permanent contracts takes into account the procedure of notification and the length of the notice period. Furthermore, information is used on severance pay, reasons for justified or unfair dismissal, length of the initial trial period before eligibility for EPL arises, and compensation or possible reinstatement following unfair dismissal. The indicator for fixed-term contracts is composed of information on valid reasons for the use of this contract type, and on the maximum number and accumulated duration of successive fixed-term contracts. The temporary work agency indicator is made up of the types of work for which temporary work agency employment is legal, the possible number of renewals and the maximum accumulated duration of temporary work agency

Table 6: Summary indicators of the strictness of employment protection legislation

	Regular employment			Fixed-term contracts			Temporary work agencies			Overall EPL*
	late 1980s	late 1990s	2003	late 1980s	late 1990s	2003	late 1980s	late 1990s	2003	2003
Denmark	1.5	1.5	1.5	2.3	2.3	2.3	4.0	0.5	0.5	1.8
Germany	2.6	2.7	2.7	3.5	1.8	1.8	4.0	2.8	1.8	2.5
Spain	3.9	2.6	2.6	2.0	2.5	3.0	5.5	4.0	4.0	3.1
UK	0.9	0.9	1.1	0.0	0.0	0.3	0.5	0.5	0.5	1.1
range	0.2–4.8	0.2–4.3	0.2–4.8	0.0–5.3	0.0–4.3	0.0–4.5	0.5–5.5	0.5–5.5	0.5–5.5	0.7–3.5

Note: * Includes information on the regulation of collective dismissal; this information is weighted at only 40 per cent of the other indicators.
Source: OECD (2004d: 112–117 (excerpt)).

contracts (for more information, see OECD 2004d). Table 6 shows the development of country indicators concerning regular and temporary employment. The last row (range) takes into account all OECD countries and therefore allows a rough assessment of the overall position of the countries under observation.

Since the late 1980s temporary work agency employment has been relaxed in all countries looked at here except for the United Kingdom, where it had already been much deregulated. Employment protection legislation on regular employment has remained more or less stable, except in Spain where EPL for permanent employment was relaxed during the 1990s from very strict regulation in line with increasing regulation of fixed-term employment. EPL on fixed-term employment has been further deregulated in Germany, while regulation slightly increased from a very low level in the United Kingdom and remained constant at an average to high level in Denmark.

The relative position of countries concerning overall strictness of employment protection legislation, as captured in the OECD indicator, has not changed a lot. Out of 19 (26) countries, the United Kingdom was ranked second in the late 1980s and in the late 1990s – thus with very lax EPL, Denmark was ranked seventh (eighth), Germany fourteenth (eighteenth) and Spain seventeenth (twenty second). Spain has one of the strictest EPL regimes in the OECD.

Table 7, taken from OECD (2004d: 119–120), gives a condensed overview of important developments in EPL legislation in the different countries from the late 1980s onwards; it will be further commented on in the next part. The minus, plus and equal signs show the direction of the effect of specific reform measures on employment protection legislation on permanent or temporary jobs and on overall employment protection legislation.

Table 7: Development of employment protection legislation*

	year	reform	EPL overall	EPL perma-nent	EPL tempo-rary
Denmark	**1995**	Since the mid-1990s the role of TWAs** has been recognised by the social partners and their scope has increased	–	=	–
Germany	**1985**	Fixed-term contracts were allowed without specifying an objective reason			
	1993	Notice period for bluecollar workers was extended and aligned with that of whitecollar workers	=	+	=
	1994	TWA legislation was loosened	–	=	–
	1996	The renewal period for fixed-term contracts and TWA and admissible frequency of renewals were increased	–	=	–
	2002	Maximum total duration of TWA was brought to 24 months	–	=	–
	2004	The limit on the maximum total duration of TWA was lifted	–	=	–
Spain	**1984**	Restrictions on fixed-term contracts were substantially relaxed			
	1994	Procedural requirements for dismissals for economic reasons were relaxed, notice periods shortened	–	–	=
	1994	Rules governing renewals of fixed-term contracts were tightened and temporary work agencies were permitted	–	=	–
	1997	Maximum compensation for unfair dismissal was reduced and some changes were made to the definition of fair dismissal (new permanent contract with lower firing costs)	–	–	=
	2001	Law 12/2001 tightened the rules governing valid cases for the use of fixed-term contracts	+	=	+
United Kingdom	**1985**	The period of service entitling a claim for unfair dismissal increased to 2 years			
	2000	Trial period was halved	+	+	=
	2002	Maximum total duration of fixed-term contracts was reduced to 4 years (from unlimited)	=	=	+

Note: * Index starts in 1985. The equal sign denotes that the change in a sub-item was not large enough to be visible in the overall score; ** TWA: temporary work agencies.
Source: OECD (2004d: 119–120 (excerpt)).

4.3.2 Specific regulation of temporary contracts in the four countries

At present, fixed-term contracts in Denmark are allowed for a specified period of time or for a specific task. Renewal must be based on objective reasons. There is no legal limit, but successive contracts imply the risk of a court ruling nullifying the fixed-term contract. The maximum accumulated duration is 30 months (OECD 2004c: 14). In Germany, fixed-term contracts are possible for up to two years, and four renewals can take place without specifying an objective reason. There are no limits for contracts based on objective reasons, but the objective reasons usually set the limit.[51] The latter is also true for Spain. There are nine different types of fixed-term contracts in Spain; the maximum length of the contract depends on the contract type: in case of increased workload the maximum contract duration is six months, though it can be modified by collective agreement. Work placement contracts (for university graduates and people with medium to high vocational degrees) and training contracts can last for up to four years (for more information, see Albarracín 2004). In the United Kingdom there are no restrictions on the use of fixed-term contracts for up to four years, after which the worker will be treated as a permanent employee; the maximum number of successive contracts is not restricted (OECD 2004c: 14–16).

In *Denmark* there is no general legislation covering employment protection legislation for all workers; instead, different acts cover special categories of workers. Whitecollar workers are mainly protected by legislation, while bluecollar or manual workers are usually protected under a collective agreement (van Peijpe 1998: 95). Applicable provisions vary considerably between both groups of workers; notice periods, for example, are much higher for whitecollar than for bluecollar workers (for further information, see OECD 2004c). As long ago as 1960 a clause was introduced that required the employer to state a reason for dismissal; this limited the basic principle governing Danish dismissal law: the freedom of the employer to hire and fire without the unions' intervention. In 1981 the possibility was introduced to declare an unjust dismissal null and require the employer to reinstate the dismissed worker. The constantly low number of fixed-term contracts in Denmark is at least partly attributable to the generally lax Danish dismissal law (van Peijpe 1998: 109).

Different studies reveal that job mobility in Denmark is comparatively high, average tenure is low and the share of job openings is very high, which allows most groups to rapidly re-enter the labour market (Madsen 2002a: 61–68, 101; 2002b: 51, 52). One explanation for the high level of job mobility is the low

51 In Germany, objective reasons apply, for example, if the person is employed as a substitute, if personnel requirements are temporary, if the character of the task justifies a temporary contract or if the contract is specified for a trial period.

level of EPL found in Denmark. The combination of high levels of job mobility and low levels of EPL does not lead to a widespread feeling of insecurity among the population; in contrast, satisfaction with regard to job security is very high in Denmark compared to other OECD or EU-15 countries (Madsen 2002b: 52 et seq.; Kaiser 2002: 12 et seq.). The next section will show that generous and long-lasting unemployment compensation is an important explanation of this. Labour market dynamics are thus enhanced without substantially decreasing the security situation of those affected.

In *Germany* prior to 1985 there was a judicial requirement that a reason must be stated for concluding a fixed-term contract. In the Employment Promotion Act of 1985 legislation was passed that allowed fixed-term contracts for newly employed workers without stating an objective reason for a period of 18 months (Rogowski et al. 1996: 634 et seq.). This period was extended to 24 months in 1996; three prolongations are possible within this time frame. From 1996, until a recent decision by the European Court of Justice, unlimited fixed-term contracts without stating an objective reason were possible for people older than 60 years (58 between 2001 and 2003 and 52 thereafter).[52] This was to enhance the re-employment possibilities of the elderly, who have comparatively low employment rates in Germany. Since 2004, newly founded firms can hire persons on fixed-term contracts for up to 4 years without stating an objective reason (compare TzBfG, §14(2a)). It should be noted that in Germany employees in small enterprises with fewer than 10 employees are in a very similar position to fixed-term contract holders because regular employment protection legislation does not apply to small businesses.[53]

The strong increase of temporary employment in *Spain* can be traced back to the Spanish government's liberalisation of temporary contracts in 1984. The 1980 Workers' Statute, which created the main labour market regulations that currently exist in Spain, established a clear preference for permanent contracts with exceptions only for specific situations and initial contracts for young employees. In 1984, in order to reduce labour market rigidity and counter high unemployment, the use of fixed-term contracts was extended to regular activities: fixed-term contracts were to last a minimum of 6 months and a maximum of three years and could be renewed up to this maximum (Toharia 1999: 7). Dismissal costs in the case of termination of a fixed-term contract were and are

---

52 The European Court of Justice decided at the end of 2005 that the exemption of people over the age of 52 from the general requirements for permitting fixed-term employment did not comply with the age discrimination provisions of the EU Equal Opportunities Directive.

53 In 1996 the business size for this rule was increased to 10 employees; in 1999 – under the new Social Democrat–Green government – it was lowered to its former size of 5 employees; in 2004 it returned to 10 employees. According to Bauer et al. (2004) modifications in these regulations have not significantly changed employment dynamics in the affected firms.

much lower than at the termination of a permanent contract (Dolado et al. 2002: 270). According to Bentolila et al. (1994: 67) the considerable employment growth of the boom period from 1986 to 1990 was mainly achieved through the creation of fixed-term employment. Toharia (1999), on the other hand, states that the influence of the 1984 reform on employment was limited, but that it significantly increased labour turnover. As a consequence of the growing notion of dual labour market structures, from the mid-1990s onwards the Spanish government tried to limit temporary employment via a succession of labour market reforms that lowered firing costs under permanent contracts, subsidised hiring under permanent contracts and supported the conversion of temporary contracts into permanent ones by means of reduced social security contributions (for more information, see Dolado et al. 2002: 274, 291–292).[54] As seen in Chapter 3, the countervailing reforms have not been very successful: the overall share of temporary employment in Spain slightly decreased, while the absolute numbers – until very recently – further increased in line with growing employment rates. Toharia (1999) associates the 1997 reform, which created incentives to hire on the basis of permanent contracts, with high deadweight losses. Reducing temporary employment is still on the government's agenda; in April 2006 it signed a preliminary agreement with the social partners that aims to curb the widespread use of temporary contracts (Castellanos 2006).

In line with the lax employment protection legislation the share of fixed-term contracts in the *United Kingdom* has been relatively low and rather stable. Until the 1960s, legislation on dismissal protection did not exist. In 1965 the Redundancy Payments Act for the first time granted compensation on a legal basis to some categories of laid-off workers who had been working at a firm for more than two years. In 1971 an unfair dismissal provision was introduced with the Industrial Relations Act (Fink 1999b: 172 et seq.). The minimum qualifying period that was necessary before a claim could be brought before the courts was raised from 6 months to one year in 1979, and to two years in 1985. After a court decision in 1995 the hours threshold limiting employment protection to people working more than 16 hours a week with two years' tenure, and more than eight hours with five years' tenure was abolished (Fink 1999b: 174). Via the Employment Relations Act of 1999 the Labour government somewhat strengthened employment protection legislation by again reducing the qualifying time to one year and by introducing higher levels of compensation in case of unfair dis-

54 The main reforms took place in 1994 and 1997. Since 1997, employers' social security contributions have been reduced if they employ workers from disadvantaged labour market groups, such as women, unemployed, elderly and mothers on the basis of permanent contracts. The reductions at present range from 20 to 100 per cent, and they usually apply to either the first or the first and second years (Toharia 1999: 10; Ministerio de Trabajo y Asuntos Sociales 2005).

missal; compensation nevertheless remains low in international comparison. According to Smith (2003: 301 et seqq.) the introduction of the 1999 laws reflects the minimalist nature of EPL in the United Kingdom and the tendency of the British government to comply with only the minimum requirements when implementing EU directives. Prior to 2002, fixed-term contracts could last for an unlimited time period; the maximum statutory duration is now four years, and unless the use of fixed-term contracts beyond this limit is justified on objective grounds, no maximum number of successive contracts is specified (OECD 2004c; I. Schömann et al. 2003).[55]

4.4 Implications for the empirical analysis

The above information calls for carefully constructed empirical models. The importance of non-standard employment varies between different labour market groups and, especially in the case of part-time employment, also depends on the household situation. Furthermore, non-standard employment plays different roles in the countries examined here.

At least in the initial stage of analysis temporary employment should be decomposed into casual work and fixed-term employment (there is no separate category for temporary work agency contracts in the data). In the analysis of part-time employment special attention has to be paid to marginal employment, which is often automatically excluded from benefit receipt. It can also be expected that marginal employment is more likely to lead to exclusionary transitions than regular part-time employment, which is probably more likely to act as a bridge to regular employment.

For the mobility analysis that is to capture downward and upward mobility of non-standard workers, demographic characteristics (gender, age), as well as job and qualification characteristics (occupation, sector, business size, qualification level) and, in the case of part-time employment, household characteristics (children, child-care and marital status) should be introduced as independent variables.

Individual and job characteristics of non-standard workers should generally have no direct influence on unemployment benefit receipt. Instead, differences in coverage should result exclusively from design features of unemployment insurance systems, such as minimum contribution requirements or hours and earnings

55 The four-year limit was specified in the Fixed-term Employees Regulations that transpose the EC Directive on fixed-term work into UK legislation. It remains a very lax requirement because it applies only to successive fixed-term contracts (compare I. Schömann et al. 2003: 42, 43).

thresholds. The household context will be important in countries that operate with means-testing and/or derived benefits. Design features and characteristics of unemployment insurance systems that either restrict or enhance the access of non-standard workers to benefits will be treated in Chapter 5. This information should allow us to derive assumptions for the empirical analysis and will help us to choose the institutional variables to be included in the cluster analysis and the multi-level analysis in Chapter 6.

5 Are unemployment insurance systems adapting to non-standard employment?

This chapter will discuss the features of the countries' unemployment insurance systems that are important in respect of the benefit receipt of non-standard workers. The first, more theoretical part on the male breadwinner model will take up the second hypothesis, that countries vary concerning the connection between social insurance and standard employment. We shall address the following questions: Why do unemployment insurance systems fail to cover certain groups? And have there been developments to better cover groups that are excluded from or disadvantaged in unemployment insurance systems? In order to answer these questions we shall examine and compare the unemployment insurance schemes of the four countries. After briefly discussing the main principles and developments we shall focus on the design features that potentially influence the coverage of part-time and temporary workers.

Part-time workers can be excluded from benefits due to hours or earnings thresholds; in some instances the qualifying period also varies between part-time and full-time workers. The calculation of replacement rates often takes into account the former wage level, which leads to lower benefits for former part-time workers. On the other hand, some countries have introduced regulations that favour part-time workers when it comes to benefit coverage in order to support this employment form. Temporary workers are most likely to be excluded on the basis of minimum contribution periods, but in some instances they are also disadvantaged when it comes to the duration of unemployment benefits.

Since our discussion of unemployment insurance systems will form the basis of the following empirical analysis, in line with the data span of the ECHP the focus will be on developments during the 1990s. The present circumstances are of course also considered in order to get an idea of the direction in which countries are heading. The last part of the chapter will outline the institutional features that will be included in the empirical analysis.

5.1 The male breadwinner model and standard employment

By considering the traditional division between male and female tasks, characterised by such terms as the 'male breadwinner model' and 'standard employment', in this part we will frame the following institutional analysis. Since most information is drawn from German studies – Germany being one of the prototypes of the male breadwinner model – a German viewpoint is adopted. The other three countries will be located in terms of the concepts outlined here.[56]

Labour market institutions and social policies are drawn up in specific national settings. A country's self-conception rests upon a more or less explicit social contract that is influenced by the traditions and values of a specific society and is therefore path dependent. The social contract is usually made up of a gender contract and an employment contract (Holst et al. 1998). In Germany the gender contract has traditionally been characterised by the male breadwinner model (male provider and housewife), and the employment contract by so-called 'standard employment' (*Normalarbeitsverhältnis*), that is, dependent, permanent and full-time employment with high continuity and stability (for a comprehensive definition, see Hinrichs 1996: 103). In this constellation standard employment mainly applies to men. It is evident that this social contract no longer reflects reality adequately since women's labour market participation has increased considerably. Depending on the country, today one would rather use the labels 'male breadwinner and secondary earner' (or 'extended male breadwinner model') (West Germany), 'double earner/double carer' (Netherlands) or 'double bread-winner with public service support' (Scandinavia) (Holst et al. 1998: 515).

Many labour market and social institutions in Germany are still based on the traditional division between male labour and female household work and are therefore centred on standard employment contracts. German social insurance is usually beneficial for people in stable full-time employment; it often takes into account household composition and derived rights for married partners (mostly women) are frequent.[57] Similarly, for the British context, Sainsbury (1996: 55 et seqq.) states that the male breadwinner model has left its imprint on post-war reforms: the adult dependent allowance and the possibility for married women to

56 There is also a considerable Anglo-American literature that criticises the gender bias of the welfare state (Rubery et al. 1998b: especially chapters 5 and 6; Jepsen et al. 2002; Sainsbury 1996).

57 In Germany, health insurance for non-working partners of employees is free of charge; there are also widow's pensions, and 'tax splitting' financially privileges households with only one worker. Additionally, replacement rates in unemployment insurance are higher for recipients with children.

not pay national insurance contributions but to rely on their husband's entitlements instead are recalled; both have been abolished.[58] Social benefits that are based on standard employment and the concept of a dependent partner not only manifest women's dependency and discriminate against deviating lifestyles, but they also create disincentives to labour market participation and, most importantly in the context of this paper, can lead to unequal outcomes in social insurance coverage (compare, for example, Holst et al. 1998: 507 et seqq.; Bennett 2005: 29 et seqq.).

Geissler (1998) carries this discussion further and labels the coupling of standard employment and statutory social insurance a particular German employment model of the industrial society. This employment model is socially constructed and encompasses three pillars: living standard security via equivalence between earnings and benefits; security of employment continuity via benefit receipt in times of transition; and family and job planning security, derived from the continuity promise. At present, fewer and fewer people are falling under this employment model, which is leading to a shift from employment-related security to second class security with a welfare character, visible in the form of growing numbers of social assistance recipients. The problem is thus merely being transferred to the welfare system, which is less centred on employment and more on inactivity. The weak position of non-standard workers, accordingly, is not being compensated, but rather labour market segmentation is being reinforced. On the other hand, this division strengthens social insurance systems because it relieves them of 'bad risks' with discontinuous, low and short contributions, coupled with potentially long benefit receipt.

What are the options that might make social insurance systems more open to non-standard workers? With reference to the German system the equivalence principle and, therewith, status maintenance are frequently called into question (H.-G. Petersen 1989: 95–99; Rolf et al. 1988: 527–531). Hinrichs (1996: 106 et seq.), for example, raises the question of whether more inclusive social insurance might not entail a lowering of ceilings on benefits in order to achieve financial sustainability. This would call for concessions on the part of standard workers so as to allow a broader group of employees to have access to social insurance benefits.[59] A further, more radical possibility is basic or minimum insurance for

58 By not paying contributions married women forfeited claims in their own right, which resulted in a loss of pensions, sickness allowance, unemployment benefits, and the like. In the early 1970s about three quarters of married women made use of this possibility. The adult dependant allowance was phased out by April 1997; the possibility to opt out of national insurance was abolished as early as 1977.

59 A possible downside often mentioned in this context could be lower legitimacy for social insurance and less willingness to pay contributions (compare, for example, Hinrichs 1996: 106; Eisen 1988: 117).

all. But minimum insurance is problematic due to means testing and thus non-compliance with more individualised benefit receipt. More women than men cannot establish entitlement to means-tested benefits because their partners' earnings exceed the threshold (Luckhaus 2000: 162). This not only strengthens dependence but, by creating unemployment or inactivity traps, means testing can turn out to be more costly than universal benefits (Clasen et al. 2002). Individualised benefits based on universal principles that encourage labour mobility and participation might thus be more suitable for flexible work forms. Individualisation of entitlements could be achieved by abolishing derived rights and family components within social insurance. Benefits granted independent of family circumstances not only free financial resources for more comprehensive social insurance but, by countering possible disincentives to work, can also generate additional financial means. Gradual individualisation of social insurance entitlements is also called for in order to bring about a modern and egalitarian gender contract that would allow the establishment of a new standard employment situation within reach of both men and women (Klammer 2001: 152 et seq.). This new standard employment situation could entail more flexible elements as long as sufficiently high wages and social insurance benefits, and therewith the financial independence of women, were attained.[60]

According to Luckhaus (2000) women are the main problem group when it comes to income security and social protection. Due to unpaid care activities a part of them are excluded from paid employment in the first place; social protection in this case is possible only via a breadwinner (derived rights). Sainsbury (1996: 72) identifies this dependence on the husband as the major shortcoming of the breadwinner model. Another group of women who lack income security are those who move back and forth between periods out of and periods in employment – often in part-time or low-paid work. Social insurance entitlements in this case can be restricted due to earnings or hours thresholds. Furthermore, if calculation of benefits and earnings are closely linked, social insurance payments will be low. Therefore social protection systems tend to reproduce women's disadvantages in the labour market – often brought about by care obligations – rather than remove them. Luckhaus (2000: 174 et seqq.) emerges with two possible notions of women's social protection. The first takes up women's disadvantages in social protection arising from their engagement in unpaid work; the

60 Especially in the German context the focus should be redirected from supporting non-employment through social policy and tax arrangements. This would release money to better secure those who are willing or forced to take up forms of non-standard employment in order to participate in the labour market. A new standard employment relationship would call for concessions by men, who would have to reduce their employment to be able to participate more equally in household and care activities.

second focuses on financial independence from a partner. In theoretical debates both principles are treated exclusively and are even pitted against each other. Concerning unpaid care work, Luckhaus argues against dependency-related provisions in social insurance and instead calls for caring credits, caring allowances or improved child-care services that may be combined with individualisation of entitlement. Although this would generate a better and more stable position for women, this combination would not provide a solution to the income insecurities experienced by part-time workers and low-paid workers that are not linked to unpaid work activities.

What, then, are the possible solutions for improving the security situation of non-standard workers? Before looking at the design features of unemployment insurance systems that are beneficial or detrimental to non-standard workers we shall characterise the four countries from a theoretical viewpoint by using some of the abovementioned concepts. Germany, as the prototype of continental European countries, seems to be especially ill-suited to labour market flexibility and women's economic independence (compare, for example, Esping-Andersen 1995: 68). This is mainly due to the prevalence of the equivalence principle, derived rights and benefits based on household composition. Relatively generous benefits are thus paid to labour market insiders, while outsiders have to rely on minimal state support as a last resort (Kvist 1998: 34). The situation is similar in Spain: the male breadwinner model, coupled with deficient child-care and low labour market participation of women, is still very strong and social insurance is heavily targeted on standard employment (compare Fassler-Ristic 1999). In Denmark, on the other hand, equal rights of women to participate in standard employment have for a long time been supported by means of comprehensive child-care and individualised entitlements (compare, for example, Holst et al. 1998: 507; Esping-Andersen 1999). The United Kingdom's social insurance system incorporates some elements of minimum insurance: for example, flat-rate unemployment benefits. Private insurance, with its discriminating effects on low income workers, is therefore more important there than in other countries (Fink 1999b). Derived rights in social insurance have been common but have gradually been reduced since the mid 1990s; means testing, on the other hand, remains an important component of the British insurance system (Jepsen et al. 2002: 112 et seqq.).

The interdependence of the male breadwinner model, standard employment and social insurance applies only indirectly to temporary workers. Temporary employment affects women and men in more or less equal parts – the male breadwinner model therefore is not applicable. Nevertheless, (male) standard employment is characterised not only by full-time employment but also by permanent positions at a specific employer. Neither temporary nor part-time employment forms thus comply with 'standard male breadwinner' employment.

5.2 Unemployment insurance

In this section we shall analyse the features of unemployment insurance systems that influence the benefit coverage of non-standard workers. Before examining specific regulations we shall briefly describe the countries' unemployment benefit systems in order to frame the detailed analysis. We give some background information on the main principles and outline the broad developments of recent years.

Denmark and the United Kingdom initiated comprehensive labour market and unemployment insurance reforms in the early to mid-1990s that were followed through over the 1990s (for Denmark, compare Madsen 2002b; Westergaard-Nielsen 2001; Frenzel 2003; for the United Kingdom, compare Davy 2000; Mohr 2004; Donnelley et al. 1998). The focus in both countries was clearly on activation but the connotation of activation and the corresponding measures varied considerably. Although in Germany some benefit system regulations were modified in the 1990s, comprehensive labour market and unemployment insurance reforms commenced only in 2002 (Mohr 2004; Rabe 2001; Seifert 2005). In Spain, a substantial reform of unemployment protection took place in 1992 in response to severe financial strains on the system brought about by numerous rotations between short employment contracts and unemployment (Toharia et al. 2000: 320 et seqq.). In 2002, another unemployment insurance reform aiming at enhancing job search was initiated and – after a period of heavy protests by the unions – followed through on the basis of a compromise (OECD 2003b).

5.2.1 Active line reforms in Denmark

The Danish government passed its first act on unemployment insurance in 1907. At that point a number of trade unions were already running voluntary unemployment insurance funds that from then on were supported by government subsidies. Since the 1970s benefit recipients have had the right and obligation to participate in employability measures (Danish Ministry of Labour 2001). Obligations concerning activation were strengthened during the 1990s reforms. The current statutory basis is the Unemployment Insurance Act No. 874 of 2005.

The Danish system is administered by more than 30 independent unemployment insurance funds that cover different sectors and occupations, and are closely associated with the trade unions but subject to direction by the Ministry of Employment. Sector-specific insurance funds are advantageous due to their specific knowledge of training needs and training opportunities and their connections to companies in the relevant sector. Potential disadvantages of this decentralised system are a lack of transparency and possibly also less control of performance. Since September 2002, cross-sectoral unemployment insurance funds have been permitted. It is expected that this development will increase competition between the different funds, possibly put pressure on contribution rates and increase the need for more transparent and comparable services (Askgaard Hyldtoft 2002). The government's proposal to install an alternative state unemployment insurance fund was withdrawn due to a lack of political support.

Unemployment insurance in Denmark is voluntary; about 80 per cent of the labour force is insured against unemployment. The problem of free-riding has already been discussed in Chapter 2. The municipalities are responsible for the labour market integration and social security of people who are not insured and people who do not qualify for insurance benefits. A recent reform initiative involved moving responsibility for social assistance from the Ministry of Social Affairs to the Ministry of Employment. Rules for both benefits are to be harmonised (Bertelsmann Foundation 2003a: 49 et seqq.). The unemployment insurance funds in Denmark are open not only to employees but also to people who participate in apprenticeship training or military service (both groups receive reduced benefits), civil servants and the self-employed. Admission to one of the funds may take place on a full-time or a part-time basis; a minimum of one year's membership is a precondition for access to unemployment benefits; the self-employed have to fulfil a waiting period of four weeks before they are eligible for benefits (European Commission 2004c: 276–301).

The financing of unemployment insurance takes place by way of the unemployment benefit fund. Its financial means derive from various sources, such as income-related contributions paid together with income tax by employees and the self-employed and, since 1997, also employers' contributions to the unemployment insurance funds plus an administration fee (both independent of income but dependent on status [full-time or part-time]),[61] contributions from employers in the form of a special value-added tax of 3 per cent and transfers from the state. In 2000, total labour market contributions to the three labour market funds, one of which is the unemployment benefit fund, amounted to 8 per cent of earned income and profits from self-employment. Earnings-related contributions are also paid by non-insured persons (Danish Ministry of Labour 2001).

61 In 2006 the contribution was DKK 3204 (€ 430) for full-time insured members.

Comprehensive labour market reforms aiming at activation were initiated in 1993. They cover both insured and uninsured unemployed. Individualised action plans and temporary leave schemes were introduced, labour market policies were decentralised and the right to renew access to unemployment compensation by participating in subsidised employment and training was removed (Lind 1999: 195 et seqq.). The second phase of the labour market reform, 'More People in Work', was implemented in 2003 – it directed active labour market policies towards the areas and instruments that had proven most successful. The principle of rights and obligations was gradually strengthened, young unemployed persons under 30 have a right to activation after six months' unemployment and since 1999 adults have been required to participate in active measures after one year of benefit receipt. Although the benefit period has been shortened to four years (one passive year and three active years), by international comparison it is still very long (Braun 2001: 659 et seqq.; Lind 1999: 195 et seqq.).

5.2.2 From unemployment assistance to basic allowance in Germany

The first nationwide insurance system for unemployment financed by contributions was established in 1927. The present system is based on the Social Code, Book III of 24 March 1997, which has been modified and amended several times. Unemployment insurance is obligatory for all employees (manual and white collar workers and trainees). Civil servants, most groups of self-employed and marginal workers (earning less than €400 a month) are excluded from unemployment insurance. The main responsibility for unemployment insurance and active labour market policies lies with the Federal Labour Agency. Regional labour directorates and local labour agencies are responsible for job placement and training.

Unemployment benefits have until recently consisted of unemployment insurance (*Arbeitslosengeld*), based on contributions, and somewhat lower tax-financed unemployment assistance (*Arbeitslosenhilfe*). Social assistance was payable in case of non-eligibility for the two unemployment benefits. A particularity of the German system was that not only unemployment insurance but also unemployment assistance was calculated as a proportion of the previous wage. Unemployment assistance has now been replaced by a minimum flat-rate benefit (*Arbeitslosengeld* II) for all unemployed who are capable of work and who are not – or are no longer – eligible for unemployment insurance (former unemployment assistance recipients and employable social assistance recipients).[62] Unemployment insurance and a large proportion of active labour market policy measures are financed by employer and employee contributions, which are paid in equal proportions and were reduced from 6.5 per cent to 4.2 per cent in 2007. In addition, there is deficit financing by the state. Unemployment assistance used to be financed by the federal state; the new basic unemployment benefit is financed by both federal state and local authorities.

The so-called Hartz reforms started in 2002; they comprise a wide range of measures implemented by amending the Social Code through Laws 1 to 4 on modern services in the labour market. The conversion of the federal employment office into a modern service provider, the improvement of job placement activities and the merging of unemployment assistance and social assistance into a new basic benefit at the level of social assistance are probably the most prominent features.

Coverage of unemployment benefits – either unemployment insurance or assistance (now basic benefit) – is high in Germany; between 1999 and 2004 the proportion of unemployment insurance recipients as compared to unemployment assistance recipients decreased. In April 2004, 47 per cent of all those eligible for benefits received unemployment insurance and 53 per cent unemployment assistance. The share of unemployment assistance as compared to insurance is much higher in East than in West Germany, which can be explained by, among other things, a much higher proportion of long-term unemployed in the East (Bundesagentur für Arbeit 2004: 43, 72).

5.2.3 Trade unions challenge reforms in Spain

Modern (post-Franco) Spanish unemployment insurance was established in 1980 by the Basic Employment Law (*Ley básica de empleo*). The present system is based on Royal Decree No. 625/85 of 2 April 1985, which has been amended several times. The State Public Employment Service (*Servicio Público de Empleo Estatal*, SEPEE) manages unemployment benefits. Unemployment benefits consist of unemployment insurance (*prestación contributiva por desempleo*) and unemployment assistance (*subsidio por desempleo*). Those not qualifying for unemployment benefits can access social assistance, which is administered by the autonomous communities and not uniform over the whole country. Unemployment benefits are financed by employers' and employees' contributions;

62 The basic benefit for job seekers is regulated through the Social Code, Book II, of 24 December 2003.

contributions are usually 7.55 per cent, 1.55 per cent of which is paid by the employee and 6 per cent by the employer.[63] The state covers some of the cost of unemployment benefits (European Commission 2004c: 89). Financing of passive and active labour market policies is considerably lower than in Denmark and Germany – especially if the unemployment rate is taken into account – but higher than in the United Kingdom (OECD 2003b). Since 1997 employers have enjoyed reduced social insurance contributions if they hire people with specific characteristics on the basis of a permanent contract (Bertelsmann Foundation, 2001: 40 et seqq.).

Spanish unemployment insurance was thoroughly revised in 1992, mainly due to financial strains suffered by the system – the minimum contribution period was doubled to 12 months and benefit receipt dependent on previous contribution time was shortened, though the maximum entitlement period of two years was maintained (Toharia et al. 2000: 320 et seqq.). In 2002, the conservative government proposed a comprehensive reform aimed at strengthening rights and obligations and enhancing active search for employment. The reform proposal was far-reaching; besides modernising and decentralising labour market policies, the unemployed were, for example, supposed to sign a written commitment to accept a 'suitable job', some elements of means-testing (income from assets and investments, for example) were to be introduced and unemployment benefits for part-time seasonal workers were to be abolished.[64] The trade unions, most opposition parties and a broad segment of the population fiercely opposed this reform. A strike was called by the trade unions that forced the government to renegotiate its proposal; many aspects of the original reform were completely or partially withdrawn (Bertelsmann Foundation 2003a: 58 et seqq.; 2003b: 49 et seqq.; 2004: 68 et seq.).

Unemployment benefit coverage is relatively low in Spain. The OECD (2003b: 74 et seq.) explains this not only by the high number of young unemployed who do not have access to insurance benefits if they have never worked before, but also by the high proportion of fixed-term contract workers who usually do not meet the minimum eligibility condition. The expert commission set up to make proposals for reforming the Spanish labour market has criticised the current unemployment insurance system's unequal protection, its relatively low coverage and its subsidising of groups who are not willing to re-enter the labour

63 There are seven different regimes for private sector workers and three different regimes for public sector workers, each with different contribution rules: they include the General regime, the Agrarian regime and the civil servants' regime. For more information, see Levy (2003: 41 et seq.).

64 There is a special insurance scheme for casual agricultural workers in Andalusia and Extremadura. For more information, see Ministerio de Trabajo Y Asuntos Sociales (2006).

market, such as those who have taken early retirement (Comisión de expertos para el diálogo social 2005: 110, 144 et seq.).

5.2.4 Jobseeker's Allowance and the New Deal in the United Kingdom

State unemployment insurance was introduced in the United Kingdom as early as 1911, but the system as we know it today has been strongly influenced by the Beveridge reforms of the 1940s. The present system is based on the Jobseeker's Act of 1995, which replaced unemployment insurance and social assistance with the Jobseeker's Allowance, granted to all those capable of work. Jobseeker's Allowance consists of two different benefits: contribution-based and income-based Jobseeker's Allowance. Both are administered by Jobcentre Plus within the Department for Work and Pensions; the basic flat-rate amount is the same for both benefits, the only difference being that income-based Jobseeker's Allowance is means-tested and housing costs and family allowances can be paid on top of the benefit.[65] People who are not required to work (single parents, or the sick or disabled) and who are on low income can get income support – benefits are the same as under income-based Jobseeker's Allowance.[66]

In the United Kingdom insurance is compulsory for all employees. Self-employed persons who become unemployed can claim income-based Jobseeker's Allowance, which is means-tested. The financing of unemployment insurance takes place via employers' and employees' income related contributions to National Insurance and state subsidies. A lower and upper earnings limit applies to employees' social insurance contributions; there is no upper earnings limit for employers (Sutherland 2004: 9). Due to the fact that social insurance contributions are not directly attributable to a certain benefit and benefits are paid out on a flat-rate basis, the insurance principle is very weak (Schmid et al. 1996: 243).

The New Deal programmes are an important part of the United Kingdom's current 'welfare to work' strategy. They consist of intensive job search aid, training measures and wage subsidies to employers (OECD 1998b). The New Deal

65 Eligibility for income-based JSA is only granted if the partner of the recipient does not work more than 24 hours and savings do not exceed £8000 (Department for Work and Pensions 2006). In 2004, child allowances and family additions to Income Support and income related JSA were subsumed within the Child Tax Credit, newly introduced in 2003.

66 For comprehensive information on the regulations on Jobseeker's Allowance (JSA) and on developments in the system since the early 1990s, see Social Welfare Statistics & Consultancy Branch (2005). Comprehensive statistics from 1999 to the present on the take-up of JSA, the distribution between contribution-based and income-based JSA and benefit levels can be found on the homepage of the Department for Social Development: http://www.dsdni.gov.uk/index/publications/jobseekers_allowance.htm.

for young people who have been on Jobseeker's Allowance for more than six months and the New Deal 25 Plus for unemployed who have been receiving Jobseeker's Allowance for more than 18 months are mandatory under threat of sanctions. In addition, a range of voluntary New Deal programmes also cater to those who are not claiming unemployment related benefits, for example single parents, the elderly and the partners of unemployed persons (for further information, see Cebulla 2001: 614–628).

The majority of unemployed in the United Kingdom receive income-based Jobseeker's Allowance (Kvist 2000: 14; Lister 2002: 46). In 2005, only about 17 per cent of all claimants received contribution-based Jobseeker's Allowance; insufficient contributions were by far the most frequent reason for lacking access to the non-means-tested benefit (Department for Social Development 2005). The predominance of means-tested benefits is also due to the short benefit period (six months) of contribution-based Jobseeker's Allowance. Possible disincentives generated by means-tested benefits might be countered by strategies to make work pay, such as the New Deal measures or the Working Tax Credit.

5.3 Unemployment benefits and non-standard employment

In their critical review of unemployment compensation Atkinson et al. (1991: 1688 et seq.) argue that the theoretical literature on unemployment benefits largely ignores important institutional features of social security schemes.[67] They list the following characteristics of real unemployment insurance schemes: (a) refusal of benefits on voluntary unemployment, (b) potentially no benefit payment in the initial period of unemployment (waiting periods), (c) job search and availability for work as prerequisites, (d) disqualification on refusal of suitable job offer, (e) eligibility dependent on past contribution record, with contributions related to earnings, (f) potential dependence of the benefit amount on past earnings and (g) payment of unemployment insurance benefits for a limited duration. People may thus be unemployed but not in receipt of benefits. While the first four conditions concern standard and non-standard workers to the same degree,

67 Market models of labour market and unemployment benefits are usually based on the following unrealistic assumptions: benefit payment irrespective of reason for entry, payment from the onset of the period of unemployment, independence of search for employment or availability for work, no penalty for refusing a job offer, no contribution conditions, payment at a flat rate, unlimited benefit duration and no influence of the income of other household members on eligibility for benefits (Atkinson et al. 1991: 1688).

conditions (e), (f) and (g) can have severe consequences for the latter in particular. The linking of eligibility and past contribution record (e) can be problematic for both temporary and part-time workers. Temporary employment contracts in many cases last for less than a year, often the minimum contribution time for eligibility. If there are no special rules sustaining contribution payments in case of job loss, a minimum contribution time threshold can seriously affect the access of temporary workers to benefits. Two important conditions can lead to deficient benefit entitlement in the case of part-time workers: many countries use hours and earnings thresholds below which employers and employees are exempted from contributions and benefits; furthermore, depending on the design of qualifying conditions part-time workers might need more time to gain access to benefits than full-time workers (counting of working hours or days instead of weeks). The linking of the benefit level to past earnings (f) is especially problematic for part-time workers who, due to their lower hours, tend to have relatively low earnings. Modifications in this field are especially difficult because potential disincentives to take up employment generated by high replacement rates have to be taken into account. The payment of unemployment insurance benefits for a limited duration (g) affects temporary workers more than permanent workers if benefit duration varies as a function of contribution time. Part-time workers, on the other hand, are not expected to be more affected by such rules than full-time workers.[68]

Kvist (1998: 36–49) argues similarly, stating that not only neoclassical economists but also proponents of the welfare state approach usually fail to take adequate account of the complexity of filtering mechanisms that limit eligibility for benefits. The following dimensions, potentially limiting eligibility for universal or selective benefits, are presented: (a) definition of risk and population group covered, (b) definition of recipient (individual or family), (c) personal circumstance (age, work capacity), (d) labour market status (full-time/part-time, insured/uninsured, length of employment career) and (e) civil and family status (single/married, breadwinner or not). Besides limiting eligibility dimensions (c), (d) and (e) in particular also often influence the level and duration of benefits. Kvist (1998) derives three important questions from these dimensions that will be discussed below: (i) Is membership voluntary or compulsory (this has already been discussed in Chapter 2)? (ii) What are the conditions for becoming insured? (iii) How long does the insured person have to work or pay contributions before qualifying for benefits?

68 In the late 1980s, conditions (e) and (g) were the most important reasons why British unemployed did not receive insurance benefits: 31 per cent of non-recipients had insufficient contribution records, while 49 per cent had exhausted their entitlement (Atkinson et al. 1991: 1689).

5.3.1 Part-time employment and unemployment insurance

Luckhaus (2000: 152) and Rubery et al. (1998a: 156) note different barriers that may restrict social insurance entitlements for part-time workers. First, the requirement of being in paid work for a certain number of hours or earning a certain amount per week; second, eligibility conditions that require a continuous employment history; and third, a method of calculating benefit amounts that is geared closely to former earnings. These three design features of unemployment insurance systems will now be examined. In addition, specific legislation directly geared to part-time workers will be reviewed. One general problem affecting the description of insurance systems is that they are constantly evolving. The following sections will focus on developments in the 1990s and on the current situation. A synopsis of national regulations in the different fields is given at the end of the chapter.

5.3.1.1 Hours and earnings thresholds limiting access to benefits

In many countries hours and/or earnings thresholds are specified that exclude people who work few hours or earn wages below the threshold for contributions to social insurance and accordingly also for access to benefits. Employment of this kind is usually referred to as marginal employment. For international comparisons a threshold of 15 hours is often defined, although there are variations between countries and also within countries over time.

Marginal employment for the most part involves women. According to Dingeldey (1998: 869), referring to the mid-1990s, in Spain, Germany and Denmark marginally employed women constitute a substantial minority (5 to 10 per cent), while in the United Kingdom they make up about 15 per cent of the labour force. At present, income-related rules for marginal employment exist in the United Kingdom and Germany; working time–related rules formerly existed in all four countries but were abolished. Possible short-term advantages of marginal part-time employment (higher net income, lower wage cost) are offset by substantial disadvantages when it comes to sickness, maternity, unemployment and retirement. Maier (1992: 50), based on a study of six EC countries,[69] concludes that the disadvantages are especially serious in the case of unemployment insurance, which in some countries tends to exclude large numbers of part-time workers from benefit receipt.

How is marginal employment regulated in the four countries under analysis? Have there been changes during the last decade and what are the possible

69 The countries examined in this study are Belgium, Denmark, France, the Netherlands, the United Kingdom and West Germany.

outcomes of these regulations for unemployed who were formerly in marginal employment?

In *Denmark*, until January 1994, part-time workers needed at least 15 hours of weekly employment during the previous 10 weeks before being accepted as a part-time member of an unemployment insurance fund (Fink 1999a: 101; Delsen 1995: 118). At present the following groups can join the insurance funds: employees, self-employed, spouses helping the self-employed, individuals with occupational or further education of at least 18 months, and individuals doing national service (Parsons et al. 2003: 17).[70] People sign up either as a part-time member or as a full-time member – with contributions and benefits adapted accordingly. Full-time workers (37 hours a week) and the self-employed must be insured on a full-time basis. Part-time workers (at the maximum 30 hours a week, calculated as an average over one month) can choose to be either part-time or full-time insured (The National Directorate of Labour 2006).[71] If they change from part-time to full-time employment they must change to full-time insurance. In principle, participation in unemployment insurance is now possible from the first hour of work onwards; in reality, entitlement is limited by minimum qualifying requirements, as will be seen below (Braun 2001: 651 et seq.).

In *Germany*, until 1997 the hours threshold below which qualification for unemployment insurance was not possible was 18 hours per week (Maier 1992). In 1997, a uniform 15 hours threshold was introduced for health, care, retirement and unemployment insurance, and the possibility of adding up marginal employment contracts to get above the hours threshold was expanded to unemployment insurance (Neuhold 1999). In 1999, the monthly earnings threshold was fixed at DM 630 (€322) for both West and East Germany.[72] Marginal employment was newly regulated by the second Hartz law; the new rules for marginal employment came into force on 1 April 2003. The maximum earnings for marginal part-time workers were raised to €400. The 15 hours limit was abolished and a short-time job can once again be held in addition to regular employment without becoming subject to social security contributions (Bundesgesetzblatt 30 December 2002). In addition, a new form of marginal employment (the 'Midi-job') was introduced, which works in a similar way to negative income tax credit measures and is supposed to reduce the financial disincentive on earning more than the maximum earnings for marginal part-time work constituted by the sudden onset of full contributions. According to the new regulation employees pay only 4 per cent of their earnings in social security contributions

70 A waiting period of four weeks applies to the self-employed before they can receive benefits.
71 Part-time insurance is not possible in all unemployment insurance funds.
72 Before this modification, the earnings threshold was considerably lower in East Germany, at €271.

for earnings of €401; contributions increase linearly until they reach the regular amount of 21 per cent at €800. Full drawing rights are achieved. Employers pay full contributions that are somewhat lower than the contributions for marginal employment (for more information, see Rudolph 2003; Oschmiansky 2004).

Before 1993 there was no hours threshold for insurance benefits in *Spain*, and unemployment benefits were granted proportionally (Delsen 1995: 117). From 1993 all part-time employment below 12 hours a week was exempted from contributions and excluded from benefit receipt for almost all branches of social insurance. The legislation was again amended in 1998 and part-time workers once again became entitled to social security protection in proportion to their working hours, irrespective of working hours (Royal Decree No. 15/1998).

In the *United Kingdom* earnings thresholds apply to social insurance contributions and receipts. There is at present a lower earnings limit of £82 (€120 at the time of writing) a week, an earnings threshold of £94 (€138) a week, as well as an upper earnings limit of £630 (€926) a week.[73] Earnings below the lower limit are not liable to National Insurance contributions and do not give access to unemployment insurance benefits (contribution-based Jobseeker's Allowance). For wages between the lower earnings limit and the earnings threshold no contributions are paid, but employees gain entitlement to contribution-based unemployment insurance benefits. Employers as well as employees pay contributions for earnings above the earnings threshold; employees' contributions on earnings above the upper earnings limit are very low (they were zero until 2003), while they remain constant for employers (Inland Revenue 2005).

It is estimated that 19 per cent of female employees and 5.5 per cent of male employees have weekly earnings below the lower earnings limit and are therefore outside the contributory benefit system (unless they make voluntary contributions) (Equal Opportunities Commission 1998). Among men the vast majority of those concerned are younger than 25, whereas this age group accounts for only a quarter of all women with earnings below this threshold. The great majority of employees (94 per cent) who earn below the lower earnings limit work part-time, and more than a third of all women who are employed part-time earn below the lower earnings limit. In addition, men and women with earnings below the lower earnings limit are more likely to be employed in temporary jobs, and half of those working on a casual basis have earnings below this threshold (Equal Opportunities Commission 1998).

Rubery et al. (1998a: 179 et seqq.) conclude that the exclusionary impact of the earnings threshold in the United Kingdom is potentially greater than in Ger-

73 Earnings thresholds are adapted every year. In 1995, for example, the earnings threshold lay at £58 (€85) per week. The lower earnings limit was introduced in 2000 (for further information, see Davy 2000: 152–155).

many due to the higher relative level of the threshold compared to average earnings. The overall effect of earnings or hours thresholds on access to unemployment benefits thus very much depends on the size of the group affected.

5.3.1.2 Minimum contribution period as access barrier

Eurofound (2003: 69), based on comprehensive country studies, argues that the contribution period needed for entitlement or re-entitlement to benefits plays an important role in access to unemployment insurance for workers on flexible contracts. In particular, calculation methods based on full days of work risk putting part-time workers at a severe disadvantage. Do the qualifying conditions in the countries under observation discriminate, implicitly or explicitly, against part-time workers?

In *Denmark*, as part of the comprehensive labour market reforms, the contribution period was increased in 1997 from 26 to 52 weeks of employment (usually full-time hours within the same industry), within a reference period of three years. In addition, one year's membership of an unemployment insurance fund is required; only work after joining the insurance fund counts towards this requirement (Hansen 2004: 5). For part-time workers (part-time insured) the employment requirement was raised from 17 to 34 weeks of full-time equivalent[74] employment within a reference period of three years (Rubery et al. 1998a: 158; Fink 1999a: 100). This requires continuous employment of 8 hours a week during the three preceding years or shorter work periods at higher hours. Renewal of rights to unemployment insurance benefits is possible after 26 (17) weeks of work within the last three years (Hansen 2002: 28 et seqq.).

In *Germany*, until January 2006 the minimum eligibility requirement for unemployment insurance benefit receipt was 12 months of contributory employment within the three years preceding the onset of unemployment (Neuhold 1999: 64; Pennings 1990: 148 et seq.). The reference period is now two instead of three years, rendering eligibility for benefits more difficult for persons who work infrequently (SGB III, § 123, 124). Until 1999 people who had been employed subject to social insurance contributions for at least 150 days were entitled to means-tested unemployment assistance; before 1983 only 70 days in employment were required (Mohr 2004: 292). From 2000 until the end of 2004 unemployment assistance was granted only to those who had exhausted their unemployment insurance entitlement. Unemployment assistance has now been replaced by a basic allowance (*Arbeitslosengeld* II), which is granted to all people who are employable; it is subject to means-testing. Due to the fact that months and not days or hours of employment form the basis of the eligibility

74 Full-time equivalent is defined as full normal working hours within the trade or occupational field. In most cases this is 37 hours.

requirement in Germany, part-time workers who exceed the earnings threshold and thus pay social security contributions have the same likelihood as full-time employees to qualify for benefits.

Eligibility requirements for unemployment insurance are rather weak in *Spain*. People have to work a minimum of 360 days during the six years immediately preceding unemployment. Before 1993 only six months of employment within the previous four years had been necessary for gaining access to unemployment insurance benefits of very short duration (Toharia et al. 2000: 320 et seqq.). People who have no access to contributory benefits may be entitled to means-tested unemployment assistance if they have family obligations and have paid social insurance contributions for at least three months; if they have no family obligations six months of contribution payments are required (Europäische Kommission 1996; European Commission 2004c). From 1994 on, qualifying for unemployment insurance benefits became more difficult for part-time workers, especially those with low hours, because the contribution period was now calculated on the basis of real working time instead of working days. Since 1999 unemployment insurance entitlement has once again been based on days worked (Fassler-Ristic 1999: 374–379). Entitlement rules based on working days instead of weeks or months render access to benefits more difficult for people who work fewer than five days a week.[75] Recently, Spain's Constitutional Court ruled that the current regulations on the contributions required for obtaining access to social security benefits discriminate against part-time workers and indirectly also against women. The court called for the annulment of the corresponding legislation (Albarracín 2005). Taking into account working days instead of weeks or months affects not only the access of part-time workers to benefits, but also, due to the application of the proportionality rule (contribution time to benefit time), the duration of benefit receipt (Ministerio de Trabajo y Asuntos Sociales 2006a).

In the *United Kingdom*, the qualifying criteria for contribution-based Jobseeker's Allowance stipulate that in one of the two tax years prior to the calendar year in which the claim is made contributions must have been paid that amount to at least 25 times the minimum contribution (lower earnings limit) for that year. As a further requirement, contributions paid or credited[76] in each of the two tax years have to amount to at least 50 times the minimum contribution (Euro-

75 Out of all registered part-time workers in 1995, 80 per cent were in part-time employment of a horizontal kind: five days with fewer than eight hours (Fassler-Ristic 1999: 388).

76 Contribution credits are added to the contribution record when a person is unemployed, not capable of work, on a carer allowance or on Statutory Maternity pay and the like. Contribution credits are often not granted automatically and, furthermore, do not in all cases count towards the contribution requirement for contribution-based Jobseeker's Allowance (compare The Social Security Regulations 1996).

pean Commission 2004c: 845; Hansen 2002: 27, 28).[77] Contribution requirements are thus more difficult to fulfil for persons with low earnings (for instance, part-time workers). Particularly problematic is the combination of low earnings and discontinuous employment; according to Cebulla (2001: 604), in 2000 only about 16 per cent of all claimants received contribution-based Jobseeker's Allowance. Insufficient contribution payments were the main reason for lacking entitlement.

5.3.1.3 Are net replacement rates beneficial to former part-time workers?

The unemployment benefits of former part-time workers are in most countries lower than those of former full-time workers. Not only financing reasons are mentioned in justification, but also incentive problems concerning re-employment. There is a range of possibilities for calculating replacement rates and adapting them for part-time workers. Unemployment benefits are often determined as a percentage of the former wage (Germany, Spain); another possibility is maximum unemployment benefits that vary between former full-time and part-time workers (Denmark). Uniform unemployment insurance benefits of a flat-rate nature (United Kingdom) are rare; they are neutral in terms of work incentives if they are very low or combined with strict reemployment or activation requirements.

Groups with low average earnings receive lower benefits than high-wage groups in countries in which benefits are calculated as a direct proportion of previous earnings. Upper thresholds that cap the benefit level at a specific point can modify this effect and redistribute benefits towards lower income groups (Denmark). More equitable treatment of lower income groups takes place in systems in which benefits are paid as a fixed amount or a minimum or maximum replacement income is granted. Equitable compensation as such is not necessarily appropriate; where benefits are very low – which is usually the case with flat-rate benefits – this disadvantages all groups (compare Rubery et al. 1998a: 168 et seqq.).

If benefit levels are strongly linked to past income, part-time workers risk finding themselves with an income that does not enable them to make ends meet. This problem can be attenuated through high replacement rates, decreasing with growing income, or by way of a guaranteed minimum benefit amount that can be

77 Before the 1988 reform, contribution requirements were much less strict – the level of earnings on which a claimant must have paid contributions did not refer to the immediately preceding tax year but to any prior year. A significant amount of unemployment during one tax year now substantially reduces the probability of unemployment insurance benefit receipt – previously, periods of unemployment were credited as contributions. For more information, see Micklewright (1990: 8).

granted either directly, via the unemployment insurance system, or indirectly, by supplementing insurance benefits with social assistance.

One problem with official comparative calculations of net replacement rates is that they usually take the Average Production Worker (APW)[78] as a basis – a concept that is not in line with the characteristics of the group that represents the focus of this study. Especially problematic is the fact that the APW refers to a person who has been continuously full-time employed since the age of 18 and therefore has a full contribution record (OECD 2004b: 127). Net replacement rates calculated on the basis of the APW disregard not only diverging situations between part-time and full-time workers and temporary and permanent workers, but so far also the different earning potentials of women and men.[79]

Notwithstanding the above stated problems, net replacement rates that refer to a former income of 67 per cent of APW should come closest to a part-time income.[80] In 2002, net replacement rate levels for a single person without children, on low income and in the initial phase of unemployment were 84 per cent in Denmark, 63 per cent in Germany, 76 per cent in Spain and 63 per cent in the United Kingdom (OECD 2004b: 92–98). Comparisons with net replacement rates for single persons previous with high earnings (150 per cent of APW) reflect the rules in the four countries: net replacement rates for this group are 45 per cent in Denmark, 62 per cent in Germany, 48 per cent in Spain and 31 per cent in the United Kingdom. Due to high ceilings, net replacement rates on unemployment hardly vary between low and high income workers in Germany; they are somewhat lower for high income workers in Spain and considerably higher for low income workers in Denmark (a very high starting rate of 90 per cent, coupled with relatively low ceilings) and the United Kingdom (flat-rate nature of the benefits).

Another question concerns the specific rules governing the calculation of net replacement rates in the countries under observation – are they beneficial for former part-time workers or do they grant only low replacement income for this group of workers?

In *Denmark*, net replacement rates are high for former low income workers, at 90 per cent of reference earnings. There are no ceilings for contribution pay-

78 The APW concept is often used to present replacement rates. An APW is an adult full-time production worker in the manufacturing sector whose wage earnings are equal to the average sectoral wage earnings. For a more comprehensive definition, see OECD (1999b: 59–67). The use of APW levels as a reference category can be criticised because it hides strong variation, for example due to different qualification levels and age categories. The OECD net replacement rates include housing benefits.

79 Rubery et al. (1998a: 171) present calculations of net replacement rates for women.

80 The following paragraphs will show that there are sometimes special rules concerning the level of benefits for former part-time workers, so the above results are only an approximation.

ments but the maximum benefit amount is currently DKK 3335 (€447) per week, which leads to net replacement rates that decrease inversely in relation to previous income (European Commission 2006: 110). Benefit levels are lower for young unemployed who gain access to benefits after a minimum of 18 months of training. Calculation of net replacement rates is usually based on the average earnings of the preceding 12 weeks. Part-time insured persons pay two-thirds of the contributions to the unemployment insurance fund, and the ceiling for their benefits lies at two-thirds of the maximum rate of a full-time insured person (Parsons et al. 2003: 16; Jensen 1999: 2). At present, the ceiling for part-time insured is DKK 2225 (€298) per week (The National Directorate of Labour 2006 (February): 10).

According to Hansen (2002: 32), Denmark probably has the narrowest gap between the maximum and the minimum benefit levels – benefits are therefore quasi flat-rate. Concerning net replacement rates of former part-time workers it must be taken into account that the minimum benefit is applicable only to persons continuously full-time employed for three years before becoming unemployed (Fink 1999a: 103). There is no unemployment assistance in Denmark, but those who are not insured or who do not gain access to unemployment insurance can claim means-tested social assistance benefits.[81]

In *Germany*, net replacement rates vary with family circumstances. At present, people without family obligations receive 60 per cent of former net earnings; people with children receive 67 per cent. Replacement rates for unemployed without children had been lowered from 68 to 63 per cent in 1986, and reduced again in 1994 to the present level (Rubery et al. 1998a: 174). Compared to Denmark, earnings ceilings are very high at €5150 (€4350) per month in the old (new) *Länder* (European Commission 2004c: 284). Whereas in Denmark net replacement rates visibly decrease with growing former earnings (low income is compensated with higher net replacement rates), high ceilings in Germany lead to constant net replacement rates over a large income margin.

Until recently, unemployment assistance – subject to means-testing – has been paid at a rate of 57 per cent of net earnings for people with children and at 53 per cent for people without children. Unemployment assistance was thus based on previous earnings, although it was tax- and not contribution-financed. Since 2005, a low uniform flat-rate benefit (*Arbeitslosengeld* II) at the level of social assistance has been paid to people who have exhausted their unemployment insurance entitlement, to unemployed persons who do not qualify for insur-

81 Social assistance payments for individuals with dependent children stand at about 80 per cent of the maximum unemployment insurance benefit; for others they amount to about 60 per cent of the maximum unemployment insurance benefit (OECD 2004a: 4).

ance benefits in the first place and to former social assistance recipients capable of work.

In *Spain* until 1991 the net replacement rate was 80 per cent of previous earnings during the first six months of unemployment, 70 per cent for the next six months and 60 per cent thereafter. In the 1992 reform the replacement ratio was cut to the present 70 per cent, which is paid for the first six months of unemployment and is then reduced to 60 per cent (Bover et al. 2002: 258). As in Germany, unemployment insurance benefits take into account not only former earnings, but also the family situation. There are minimum and maximum unemployment insurance benefits. Since July 2004, the minimum benefit for recipients with dependent children has been 107 per cent; without dependent children it is 80 per cent of the Public Indicator of Multiple Effects Income (IPREM).[82] The maximum benefit ranges from 175 to 225 per cent of the IPREM, depending on the number of children (if any) (Ballester 2005).[83] The minimum unemployment insurance benefit for part-time workers is reduced proportionally to hours worked (Ministerio de Trabajo y Asuntos Sociales 2006a). The maximum benefit in Spain is about 64 per cent of the earnings of a single APW; in Germany it is about 103 per cent and in Denmark only about 52 per cent (OECD 2004b: 21–24).[84] Reference earnings are usually average gross earnings over the last six months.

Means-tested unemployment assistance is granted either as a follow-up benefit to unemployment insurance (in specific cases) or, in case of an insufficient contribution record, as an alternative to unemployment insurance. It is granted at a rate of 80 per cent of the IPREM, though elderly long-term unemployed with long contribution records and responsibility for children can receive up to 107 per cent of the IPREM (Comisión de expertos para el diálogo social 2005: 85). The duration of unemployment assistance ranges from 3 to 30 months (Ministerio de Trabajo y Asuntos Sociales 2006c).

The *United Kingdom* is the only country in this sample that grants flat-rate unemployment benefits instead of a replacement income related to previous earnings. Low flat-rate benefits are usually paid in combination with housing benefits. In the case of unemployment insurance (contribution-based Jobseeker's

---

82 IPREM substitutes the minimum wage that was used as reference category before July 2004. This allows raising the minimum wage without affecting social insurance benefit minima or maxima. IPREM is revised every year; in 2005 its annual amount was €6.58, while the minimum wage was €7.18.

83 The minimum insurance benefit for unemployed persons without children is €447; for unemployed with children it is €598. The maximum monthly benefit is €978 (unemployed without children) and €1258 (unemployed with more than two children) (Ministerio de Trabajo y Asuntos Sociales 2006a).

84 The different purchasing power parities make such static comparisons difficult.

Allowance) the amount of the flat-rate benefit depends exclusively on the age of the recipient; the benefit is lower for recipients who are younger than 25 years. Unemployment assistance (income-based Jobseeker's Allowance) depends on age and household situation (for example, the number of hours worked by the partner). The unemployment insurance system was thoroughly reformed in 1996; supplements for dependents, for example, were abolished (Jepsen et al. 2002: 112 et seq.). The flat-rate amount is the same for unemployment insurance, unemployment assistance and social assistance; variations occur only due to means-testing and inclusion of the household situation in the latter two cases (Department for Work and Pensions 2006).

The level of flat-rate compensation does not vary between former full-time and eligible former part-time workers, but it is very low by international comparison (Mohr 2004: 294–298). In 2006, unemployed persons aged 25 years or over received £57.45 (€84) per week, those between 18 and 24 years received £45.50 (€66) and those aged 16 to 17 years received £34.60 (€50) per week (Department for Work and Pensions 2006). There is no increase for dependents, but unemployment insurance benefits can be topped up with social assistance if they are not sufficient, given the household situation (OECD 2004b: 1999). The low benefit level weakens possible disincentive effects.

5.3.1.4 Specific legislation benefiting former part-time workers

In some countries special rules which are beneficial to part-time workers are in place when it comes to unemployment insurance benefits. A prominent example is the possibility to base unemployment benefits on former full-time employment earnings instead of actual part-time earnings for a transitional period. This possibility has been introduced in some countries to encourage full-time workers to switch to part-time employment. Furthermore, specific rules often exist that allow the combination of unemployment benefit receipt and part-time employment. These rules are usually rather restrictive in order to prevent abuses or disincentives. The following section discusses some of the current regulations in the four countries. Special regulations for part-time employment as a transition route to retirement or as an alternative to early retirement will not be considered here.

In *Denmark*, a person who becomes partially unemployed or who starts a part-time job may receive complementary unemployment benefits if he or she is available for full-time work (or for 30 hours' employment if part-time insured) (The National Directorate of Labour 2006: 11). Danish insurance data from the 1980s and early 1990s demonstrate that considerably more women switched from part-time to full-time insurance than from part-time to full-time employment, which suggests that many women engage in part-time employment with supplementary benefits while seeking full-time work (Rubery et al. 1998a: 161).

In *Germany*, there are a number of grounds for qualification for partial unemployment. Partial unemployment benefits can be granted in the event of short-time work (*Kurzarbeit*), but in some sectors also due to weather conditions (*Schlechtwettergeld*). One interesting but restrictive regulation is that persons who had two jobs under compulsory insurance coverage, but lost one of them and are now searching for a new additional part-time or full-time job have a right to supplementary unemployment benefits. In order to prevent abuse this benefit is restricted to 6 months and is paid only if the job that was lost was held for at least 12 months within the last two years. The benefits granted are based on lost earnings and calculated in accordance with regular unemployment benefits (SGB III, §150) (European Commission 2004c: 292).[85]

Since August 1994 transitions from full-time to part-time employment have been supported through a range of measures that – for a limited period – lead to protection of the status quo on benefit receipt. If a person has received unemployment insurance or assistance benefits during the three (from February 2006 onwards, two) years preceding a new unemployment spell, the benefit amount will conform to the old claim if it was higher than what the unemployed can expect based on his or her new earnings. This should strengthen incentives to escape unemployment by taking up part-time employment. Furthermore, if a person has reduced his or her working time to less than 80 per cent of former working time, but has, during the three and a half years preceding unemployment, worked full-time for at least six continuous months, the claim will be based on full-time employment. A third rule is beneficial to those who, within a framework of two years, have mainly been full-time employed, but were part-time employed directly before the onset of unemployment – in this case the claim can be based on two years instead of one, so that the full-time income is also taken into account (SGB III, §130 and §131) (Rabe 2001: 407–409). For an interpretation of these specific laws, see Wissing (1996: 6, 7) and Stascheit (2004).

In *Spain*, unemployment is regarded as partial when the worker's usual working day and wage is temporarily reduced by at least one third. Entitlement depends on the decision by the labour administration within the framework of a reorganisation plan. The benefit, if granted, is calculated as for total unemployment but in proportion to the reduction in working time (European Commission 2004c: 293–295). Since 1999 remuneration deriving from overtime that is liable to social insurance contributions has served as additional basis for calculating social benefit premiums. This rule applies only to permanent part-time workers;

85 The downside is that the entitlement to unemployment benefits that arises within two years of receiving supplementary unemployment benefits is shortened by one day for every two days that the supplement was paid out (SGB III, §128).

full-time workers, on the other hand, pay contributions on overtime but since 1999 overtime no longer increases their benefits. Part-time workers with temporary contracts can work overtime only in exceptional cases (Fassler-Ristic 1999: 372).

There are hardly any special regulations for part-time workers in the *United Kingdom*. One of the conditions for receiving Jobseeker's Allowance is that the claimant is not engaged in work for more than 16 hours a week. The withdrawal of all additional earnings above £5 provides no incentive to combine part-time work with unemployment benefits. From 1996 until the end of 2004 it was possible to reclaim part of the 'lost' earnings (deriving from a job held in addition to benefit receipt) up to a limit of £1000 as a back-to-work bonus (Department for Work and Pensions 2002 (May): 100). The fact that flat-rate benefits rather than earnings-related benefits are paid renders regulations of the kind existing in Germany unnecessary.

5.3.2 Temporary employment and unemployment insurance

While hours and/or earnings thresholds, as well as the calculation rules for net replacement rates, potentially influence the unemployment benefit receipt of part-time workers, neither are usually a problem for workers with temporary contracts.[86] Minimum contribution periods, on the other hand, can seriously restrict access to benefits for temporary workers. The longer the minimum contribution period and the shorter the reference period, the less likely temporary workers are to qualify for benefits. Those who qualify for benefits in the first place are also disadvantaged in insurance systems that link the duration of benefits to the length of former contribution periods.

5.3.2.1 Minimum contribution period as an obstacle to entitlement

The implications of minimum contribution periods for benefit entitlement have already been discussed for part-time workers. In the case of temporary workers this regulation not only works more directly but should also affect a larger group because one of the specific characteristics of fixed-term or casual contracts, in contrast to permanent contracts, is their relatively short duration. In most countries, the required qualifying period is at least one year, whereas – as we saw in Chapter 3 – the average duration of temporary contracts is less than a year in the

86 There is sufficient evidence that temporary workers on average earn lower wages than permanent workers, at least in some countries (for Germany and the United Kingdom, see Giesecke et al. 2005; for Spain, see Jimeno et al. 1993). In many unemployment insurance systems this leads to lower benefit levels.

majority of cases. How far-reaching access restrictions are depends not only on the required minimum contribution period, but also on the reference period. In most countries, as regards meeting minimum contribution periods for claiming benefits, separate spells of employment can be accumulated, albeit over a relatively limited time period (OECD 2002c: 144–150). This implies that temporary workers, who alternate between short spells of employment and unemployment, may be able, at least after a certain time, to draw benefits not tied to a specific job. The longer the reference period during which the employment requirement can be fulfilled, the more beneficial the regulation is for temporary workers. In a country characterised by frequent transitions between employment and unemployment instead of direct transitions from one (temporary) job to another even a long reference period will not be of help because a new reference period usually starts after each period of unemployment benefit receipt (for Germany, see, for example, SGB III, § 124 (2)). Some of the relevant information on minimum contribution periods in the specific countries was discussed in the section on part-time employment and will not be repeated here.

While prior to 1995 the minimum contribution period was 26 weeks in *Denmark*, at present it is 52 weeks of insured employment within the preceding three years. Access for (temporary) workers has accordingly become more difficult. A further disadvantage is that the minimum benefit applies only to persons who were continuously employed during the three years preceding unemployment. On the other hand, temporary workers benefit from the possibility to renew the right to benefits after 26 weeks of work within a three-year period.

In *Germany*, qualification for unemployment insurance benefits now requires 12 months of work within the preceding two years; before January 2006 the reference period was three years (SGB III, §§123, 124). The shorter reference period penalises people with discontinuous employment careers. One rule benefiting workers who have received benefits within the preceding four years is the possibility to use remaining benefit entitlement in the case of a new unemployment spell (Stascheit et al. 2004: 192–201). The reduced minimum contribution period of six months that had been in place for seasonal workers[87] was also abolished (European Commission 2003c).[88] Seasonal employment is termed marginal employment if it is shorter than two months or 50 working days within one year.

87 The following definition applied to seasonal workers: a person who has worked for at least 180 days at a seasonal establishment during the preceding 16 months, or a person who has received unemployment insurance benefits for some time during the preceding 16 months and who has, in addition, worked at least 120 days (Stascheit et al. 2004: 95). This rule also applied to basic military or civil service personnel.

88 Prolonged reference periods for newly self-employed and carers will also be abolished which can be compensated to a certain degree by the new possibility of voluntary insurance during times of non-eligibility for compulsory insurance.

It is exempted from social security contributions and benefit receipt (SGB IV, §8). The abolition of primary unemployment assistance in 2000 has, according to Trube (2002), mainly excluded non-standard workers from wage-related unemployment assistance and referred them to social assistance. With the introduction of the new basic benefit (ALG II), wage-related unemployment assistance has been completely abolished.

In *Spain*, the qualifying condition is 360 days of insured work within the last six years. Contributions that have not been exhausted during an unemployment spell are carried forward if the employer is changed (Eurofound 2003). The short benefit duration that, furthermore, depends on the beneficiary's contribution record limits the effectiveness of this rule. According to Fassler-Ristic (1999: 274), after the minimum contribution time was doubled from 6 to 12 months in 1992 a large part of temporary workers no longer had access to insurance benefits, but only to means-tested, very low and short-term unemployment assistance.[89]

In the *United Kingdom*, the rules that govern entitlement to contribution-based Jobseeker's Allowance are beneficial to those with moderate wages who work continuously but also to workers with discontinuous employment and high wages. This is due to the fact that entitlement to benefits does not depend on a specific contribution period but on a certain level of contributions paid or credited. Problems of access to contribution-based Jobseeker's Allowance can arise for temporary agency workers because they are often treated as self-employed for the purpose of employment legislation (K. Schömann et al. 1998: 69, 86; Slater 2003: 12 et seq.). The fact that unemployment insurance, unemployment assistance and social assistance in the United Kingdom grant the same low benefit level renders a lack of access to contribution-based Jobseeker's Allowance problematic only in cases in which means-testing makes a difference.

5.3.2.2 Duration of unemployment benefits

Linking the duration of benefit payments to the length of previous employment puts workers with discontinuous employment periods at a disadvantage. Rubery (1998a: 165) notes a further problem, namely the shorter the duration of unemployment benefits, the sooner unemployed workers have to rely upon unemployment assistance or social assistance. Unemployment assistance and social

89 In fact, one of the arguments that the government brought forward in order to justify the comprehensive revision of the unemployment protection system was that the system's financial problems had been caused by the possibility of linking short employment contracts with benefit periods (Toharia et al. 2000: 321). In line with the objectives of the 1992 reforms, benefit coverage, which had risen from 23 per cent in 1984 to 50 per cent in 1992, had again fallen, to around 37 per cent in 2001 (Bentolila et al. 2003).

assistance benefits are usually means-tested; a loss of benefit entitlement often also leads to a lack of access to the whole range of active labour market programmes. Compared to other European countries, Denmark is characterised by a uniform long duration of insurance benefit payments, while payments of insurance benefits in the United Kingdom are of equally short duration for all recipients. In Germany, the age of the recipient and the length of insured employment are taken into account when determining benefit duration. In Spain, the duration of unemployment insurance is a proportional function of contribution time. Contribution time, age, as well as family composition are taken into account when determining the duration of unemployment assistance.

In *Denmark*, until 1993 unemployment insurance benefits were paid for 30 months and re-qualification for benefits through the acceptance of a subsidised job or training offer was possible. The labour market reform that came into force on 1 January 2004 abolished the latter possibility; furthermore, a two-period benefit system was introduced with an initial passive period of four years (with optional activation) and a subsequent activation period of three years. Further reforms during the 1990s shortened the passive and the overall period. In 1996 the passive period was reduced to two years, and to six months for young unemployed. In 1999 it was shortened to one year, followed by an activation period of three years with simultaneous benefit receipt (Madsen 2002a: 75 et seq.). Benefit duration is the same for all beneficiaries.

In *Germany*, the duration of unemployment insurance benefits has so far varied according to age and length of previous insured employment within the prolonged reference period of seven years.[90] The ratio of contribution time to benefit period was 2:1; a person with a contribution record of 12 months during the preceding seven years could draw benefits for six months. This entitlement period could rise to up to 32 months for persons older than 57 who had been employed subject to social insurance contributions for at least 64 months within the seven-year reference period. For all recipients younger than 45 the maximum benefit period was 12 months. With the reform of 2003 the maximum duration of unemployment insurance benefits was cut to 18 months for people older than 55; the maximum duration for all others is now 12 months. The ratio of 2:1 still applies, while the prolonged reference period is now three years; the minimum duration remains six months. The new regulation has applied since February 2006 (Stascheit et al. 2004: 192–197) (SGB III, §127).

Primary unemployment assistance, which existed until December 1999, was particularly beneficial to people with short contribution records – for instance, workers with fixed-duration contracts – because it granted 312 days of wage-

90 In order to calculate benefit duration the reference period was extended to seven (now three) years. Every unemployment spell triggers the start of a new reference period.

related benefit receipt after a minimum contribution period of only 150 days (European Commission 2003c: 32).[91] Wage-related unemployment assistance was replaced by a means-tested flat-rate benefit at the level of social assistance that is in principle granted for unlimited duration to unemployed persons who have exhausted insurance benefits and to those who have insufficient contribution records to qualify for unemployment insurance.

As in Germany, the duration of benefit payments in *Spain* depends on the length of the contribution period, which is disadvantageous for temporary workers with short contracts. Prior to the reform of 1992 each period of six months' contributions gave access to three months' benefit receipt; now the duration of benefits is only one third of the contribution time. The minimum contribution period of 12 months therefore gives rise to four months of benefit receipt. The maximum entitlement period remains two years (Toharia et al. 2000: 321). The duration of unemployment assistance that can be granted, either in case of non-qualification for unemployment insurance or as a follow-up benefit to unemployment insurance, depends on the contribution time, age and family responsibilities of the beneficiary. The maximum duration is two and a half years (Ministerio de Trabajo y Asuntos Sociales 2006b, c).

In the *United Kingdom*, the entitlement to unemployment insurance benefits (contribution-based Jobseeker's Allowance) was cut from 12 to 6 months in 1996. Income-based Jobseeker's Allowance, as the follow-up or alternative benefit, can be granted for an unlimited period, but is subject to means-testing. It is administered by the same authority as contribution-based Jobseeker's Allowance in order to ensure consistent activation of all employable groups. The rules for benefit duration are the same for all beneficiaries, regardless of the former insurance period.

5.4 Summary and outlook

Table 8 gives a synopsis of the four countries' insurance regulations as far as the access and coverage of non-standard workers are concerned. In all countries looked at here unemployment benefits are modelled on standard employment. The general principles on which the countries' social insurance systems are based, as well as the specific rules governing unemployment benefits, nevertheless suggest variations between the countries when it comes to the inclusion of non-standard workers.

91 Before 1994 primary unemployment assistance was granted for an unlimited period.

Table 8: Synopsis of unemployment insurance rules concerning non-standard workers

	Denmark	Germany	Spain	United Kingdom
Hours or wage threshold (only applies to part-time workers) → access	– until 1994 membership of UI* fund was not possible for persons employed for less than 15 hours a week – at present membership is possible from the first hour onwards	– until 1997 hours threshold at 18 hours (for UI and UA) – since April 1997 threshold at 15 hours and possibility to add up employment for access – since 1999 uniform earnings threshold of €322 – Hartz reform: hours threshold was abolished, earnings threshold of €400	– before 1993 no hours threshold applied – between 1994 and 1998 part-time employment below 12 hours was excluded from unemployment insurance benefit receipt – it was re-included at the end of 1998 (pro rata temporis)	– an earnings threshold applies – since 2000 there has been a small earnings bracket in which persons do not have to pay National Insurance Contributions but gain entitlement to benefits
Minimum contribution period → access	general: – one year membership in UI fund – until 1996 26 weeks insured employment within preceding 3 years after joining fund – from 1997 52 weeks in last 3 years (full-time employment), renewal of rights after 26 weeks part-time insured: – before 1997 uniform 26 weeks – from 1997 on 34 weeks full-time equivalent instead of 52 weeks, renewal of rights after 17 weeks temporary workers: – access has become more difficult due to prolonged insurance period requirement, but lax renewal rule applies	general: – UI: 12 months of insured employment during last 3 years; from 2006 on during last 2 years – UA** until 1999: 150 calendar days of insured employment, until the end of 2004 only as follow-up benefit – since 2005 low flat-rate benefit (ALG II) for all employable persons without a contribution requirement part-time workers: – no disadvantages temporary workers: – primary UA that was beneficial to temporary workers was abolished – shortening of reference period from 3 to 2 years problematic – remaining entitlements can be carried forward	general: – UI: at least 360 days of insured employment in the 6 preceding years – UA: at least 90 days part-time workers: – from 1994 contribution has been based on time actually worked – since 1999 every working day counts towards contribution period independent of hours worked (more difficult to enter for those who work less than 5 days per week) temporary workers: – remaining entitlements can be carried forward but due to comparatively short benefit duration this is not so effective	general: – UI: 25 times the minimum contribution in the preceding year, additionally, in the 2 preceding years at least 50 times the minimum contribution – UA: no conditions, but means-tested part-time workers and temporary workers: – no direct disadvantages but difficulty gaining entitlement to contribution-based JSA*** for persons with low earnings (part-time) and/or discontinuous employment

	Denmark	Germany	Spain	United Kingdom
Dependence on former wage level **Only applies to part-time workers** **→ level**	– yes, replacement rate is 90% combined with low ceilings part-time insured: – can at most receive 2/3 of maximum benefit; the minimum benefit does not apply to former part-time employed – low ceilings lead to redistribution from high to low incomes	– yes, UI: 67% (60% without children) combined with high ceilings – UA: formerly 57% (53%), now low flat-rate basic benefit part-time workers: – special rule for those who change from full-time to part-time: for a certain period they can receive UI benefits, depending on their former wage	– yes, UI: 70%, after 6 months 60%, – no, UA: between 80% and 225% of IPREM depending on age, contribution time and children part-time workers: – upper benefit limit and minimum benefit (UI and UA) are reduced for former part-time employed proportional to their hours	– no, UI and UA are low flat-rate benefits
dependence on former contribution time and age **→ duration**	– no, UI is granted to all those entitled, for 4 years (1 year passive, 3 years active) – UA does not exist but social assistance is paid at a relatively high level	– yes, UI: contribution time and age are taken into account; ratio: 12 months of contribution = 6 months of entitlement – UI: maximum 12 months (18 months for elderly) – no, UA (now basic benefit): indefinite but subject to means-testing temporary workers: – disadvantaged if short contract duration (see above)	– yes, UI and UA – UI: contribution time is taken into account in a proportion of 3 (contribution months) to 1 (entitlement); before 1992 the proportion was 2 to 1 – UI: maximum 24 months – UA: 3 to 30 months; ratio in some cases 1 to 1 temporary workers: – disadvantaged (see above) part-time workers: – disadvantage for those working less than 5 days a week (see minimum contribution period)	– no, UI: 6 months for all – UA: indefinite but subject to means- testing

Note: * Unemployment insurance; ** Unemployment assistance; *** Jobseeker's Allowance.
Source: Own synopsis drawn from various sources (see above).

The theoretical part has already revealed that the Danish and British unemployment insurance systems incorporate welfare principles more strongly, while the German and Spanish systems favour insurance principles. The above analysis has further strengthened this assessment. Flat-rate benefits independent of former wages (United Kingdom) and low upper ceilings combined with high net replacement rates (Denmark) clearly support the welfare principle. The same is true for the uniform duration of benefit receipt independent of contribution time (both the United Kingdom and Denmark). In Germany and Spain, on the other hand, certain rules in the unemployment insurance system clearly work in favour of the insurance principle. In Germany, earnings ceilings are high, leading to strong equivalence between former earnings and benefits, in Spain and, to a lesser degree, Germany there is a strong connection between contribution periods and the duration of benefit receipt. The hypothesis that systems based on welfare principles are more favourable to non-standard workers than systems that are more strongly based on insurance principles might hold in general, but the systems are in practice much more complicated than those two theoretical principles suggest.

There is a variety of specific rules that influence the coverage of non-standard workers directly or indirectly. Examples are specific maximum benefits for part-time (insured) workers in the Danish and the Spanish system, and strong links between former wages and replacement benefits. Such rules not only counter possible disincentives to take up new employment but also make the systems financially more viable. The British system does not require specific rules for non-standard workers who have entered the system because benefits in general are very low, of short duration or subject to means-testing, and therefore pose neither serious financial nor incentive problems.

Restrictions on benefit access for specific groups of unemployed exist in all four countries. The clearest and most exclusive rules are those for marginal part-time workers. A regulation that operates less directly is the minimum contribution period that is usually disadvantageous for persons in discontinuous employment or, in certain cases, for persons with fewer than five working days per week (Spain). As far as special rules (easier access or higher benefits) are concerned, they apply mostly to part-time workers (Denmark and Germany). This can be explained by the political intention to create more part-time employment by providing incentives to take up this kind of employment. At least in the German case this line of argument has been used when allowing part-time workers to base unemployment insurance claims on former full-time employment for a limited period.

All in all, no clear trends can be discerned towards better inclusion of non-standard workers in the countries under analysis. Hours thresholds in Germany and Denmark have been relaxed, but the earnings threshold for marginal employment in Germany is still in place and has even been raised.[92] In Spain an hours threshold for part-time employment was in place for about four years, but in an attempt to make part-time work more attractive it has been abolished again. Modifications in qualifying and reference periods (Denmark, Germany and Spain) have impaired the access to benefits of non-standard workers in particular. In all four countries benefit duration has been shortened, but these developments affect non-standard workers disproportionately only in Germany and Spain. Net replacement rates have been cut in Germany and Spain; in the United Kingdom the adult dependants allowance has been abolished and lower benefit rates have been introduced for young unemployed. These developments affect standard- and non-standard workers equally.

Based on the available information it is evident that the unemployment benefit coverage of non-standard workers has not been directly on the agenda in any of the countries under analysis.[93] Non-standard workers seem to lack adequate interest representation. There has been some union engagement in favour of the rights of non-standard workers to unemployment insurance benefits (Spain), but it only succeeded in defending the status quo and did not put more comprehensive social insurance inclusion on the agenda.

What procedures can be derived from the information presented above for Chapter 6 and what are the limits on analysis?

Concerning hours or earnings thresholds the data allow us to assess the corresponding share of workers affected by this access restriction. Problems fulfilling the minimum contribution period can be assessed by using the indicator on contract length, but complete information on this indicator is available only for Spain and Denmark. Information on weekly working hours can be used to assess access to systems that base their minimum contribution periods on working hours instead of working weeks or months. Accurate assessment of the Spanish system, which favours horizontal as compared to vertical part-time employment, is not possible because there is no information on the average number of days worked in a week. Potential net replacement rates can be calculated on the basis of the annual earnings information, transformed into monthly earnings. Differences in the duration of unemployment compensation (Germany and Spain) can theoretically be approached by taking into account the average contract duration

92 Using an earnings threshold for marginal jobs without specifying an upper hours limit can lead to a situation in which very low hourly wages are paid to marginal workers.

93 Things are different as regards retirement insurance. In Germany, since 2001 the contributions to retirement insurance of part-time workers and workers with low earnings who care for a child, as well as for non-employed who care for at least two children, have been upgraded during the first ten years after childbirth (Bäcker 2001: 477–479).

of temporary workers – no direct information on benefit duration is available in the public-use file of the data.

The existence of a range of specific rules that apply particularly to part-time workers cannot be adequately treated in the analysis, but they have to be kept in mind when assessing the outcomes. Another problem for data analysis is that unemployment insurance regulations are frequently amended: an attractive strategy would be the use of dummies capturing these changes; unfortunately, the sample size severely restricts such undertakings. Furthermore, the data do not allow us to distinguish between unemployment insurance and unemployment assistance benefits, but, with the exception of the United Kingdom, information on social assistance is available.[94]

The overall research question, which attempts to relate flexible employment and unemployment insurance coverage, points to a need to combine micro-data with institutional information. This is done in Chapter 6 by constructing proxies for institutional configurations from the ECHP data, and by merging country-level institutional information to the ECHP data and analysing this using cluster analysis and multilevel analysis methods.

Many of the shortcomings that Kvist (1998) identified in conventional approaches to social security benefits can be overcome by using panel data. Event history techniques allow us to assess the risks faced by non-standard workers when making downward (unemployment and inactivity), upward (standard employment) and sideward (education) transitions. Furthermore, entitlement to unemployment benefits can be analysed taking into account personal circumstances (age, gender) and former labour market status (part-time, fixed-term), as well as household or family situation. A more adequate account of the real operation of social security benefits should thus be possible.

94 Using country-specific administrative data that include detailed information on the recipients' employment history could be a remedy to this problem. But such comprehensive data are only now becoming available for individual countries – comparative analysis would therefore prove difficult.

6 Risk of job loss and the insurance situation of non-standard workers

This chapter will test the following two hypotheses:

1. Non-standard workers face greater risks in making transitions to unemployment or inactivity than standard workers.
2. Unemployment insurance systems that strongly incorporate welfare princeples instead of insurance principles provide better coverage of non-standard workers.

We looked at the second hypothesis in Chapter 5. The results from Chapter 5 will be further illustrated here by using data from the European Community Household Panel (ECHP).

After describing the main features of the ECHP and discussing its advantages and disadvantages, in a second part we shall consider transitions from non-standard employment to other states in order to assess the validity of the first hypothesis. The reference group is always standard workers – permanent and/or full-time employees.[95] The temporary nature of fixed-term and casual contracts in particular suggests alternations between employment and unemployment. We assume that, in general, part-time employment is not less stable than regular full-time employment. More frequent transitions to non-employment, especially inactivity, are expected, however, due to combinations of part-time employment and care responsibilities. If the hypothesis proves true, downward transitions should occur more frequently among non-standard workers than among standard workers. The third part of this chapter examines unemployment benefit coverage of standard and non-standard workers in the four countries in order to shed light on the validity of the second hypothesis. Not only benefit entitlement but also benefit levels are taken into account. According to the second hypothesis, countries with unemployment insurance systems that are to a lesser degree based on standard employment (incorporating welfare instead of insurance principles) should display more equal outcomes as regards coverage. In a last step, informa-

95 The multivariate models will take into account overlaps between temporary contracts and part-time employment.

tion on the design and financing of the four countries' benefit systems is merged with the individual-level data in order to allow broader statements on the influence of specific institutional settings on the inclusiveness of unemployment insurance systems. This is possible only on the basis of a wide range of countries with different institutions. Therefore, all countries concerning which the ECHP data contain sufficient information on the variables of interest are included in this analysis.

6.1 The European Community Household Panel

The European Community Household Panel (ECHP) provides comprehensive harmonised cross-sectional and longitudinal data for EU-15 countries. It ran from 1994 to 2001.[96] In 1994 a sample of approximately 60,500 nationally representative households, comprising about 130,000 individuals aged 16 and over, were interviewed in the then 12 member states (Eurostat 2002). Austria joined the ECHP in 1995, Finland in 1996. Sweden has provided data for the ECHP derived from the Swedish Living Conditions Survey since 1997. The data were collected by national statistical offices or research institutions, based on a common questionnaire. They were then transmitted to Eurostat, which further processed the data (editing, weighting, imputations) and created the user data base (Wirtz et al. 2002). In Germany, the United Kingdom and Luxembourg the original ECHP survey was stopped after three waves and replaced by comparable data derived from existing national panels. In Germany, ECHP variables are derived from the German Socio-Economic Panel (SOEP), in the United Kingdom from the British Household Panel Survey (BHPS). Accordingly, some variables and categories are missing in the German and the British data, and comparability is lower than between countries that used the original questionnaire.

Mainly due to data protection the information that is available in the user data base is more restricted than the original data. The occupation, industry and education categories are, for example, highly aggregated in comparison with the original questionnaire. Furthermore, the user data base provides only aggregated information on many income variables. While the survey participants were ques-

96 Due to concerns about timeliness and comparability, in 1999 it was decided to replace the ECHP with a new data base, the 'Statistics on Income and Living Conditions' (EU-SILC). The main difference with the ECHP is that existing national data sources (survey or register data) are used (ex ante output harmonisation), a rotating panel structure is adopted and new EU member states, as well as Norway and Iceland, participate (for more information, see Ehling et al. 2003). In 2007, longitudinal data for two or three waves covering the years 2003 to 2005 were available for 13 countries. Spain was the only country included in the 2007 longitudinal data release among the countries treated here.

tioned in detail on their monthly unemployment insurance and assistance benefits, the user data base contains only one variable on unemployment related benefits as an annual net amount.

Income variables (wage income as well as replacement income) are supplied in the data in national currencies. In order to make comparisons possible they are transformed into equivalent units – to reflect the relative value of wages in the four countries (eliminating price level differences). This is done by dividing the national currency amounts by the purchasing power parities (PPP)[97] provided in the data. The ECHP contains weights to take into account household and unit non-response and thereby correct for any lack of representativeness in the sample.[98]

What are the advantages of ECHP data as compared to other data sources? First, the data are very comprehensive: on the household level, information on income, accommodation, durables and children is available. The individual data include demographic information, information on current and previous jobs, unemployment and job search, income, training and education, health, social relations and migration (compare Eurostat 2003b). Second, information on partners and children can be matched to the individuals of interest. This allows us, for example, to take into account the partner's income as a proxy for means-testing. Third, the panel design of the data makes it possible to study dynamics and mobility. Unemployment insurance entitlement can be linked to the type of former employment and the employment history of an individual. Fourth, while information on benefit receipt from administrative sources is often restricted to individuals who are registered at the employment office, the ECHP data allow us to choose a broader reference group (all persons looking for a job). It can thus draw a more realistic picture of benefit coverage by also taking into account individuals that decide not to register at the employment office because they do not expect any benefit receipt in the first place. Fifth, the panel structure is beneficial for accuracy of results because it allows us to control for unobserved heterogeneity. Finally, the data provide comparable variables for a range of countries. Whereas for Germany and the United Kingdom national household panels that cover longer time periods than the ECHP would have been available for analysis, for Spain and Denmark no – or no easily accessible – panel data are available.

97 Purchasing Power Parities (PPPs) are currency conversion rates that both convert to a common currency and equalise the purchasing power of different currencies. It is recommended to use PPPs in economic comparisons to take into account the price level differences between countries. For more information, see Schreyer et al. (2002).

98 There are two types of weights: cross-sectional weights on the individual and the household level, and individual-level longitudinal weights.

As to the disadvantages of the ECHP data, the sample size restricts the accuracy of analysis. Especially if subgroups of employees, such as part-time or temporary workers, are at the centre of interest the sample size can become a problem. In the 2001 sample, between 400 (Denmark) and 1000 individuals (Germany) were part-time employed, while between 200 (Denmark) and 1370 (Spain) were fixed-term/short-term or casual employed. The linkage of this information to unemployment further reduces the sample. A viable solution to this problem is the pooling of data over all waves. For more accurate analysis of small subgroups national census data or administrative data are needed. Another problem is that most information is recorded on an annual (status at the time of the interview) and not on a monthly or a daily basis. This not only leads to underestimation of certain transitions, but also makes causal statements more difficult and imprecise. In addition, despite its comprehensive variable list certain aspects of interest to this study are not available in the data. There is, for example, no separate information on unemployment insurance and unemployment assistance receipt, and the duration of benefit receipt is not recorded either. Furthermore, typical problems associated with panel data, such as panel attrition and over- or undersampling of certain groups, have to be dealt with. Finally, but importantly, the ECHP data end in 2001 and the new EU-SILC data (Statistics on Income and Living Conditions) are not yet available for comprehensive analysis. In-depth information on the contents and construction of variables and on descriptive outcomes can be found in Annex 1.

6.2 Mobility patterns of non-standard workers

A range of recent empirical studies focus on the mobility patterns of non-standard workers. Among the data sources used for transition studies focussing on the countries under observation here are the ECHP (European Commission 2004b, 2003b; OECD 2002c; Debels 2005, 2004; Gash 2003; Golsch 2004; Muffels et al. 2005), labour force surveys of individual countries (Amuedo-Dorantes 2000; Smith et al. 2000), the British Household Panel Survey (BHPS) and the German Socio-Economic Panel (SOEP) (Bothfeld et al. 2000; McGinnity 2004; O'Reilly et al. 2002).

Most studies on temporary employment test the stepping-stone theory or the segmentation theory, or both. Studies following the assumption that temporary contracts might act as stepping stones to regular jobs usually look at transition patterns from temporary to permanent jobs; studies that follow the segmentation theory typically take into account downward transitions to unemployment and inactivity, and maintenance transitions (remaining in temporary employment). In studies that compare transition patterns in multiple countries, Denmark and the United Kingdom are usually among the countries with comparatively high (short-term) upward mobility, while Spain is located at the other end of the spectrum and Germany normally takes an intermediate position (OECD 2002c; European Commission 2004b; Muffels et al. 2005; Debels 2004).[99] The stepping-stone function of temporary jobs in the United Kingdom is also confirmed by an individual country study (Booth et al. 2002b), while the function of temporary jobs as a trap is manifested for Spain (Amuedo-Dorantes 2000). At least for young employees temporary jobs in Germany seem to act as stepping stones rather than traps (Golsch 2004; McGinnity et al. 2004). A longer-term perspective (a five-year period) reveals considerable downward transitions from temporary employment in all four countries: unemployment or inactivity affected more than 10 per cent in Spain and Germany, while in Denmark and in the United Kingdom considerable proportions (about 15 and 20 per cent, respectively) of temporary workers in 1995 were inactive in 2000 (European Commission 2003b: 133).

Studies on transitions to and from part-time employment usually test alternative assumptions according to which part-time employment either acts as a bridge to regular full-time employment or leads to further segmentation of the labour market. In the latter case, part-time employment provides only transitory employment integration with higher propensities for part-time than for full-time workers to return to non-employment. The focus of these studies is clearly on women and their household context. Most studies conclude that the employment (re)integration of women often takes place via part-time contracts, but that part-time employment is also more volatile than full-time employment in leading more often to exclusionary transitions (compare, for example, Gash 2003; O'Reilly et al. 2002; OECD 2002d; Smith et al. 2000). Based on ECHP data, Chaupain-Guillot et al. (2004) show that short-term (t+1 and t+2) downward transitions to non-employment from all persons who took up part-time employment in year t are considerably more frequent in Spain and Germany than upward transitions to full-time employment. In Denmark, they are somewhat more frequent and in the United Kingdom the proportions are more or less equal. In terms of longer term trends (four years) and based on individuals between 20 and 50 who had been part-time employed in year t, the above results prove true only for Spain. In addition to these results, transitions from part-time to full-time employment are in most countries more likely for men than for women (Smith et al. 2000). According to Chaupain-Guillot et al. (2004) the gap between men and women is especially large in the United Kingdom, but non-existent in Denmark.

99 A good comparative overview of transitions from temporary to permanent jobs is given in European Commission (2004b: 160, 161).

Household composition plays an important role in explaining downward transitions of part-time workers. Bothfeld et al. (2000: 151–157) demonstrate that in Germany and the United Kingdom child-care responsibilities push part-time employed women into non-employment. Chaupain-Guillot et al. (2004) confirm the strong influence of children on the probability of non-employment in Germany and the United Kingdom, but according to their analysis this is not a major factor in Denmark and Spain. The trends for the United Kingdom and Denmark are also supported by Gash (2003).

The methods used in the above studies include simple transition matrices for different reference groups, descriptive event-history techniques such as Kaplan-Meier survival estimates and sophisticated multivariate models. Most studies make use of multinomial logistic regression in order to model competing events such as upward and downward transitions or transitions to different states (compare, for example, Muffels et al. 2005; Golsch 2004; European Commission 2004b; Amuedo-Dorantes 2000; Smith et al. 2000; Chaupain-Guillot et al. 2004). Some studies use event-history models (some also in combination with multinomial regression models) that take account of specific problems such as right-censoring[100] and time-varying covariates (compare, for example, Amuedo-Dorantes 2000; Booth et al. 2002b; Debels 2005; Bothfeld et al. 2000; Lauterbach 1994; McGinnity 2004).

6.2.1 Year-to-year transitions

What trends in the mobility patterns of standard and non-standard workers are revealed if year-to-year transitions are compared between the four countries? Are there pronounced differences in downward trends to non-employment between standard and non-standard workers as expected in the hypothesis, and are there higher shares of non-standard workers that make transitions to inactivity instead of unemployment?[101] If yes, what inactivity categories stand in the foreground?

Tables 9 and 10 reveal that full-time workers and workers with permanent jobs in year *t* are in all countries more likely than part-time workers or temporary workers still to be employed one year later. Part-time employment is rather persistent in Denmark, Germany and the United Kingdom: more than 60 per cent of

100 Right censoring describes the case in which a person participates in a study for a certain time and thereafter is no longer observed. This is the case if the event or transition has not occurred for some person at the end of the study or if a person withdraws prematurely from the study (Cleves et al. 2002: 31).

101 The year-to-year transition analysis is based on the variable that codes the self-assessed main status of the respondent at the time of the interview (see Annex 1).

part-time workers are still in the same state one year later (Table 9). Consistently, only around one-fifth of part-time workers make upward transitions to full-time employment in these three countries. In Spain, on the other hand, transitions from part-time to full-time employment are more common. We have already seen that part-time employment in Spain plays a different role than in the other three countries – it is more often exercised involuntarily and less often used to combine work with child-care responsibilities. Downward transitions are considerably more important among part-time than among full-time workers in all four countries. Except for Germany, transitions to unemployment are more common for part-time workers. Movements to inactivity are especially prevalent among part-time workers – the shares of part-time workers moving to inactivity are three to four times larger than those of full-time workers. This is not surprising because the inactivity category explicitly contains 'housework and caring' and, at least in Germany and the United Kingdom, part-time employment is often combined with care activities. The United Kingdom stands out when it comes to transitions to inactivity as compared to unemployment. Among both full-time and part-time workers, transitions to inactivity are considerably more frequent than transitions to unemployment, which might hint at more deficient unemployment insurance coverage in the United Kingdom, leading to different self-assessment behaviour. As to potentially employability-enhancing sideward transitions (movements to education), they are more important among part-time workers than among full-time workers in all four countries, particularly in Denmark and Spain. Especially in Denmark we can assume that this result is in part due to the large share of part-time workers among students. In addition, Table 9 shows that in Denmark transitions between unemployment and education play an important role; in fact, as discussed in Chapter 5, further education and activation are integral parts of the Danish unemployment benefit system.

Upward transitions from temporary to permanent employment are most common in the United Kingdom; about 45 per cent of temporary workers are permanently employed one year later (compare Table 10). In Spain, on the other hand, only a quarter of temporary workers move into permanent employment from one year to the next. Persistence of temporary employment in Spain, accordingly, is very high at around 50 per cent. It is around 40 per cent in Denmark and Germany and around 30 per cent in the United Kingdom. As expected from the hypothesis, temporary workers are more likely than permanent workers to enter either unemployment or inactivity. The shares of temporary workers who are unemployed or inactive one year later lie between 13 per cent in Denmark and 21 per cent in Spain, while only between 3 (Denmark) and 6.5 per cent (Spain) of permanent workers make downward transitions. In all countries ex-

Table 9: Upward, downward and sideward transitions from and to full-time and part-time employment

t		*t*+1				
		full-time	**part-time**	**education**	**unemployed**	**inactive**
full-time	**DK**	91.43	2.17	1.58	2.88	1.94
	DE	90.40	1.84	0.86	3.92	2.98
	SP	88.36	2.28	0.40	5.64	3.33
	UK	90.82	3.10	0.46	1.97	3.65
part-time	**DK**	20.29	61.39	6.91	5.08	6.32
	DE	17.52	65.66	2.17	3.21	11.44
	SP	31.58	42.60	2.75	10.45	12.36
	UK	18.18	64.22	1.25	2.62	13.73
education	**DK**	26.69	7.44	56.55	6.96	2.36
	DE	17.88	5.19	61.89	6.17	8.89
	SP	10.00	3.34	73.75	10.20	2.71
	UK	24.13	9.13	45.11	11.55	10.08
unem-ployed	**DK**	32.19	6.29	9.38	38.38	13.76
	DE	25.26	3.16	4.30	49.77	17.51
	SP	30.16	4.81	3.31	46.68	15.05
	UK	16.46	4.24	2.08	59.03	18.19
inactive	**DK**	4.77	2.59	1.69	3.15	87.80
	DE	4.33	3.87	1.37	2.66	87.76
	SP	4.71	2.69	0.49	5.51	86.60
	UK	6.87	7.62	1.20	7.05	77.26

Source: Own calculations; age: 18–64, weighted data, 8 waves (1994–2001); employment refers to employment of more than 1 hour.

cept for the United Kingdom movements of temporary workers to self-assessed unemployment (with or without benefit receipt) are more important than movements to inactivity. Reintegration after unemployment often takes place via temporary employment – this is especially the case in Spain where unemployed persons are considerably more likely to re-enter employment by way of a temporary job than a permanent job. This route of integration is also quite important in Denmark. Interestingly, the United Kingdom, which has the lowest share of

Table 10: Upward, downward and sideward transitions from and to permanent and temporary employment

t		*t*+1				
		permanent	**temporary**	**education**	**unemployed**	**inactive**
permanent	**DK**	92.01	2.92	1.08	2.20	1.79
	DE	89.47	3.63	0.50	3.05	3.34
	SP	89.70	5.45	0.13	2.51	2.21
	UK	91.35	1.89	0.35	1.79	4.62
temporary	**DK**	39.00	38.96	9.09	7.53	5.42
	DE	38.54	38.55	3.93	13.55	5.43
	SP	24.94	53.62	1.38	15.46	4.59
	UK	45.82	30.62	6.21	7.40	9.95
education	**DK**	15.22	14.45	59.81	7.93	2.60
	DE	9.40	6.66	67.93	6.81	9.21
	SP	2.25	8.14	76.70	10.47	2.45
	UK	19.15	13.19	45.54	11.66	10.46
unemployed	**DK**	20.13	12.78	11.45	38.78	16.86
	DE	15.52	9.39	4.48	53.70	16.91
	SP	5.76	24.10	3.67	49.95	16.51
	UK	12.38	4.20	2.11	63.40	17.92
inactive	**DK**	3.36	1.86	1.82	3.14	89.82
	DE	4.73	1.81	1.39	2.75	89.31
	SP	0.75	2.92	0.47	5.08	90.78
	UK	10.22	2.32	1.27	8.17	78.02

Source: Own calculations; age: 18–64, weighted data, 7 waves (1995–2001); permanent and temporary employment in *t* refers to employment of more than 15 hours (main activity concept).

returns to employment via temporary employment, has the highest unemployment persistence (more than 60 per cent) in this sample. While transitions from permanent employment to education hardly play a role in any of the countries, transitions from temporary employment to education are rather important in Denmark and the United Kingdom, with shares of 9 and 6 per cent, respectively. While very high shares of education among temporary workers occur mainly among young workers, in all age groups temporary workers are more likely than permanent workers to move to education.

The above year-to-year transitions confirm the hypothesis of higher transitions out of employment for non-standard workers as compared to standard workers. On the other hand, we also observe more sideward transitions among non-standard workers. Sideward transitions in the form of (further) education or training could strengthen employability and thereby ameliorate the chances for reemployment and possibly even for qualitative job improvements, such as higher wages.

If longer-term transitions (t+4) are assessed, standard employment forms (full-time as well as permanent employment) are very stable in all countries. Between 80 (Germany) and 84 per cent (Denmark) of full-time workers in t were still (or again) in this state four years later. This is also true for between 77 (Spain) and 86 per cent (Denmark) of workers with permanent contracts. As to part-time workers, between 27 (Germany) and 43 per cent (Spain) were full-time employed four years later, while considerable shares had moved to inactivity (between 17 per cent in Denmark and Spain and 23 per cent in the United Kingdom). Longer-term persistency in part-time employment is greatest in Germany (47 per cent) in this sample. As might be expected, due to the greater involuntariness of this employment form and the rules governing it (limit of prolongation), persistency of temporary employment is considerably lower than persistency of part-time employment. It is by far the highest in Spain, where about 34 per cent of temporary workers in t still (or again) hold a temporary contract four years later. Movements to permanent jobs are most common in the United Kingdom, where almost 70 per cent of temporary workers hold permanent contracts four years later. This is the case for only about 45 per cent of Spanish temporary workers.[102]

6.2.2 Exits from employment

Year-to-year transitions are intuitive and frequently displayed in studies on non-standard employment and labour market mobility. While the above tables were restricted to two time-periods the following section will broaden the analysis by providing results based on longer time periods. Event-history analysis techniques are used. They correct for certain problems inherent in the data and take into account the timing of events.

102 The results are based on the ECHP data and calculated in the same manner as Tables 9 and 10.

Event-history analysis techniques are designed to describe and predict the occurrence of events at particular time points. Survival times are modelled indirectly via so-called hazard rates. This concept is related to the chances of making a transition out of a current state (here employment) at each time period (here month) conditional on survival up to that point (Jenkins 18 July 2005: 10). Depending on the underlying process, the hazard rate can take on different functional forms. Over time, the hazard rate or risk can remain constant, increase, decrease or it can be a combination of all three possibilities (serpentine shapes) (Cleves et al. 2002: 7 et seq.).[103] The survivor function is directly related to the hazard rate; it reports the probability of surviving beyond time *t* or, put differently, the proportion of units not having experienced the event up to time *t*.[104] The failure function is the inverse of the survivor function and thus allows the presentation of survival in another way. If, for example, one is less interested in the share of people who survive (remain in employment) but rather in the share of people who exit employment, one usually uses the failure function.

Two other important concepts in event-history analysis are censoring and truncation. A survival time is said to be censored if all we know is that it began or ended within some particular time interval but we do not know the total spell length. Two types are distinguished: right and left censoring. 'Right censoring' signifies that at the time of the last observation the event under study has not yet occurred in some observations – in our case, persons remaining in employment over the whole time period or persons leaving the study prematurely without having experienced the event. The term 'left censoring', on the other hand, is used when the start date or start interval of the spell has not been observed – the person was already employed when the survey started.[105] It is assumed that the process giving rise to censoring of survival times is independent of the survival time process (compare Jenkins 18 July 2005: 4, 5). The basic problem with disregarding right censoring is that if censored and uncensored cases are treated equally, parameter estimates may be misleading in that the relationship between the covariates and the duration times may be under- or over-stated (Box-Stef-

103 An example of a combination of all three possibilities is human mortality related to aging. For some time after birth the hazard of dying falls, then a long plateau sets in; thereafter it rises constantly (Cleves et al. 2002: 8).

104 $H(t)$ being the cumulative hazard function – the total amount of risk that has been accumulated up to time t – and $S(t)$ being the survivor function, the relationship between both functions can be described as $S(t) = \exp[-H(t)]$. For a formal discussion of the concepts underlying survival analysis, see Cleves et al. (2002: 7–11), Jenkins (18 July 2005: 13–24) and Box-Steffensmeier et al. (2004: 12–15).

105 This definition of left censoring is most commonly used in economics; biostatisticians usually use another definition – to them, left censoring means that the event occurred before the observation date.

fensmeier et al. 2004: 16–19). While right censoring can be dealt with in a straightforward way in event-history analysis, most event-history methods are not designed to handle left censoring.

Left truncation means late entry to the risk set: an individual has not been in employment during the first observation period or has not been observed at that time point but entered employment at a later time. Left truncation can be dealt with relatively easily in event-history modelling. Right truncation is not relevant for the data used here.[106]

In order to use event-history methods the data have to be reorganised into a longitudinal record that contains information on the length of a spell, the time when the event occurred to an individual or a group of individuals, and information on the type of event. In the following models the time to event is the length of employment (spell) and the event (exit) is non-employment. The descriptive methods used below do not, for the most part, differentiate between different exits. The discrete time multivariate models, on the other hand, look at competing exits: unemployment, inactivity, housework/carer, education, and other (retirement and other). The data used do not contain information on the exact timing of events; only month-to-month transitions (grouped or interval censored data) are observed. Standard methods for continuous event-history data, such as Weibull models, Exponential parametric models or Cox's proportional hazard models, are therefore not appropriate. Instead, discrete time multivariate models are used.

The basic idea of discrete time multivariate models is to create one record for each time unit that an individual is observed in employment. For each one of these records a dependent variable is generated that is coded 0 in every record but the last. The last record is coded 1 (in the case of multiple events, 1 to *n*) if an event occurred and 0 otherwise (censored). Furthermore, a time variable is created that is introduced into the models as a covariate in order to assess time dependence. Time varying covariates can be matched to the data. The ECHP data only provide annual information on covariates. They are assigned to every corresponding month of the specific year. On the reorganised data, standard logistic regression methods can be used. One thereby obtains maximum-likelihood estimators of models that are analogues to those for continuous-time data (compare Allison 1982: 94). As suggested by Box-Steffensmeier et al. (2004) multiple spells per person instead of only the last spell are taken into account for the de-

106 Only people who have experienced the event at a particular time point are included in the sample (for example, outflow sample from the unemployment register). Long survival times are therefore systematically excluded.

scriptive and the multivariate analysis.[107] In the multivariate models possible dependence of events is controlled for via a person identifier.

6.2.2.1 Comparative exit patterns

Exits from employment to non-employment, displayed as the cumulated failure rate,[108] are most common in Spain and least common in Germany (Figure 18). If different exit types are considered, exits to unemployment are by far the most important; they make up about two thirds of all exits. Transitions to unemployment are by far the most pronounced in Spain, followed by Denmark. Exits to inactivity, household/carer activities and education are of similar importance. Transitions to household/carer activities are most pronounced in the United Kingdom and, compatible with the findings in Chapter 4, least pronounced in Denmark. In Denmark, on the other hand, exits to education are comparatively high.

Figures 19 and 20 contrast transitions from employment for standard and non-standard workers – all exit types are combined.[109] In all countries, non-standard workers exit employment to higher degrees than standard workers, but countries vary markedly in the extent of the differences.[110] Failure rates of full-time and part-time workers are closest in Germany, followed by the United Kingdom, while part-time workers show much higher exit rates than full-time workers in Denmark and, especially, Spain (see Figure 19). The hazard of exit is very high during the first 24 month of recorded employment, which might be especially problematic because people might not have spent enough time in em-

---

107 Taking into account only the last spell per person leads to considerably lower cumulated failure rates, especially among non-standard workers. This indicates that a non-negligible part of workers, and especially of those with non-standard contracts, is faced with repeated transitions from and to employment.

108 The estimated failure function cumulates period-by-period risks of even occurrence and provides maximum-likelihood estimates of the probability that an individual randomly selected from the population will experience the event (make an exit from employment) (Singer et al. 2003: 326 et seq.).

109 In order to be able to directly contrast transitions to non-employment for part-time and full-time employees and for workers with fixed-term and permanent contracts, respectively, individuals are treated as censored as soon as they make a transition from fixed-term employment (part-time employment) to permanent employment (full-time employment), and vice versa. As soon as missing values appear in the covariate the individual is also treated as censored. Specifying changes in the covariates of interest as censoring seems to provoke somewhat higher failure rates for non-standard workers during the first two years and an assimilation of both failure rates thereafter; the general tendencies and pronounced differences between countries, as well as between standard and non-standard workers, are very similar, independent of specification.

110 The differences between countries are supported by the log-rank test for equality of survivor function (compare StataCorp 2005b).

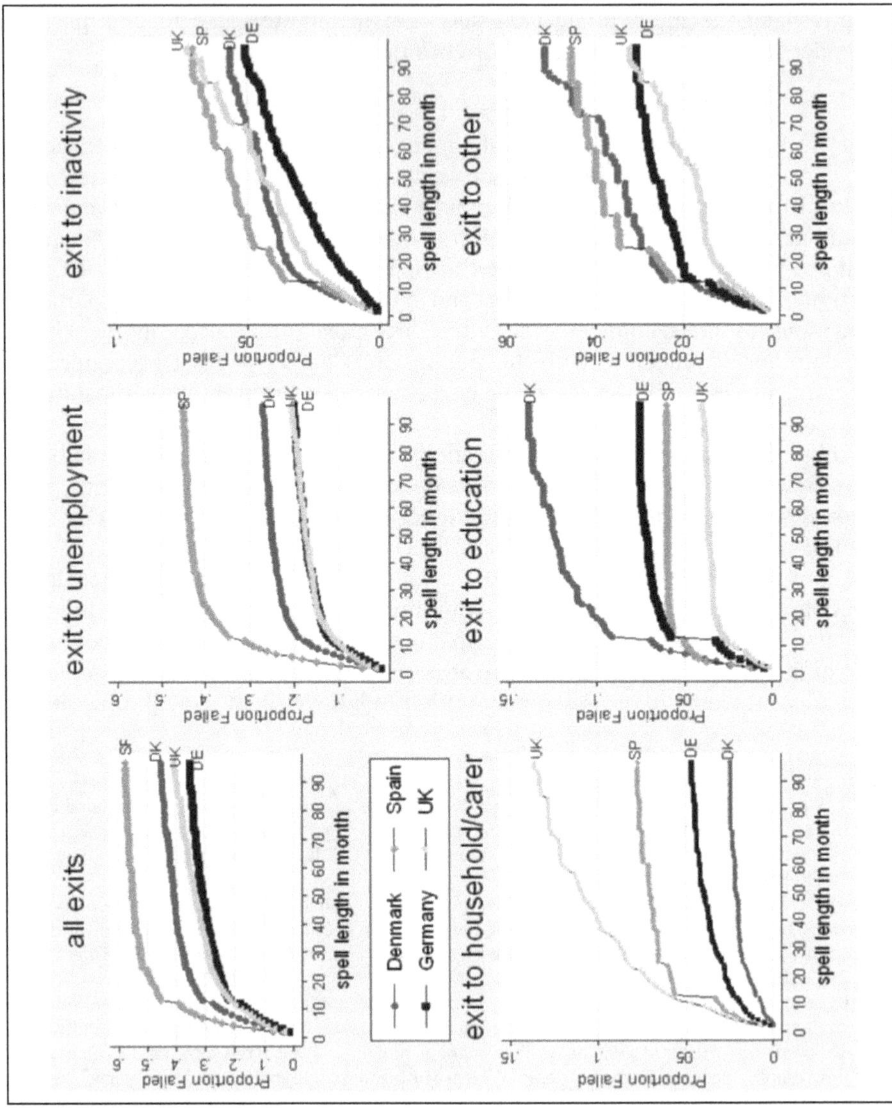

Figure 18: Comparison of importance of exit types by country (cumulated failure).

Source: Own calculations based on ECHP data (8 waves); multiple spells per individual are possible; age: 18–64. The category 'other' combines 'exits to other' and 'exits to retirement.

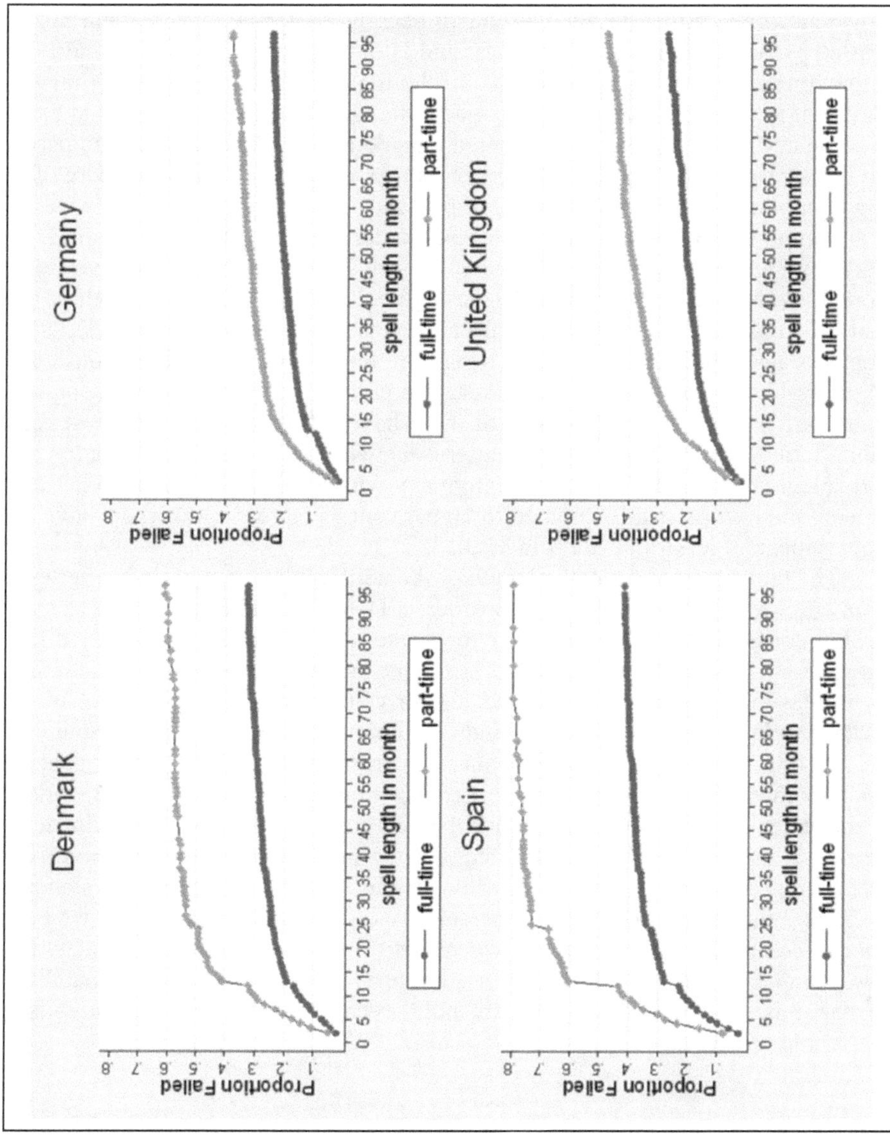

Figure 19: Exits from employment for full-time and part-time workers.
Source: Own calculations based on ECHP data (8 waves); multiple spells per individual are possible; age: 18–64.

ployment to be entitled to unemployment benefits. After two years about 50 per cent of part-time workers in Denmark and about 70 per cent in Spain have left employment, at least for a short period. The higher incidence of exits from employment to non-employment among part-time workers in Denmark and in Spain as compared to Germany and the United Kingdom might be due at least in part to the fact that part-time contracts in Denmark and, especially, Spain are more often of a temporary nature (see Table 30, Annex 1).

Temporary workers show similar exit patterns to part-time workers in Denmark and Spain – they are considerably more likely to exit employment than workers with open-ended contracts (see Figure 20). After two years about 60 per cent of temporary workers have left employment at least for a short period in Denmark and Spain. In the United Kingdom, temporary workers are considerably more likely than permanent workers and part-time workers to leave employment – after two years, about half of them have left employment at least for a short period. Differences in exit patterns between workers on temporary and permanent contracts are smallest in Germany where, after two years, 25 per cent of temporary workers as compared to 10 per cent of permanent workers have left employment, at least for a short interval.

The tables do not show the length of the non-employment periods after exits from employment take place. Exit profiles in Denmark and Spain might be similar, but considerably lower unemployment rates in Denmark suggest very different re-entry profiles (much faster in Denmark than in Spain). Lower unemployment rates in Denmark are, of course, also driven by the fact that in Denmark far fewer people are affected by non-standard employment patterns than in Spain.

In line with the year-to-year transition matrices the above results confirm our hypothesis that non-standard workers are more likely than standard workers to make exits from employment, but they do not control for other influencing factors. It may be that higher exit rates among non-standard workers are driven by different age or occupational profiles pertaining to non-standard and standard workers – this might also explain the country differences. Furthermore, we have not yet controlled for overlaps between part-time and temporary contracts. Below, competing risk models will be used to test whether higher exit probabilities of part-time and temporary workers hold even if we control for individual, household and job characteristics.

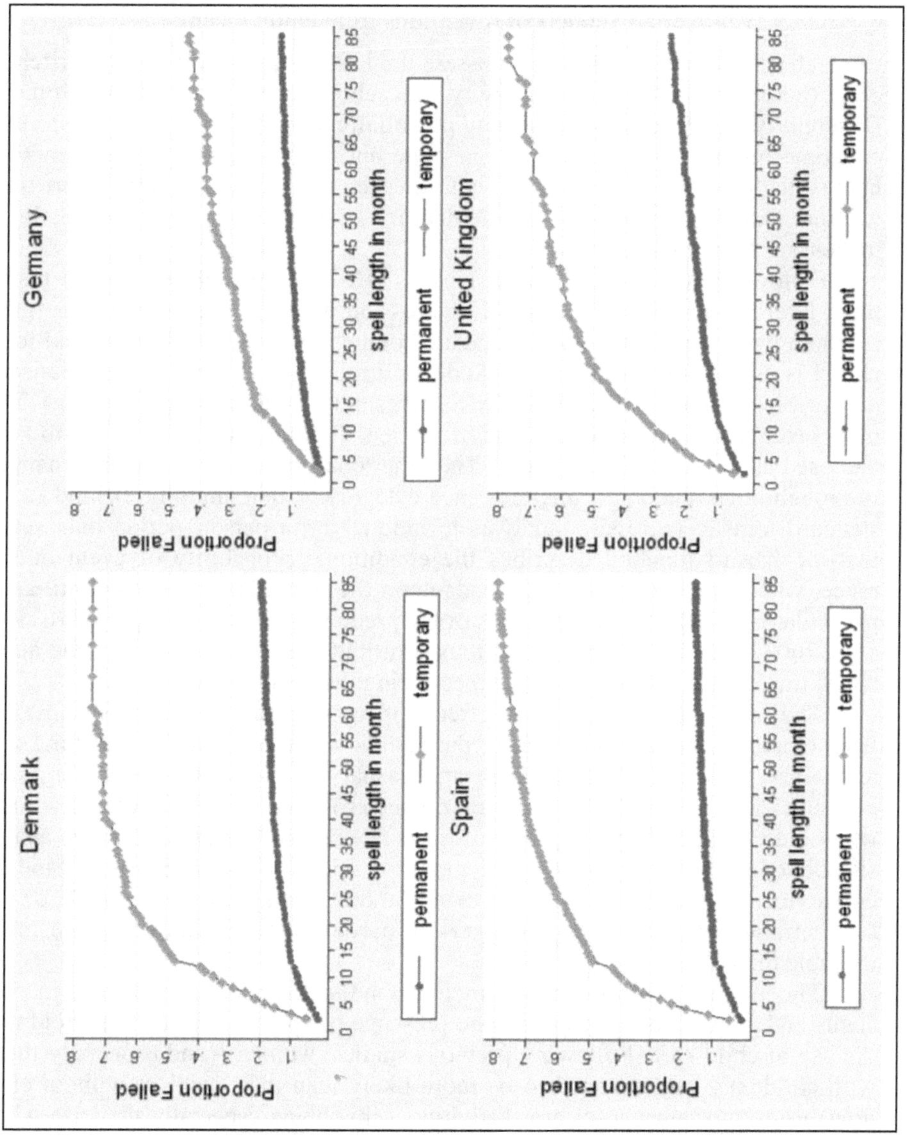

Figure 20: Exits from employment for workers with permanent and with temporary contracts.
Source: Own calculations based on ECHP data (7 waves); multiple spells per individual are possible; age: 18–64.

6.2.2.2 Multivariate models of transitions from employment

Competing risk models allow us to assess the influence of covariates on different exits (here: unemployment, inactivity, household/carer, education and other). Different types of exits or events may potentially have different causes; a certain covariate might influence exits to one state but not to another. The assumption here is that exits to household/carer activities are more common among part-time workers than among persons with temporary contracts, who are more likely to make transitions to unemployment.

Following Allison (1982) and Jenkins (18 July 2005: 93 et seq.), a maximum likelihood multinomial logistic regression model is used on data reorganised in a person–month form to calculate competing events. A multinomial logit model is essentially a series of 'linked' logit models and the parameters are interpretable as logit coefficients (Box-Steffensmeier et al. 2004: 173 et seq.). The model can be calculated only if one of the sets of parameters is set equal to zero and used as the reference category. The other coefficients then measure changes in probabilities relative to this reference category.[111] The intuition behind using standard logistic regression analysis techniques on a person–period data set is that the hazard function describes the conditional probability of event occurrence, where the conditioning depends upon the individual surviving until each particular time period and the values of the predictors in each time period (Singer et al. 2003: 381–384). Each person thus contributes as many records as the number of times he or she is at risk of experiencing the event.

The main interest lies in the effects of non-standard employment on exits from employment; interpretation of the results will thus focus on part-time and temporary employment (fixed-term and casual employment). The other independent variables are used to control for heterogeneous profiles of individuals who hold these contracts. Higher exit rates, as observed in the descriptive analysis above, and differences between countries might not be due to non-standard employment contracts as such, but could be due to a specific age profile or the concentration of non-standard workers in particular occupations that are more unstable than others.

The individual level variables included in the model are gender, age, marital status and a variable that captures the presence of children in the household and the use of child-care. Following previous studies, women – and especially those with children – are expected to be more likely than men (with or without children) to exit to household/carer activities – this being especially the case when

111 One potential disadvantage of estimating the model using standard software multinomial logit programmes is that these typically require that the same set of covariates appears in each equation, even though it can easily be imagined that assumptions about the type of influencing factor vary with exit type (Jenkins 18 July 2005: 96, 97).

no child-care is used. Marital status is to capture possible effects of the male breadwinner model on exits from employment. Age is taken into account because the importance of temporary and part-time employment varies between age groups. The second group of independent variables captures human capital and job-related aspects, such as qualification levels and occupations, which – as has been shown – vary between standard and non-standard workers. In general, people with higher qualification levels are expected to exit employment more seldom; the same holds true for occupations. Since it is assumed that previous unemployment periods have a positive effect on exits from employment, especially to unemployment, a variable is included that captures previous unemployment spells. Duration dependence in exit patterns is controlled for in the model by including the natural log of the number of months in employment as a covariate.[112] All covariates except for gender are time-varying and thus take on different values in different time periods. While individual and household characteristics are assumed to have a stronger influence on exit patterns to household/care activities, job-related aspects are assumed to be more important for exits to unemployment.

The following tables and interpretations will focus on the coefficients that capture non-standard employment, controlled by the other independent variables (the full regression table can be found in Annex 2, table 37). The effects of interest are displayed in the following tables under two headings: (1) types of exit (unemployment, inactivity and household/carer, as compared to remaining in employment), and (2) employability (exits to education).[113] Instead of beta coefficients, odds ratios are displayed and used for interpretation.[114]

In the *country comparison*, the Spanish and Danish survey populations are about 1.4 times more likely, and the British about 1.9 times more likely than the German one (reference) to exit to unemployment, relative to staying in employment (see Table 11). Concerning transitions to inactivity only the effect for the United Kingdom is significant; British citizens are 1.6 times more likely than

112 Transforming the values of the duration time instead of merely including dummy variables can lead to a better characterisation of time dependency in the hazard. The log transformation rescales the duration times, which results in a smooth, monotonic transformation (Box-Steffensmeier et al. 2004: 75–77).

113 In order to compare the effect of the main variables of interest between different pairs of outcomes (not only between unemployment and remaining in employment but also between unemployment and inactivity, for example), the 'listcoef' option implemented as Stata ado-file by Long and Freese (2006: 261) is used.

114 They are the exponential of the coefficient and can be interpreted in the following way: 'For a unit change in x the odds are expected to change by a factor of $\exp(b)$, holding all other variables constant.' For $\exp(b) > 1$ the odds are exp(beta) times larger. For $\exp(b) < 1$ the odds are exp(beta) smaller.

Table 11: Odds of different exit types compared between countries: reference Germany

Odds ratios	DK	SP	UK
	Types of exit		
Unemployed – remaining employed	1.46**	1.40**	1.88**
Inactive – remaining employed	1.04	0.89	1.61**
Household – remaining employed	0.93	2.81**	6.98**
	Employability		
Education – remaining employed	4.40**	1.05	1.28
p^2_{MF}[115]	0.19		
Independent variables: part-time employment, type of contract, gender, marital status, age, qualification level, occupation, previously unemployed, children in the household and, if yes, childcare or not.			
+ significant at 10%; * significant at 5%; ** significant at 1%			

Note: The data for the four countries are pooled. Germany is used as the reference category. *Source*: Own calculations based on ECHP data.

Germans to exit to inactivity. Exits to household activities relative to staying in employment are considerably more likely in the United Kingdom (7 times greater) and in Spain (2.8 times greater) than in Germany. The coefficient is not significant for Denmark. The odds on exit to education are significant only for Denmark and are about four times greater than in Germany. This shows the importance of employability strategies when it comes to bridging non-employment periods in Denmark.

For all countries and all exit types, the odds on exit from employment as compared to remaining in employment somewhat decrease with time in employment. Furthermore, in all countries exits to unemployment relative to remaining in employment are strongly and significantly associated with former unemployment spells, while exits to education relative to remaining in employment are negatively associated with former unemployment spells (compare Table 40, Annex 2).

In contrast to the descriptive analysis and in line with our expectations, the coefficients for *part-time vs full-time employment*[116] on exits to unemployment

115 Pseudo r^2 (p^2MF) cannot be interpreted analogous to r^2 from linear regression. In practice, p^2MF values are lower than r^2 values, all one can say is the higher p^2MF the better the model fits (Kohler et al. 2001: 272-273).

116 Models that used different hours categories (1–14, 15–19, 20–29, 30–34 and 35+) to proxy marginal employment instead of the dichotomous part-time/full-time variable did not generate any significant effects on the different hours categories.

Table 12: Odds of different exit patterns for part-time workers as compared to full-time workers (reference)

Odds ratios	DK	DE	SP	UK
PART-TIME WORKERS VS FULL-TIME WORKERS				
Types of exit				
Unemployed – remaining employed	0.91	1.07	0.86⁺	1.33**
Inactive – remaining employed	2.16**	0.45	2.17**	1.03
Household – remaining employed	2.80*	2.43*	1.05	1.28*
Employability				
Education – remaining employed	2.03**	2.18⁺	3.20**	3.59**
Education – unemployed	2.24**	2.03⁺	3.70**	2.70**
p^2_{MF}	0.17	0.14	0.21	0.19
Independent variables: part-time employment, type of contract, gender, marital status, age, qualification level, occupation, previously unemployed, children in the household and, if yes, childcare or not.				
+ significant at 10%; * significant at 5%; ** significant at 1%				

Note: Separate models are calculated for each country.
Source: Own calculations based on ECHP data.

are not significant except for the United Kingdom, where part-time workers are somewhat more likely than full-time workers to make a transition to unemployment (Table 12). Transitions to household/carer activities relative to remaining in employment are in all countries significantly greater among part-time than among full-time workers. The coefficient is not significant for Spain, however, once again supporting the finding that part-time employment exercises a different function in Spain than in the other countries. Nevertheless, part-time employment in Spain is less stable than full-time employment; transitions to inactivity relative to remaining in employment are more than twice as likely for part-time than for full-time workers. In Denmark, part-time workers are not only more likely than full-time workers to make transitions to household/carer activities relative to staying in employment, but they are also more likely to make transitions to other inactivity.

Participation in education can be seen as a sustainable strategy for bridging non-employment periods because it helps in maintaining employability and work-readiness. The year-to-year transitions already revealed that the share of part-time workers that make transitions from employment to education is higher than that of full-time workers in all countries. This also holds true when controlling for additional characteristics; in fact, the odds of part-time workers making transitions from employment to education relative to remaining in employment and relative to becoming unemployed are two to four times greater than those of full-time workers. As to the male breadwinner model, independent of holding a full-time or a part-time contract women and parents are considerably more likely to exit to housework/carer activities than men and childless people. Surprisingly, the gender effect is not significant for Germany. The child-care effect shows the expected direction (though insignificant) in all countries except for Spain: people who make use of child-care facilities are less likely to exit to household/carer activities than people without child-care facilities (see Table 40, Annex 2).

How do *temporary and permanent workers* compare if we look at their exit patterns? Since the strength of effects varies considerably between fixed-term/short-term workers and casual workers, tables for both groups are displayed separately (Table 13). Controlling for individual, household and job characteristics, the odds of making transitions to unemployment relative to remaining in employment are 2.7 to 4.1 times greater for workers with fixed-term contracts than for workers with permanent contracts. Effects are of similar size for casual workers, but not significant in Germany. The status of workers with casual contracts is even more volatile than that of workers with fixed-term contracts; the effects of fixed-term contracts on exits to inactivity are significant only for Spain (odds of 2), while casual workers are 2.3 (UK) to 4.8 (Germany) times more likely to exit to inactivity than workers with permanent contracts. As to household/carer activities, German and Spanish fixed-term workers are much more likely than permanent workers to take up household/carer activities relative to remaining in employment. The situation is even more pronounced for casual workers in Spain; their risk of exit to household/carer activities is nine times greater than that of permanent workers.

What about the employability dimension? In all countries, the odds of making transitions to education relative to remaining in employment are significantly greater for fixed-term and casual workers. In contrast to part-time workers, the odds of making transitions to education relative to becoming unemployed do not significantly vary between workers with temporary and workers with permanent contracts. We had earlier expected a positive relationship between low qualification levels, as well as employment in elementary occupations, and exits to non-employment. This seems to be true for the sample population, at least for exits to unemployment. Except for Germany, where coefficients take the expected direction but are not significant, occupations that require higher qualifications are associated to a lesser degree with odds of entering unemployment than elementary occupations (see Table 37, Annex 2). There are no consistent age effects, except for highly significant negative effects of age on participation in education, which applies to all countries.

Table 13: Odds of different exits for fixed-term/short-term (casual) workers compared to workers with permanent contracts (reference)

Odds ratios	DK	DE	SP	UK
FIXED- /SHORT-TERM WORKERS VS PERMANENT WORKERS				
Types of exit				
Unemployed – remaining employed	3.64**	3.68**	4.05**	2.66**
Inactive – remaining employed	1.77	0.99	1.89**	1.32
Household – remaining employed	0.55	2.85**	3.70**	1.27
Employability				
Education – remaining employed	4.03**	3.51**	2.65**	3.72**
Education – unemployed	1.11	0.95	0.66+	1.40
CASUAL WORKERS VERSUS PERMANENT WORKERS				
Types of exit				
Unemployed – remaining employed	3.26**	1.41	3.83**	3.35**
Inactive – remaining employed	3.12**	4.75**	2.80**	2.30*
Household – remaining employed	1.72	2.80	9.46**	1.30
Employability				
Education – remaining employed	3.38**	3.77*	2.51*	5.45**
Education – unemployed	1.04	2.67	0.66	1.63+
P^2_{MF}	0.17	0.14	0.21	0.19
Independent variables: part-time employment, type of contract, gender, marital status, age, qualification level, occupation, previously unemployed, children in the household and, if yes, childcare or not.				
+ significant at 10%; * significant at 5%; ** significant at 1%				

Note: Separate models are calculated for each country.
Source: Own calculation based on ECHP data.

6.2.3 Summary

Short-term and longer-term descriptive, as well as multivariate results support the hypothesis that non-standard contracts are less stable than standard employment contracts. Workers with temporary contracts are, in fact, considerably more likely to make transitions to unemployment and inactivity than workers with permanent contracts. In the longer-term perspective, movements of temporary workers to non-employment are most important in Spain and Denmark and least important in Germany. Upward transitions to permanent employment (only looked at here as year-to-year transitions) are most common in the United Kingdom and least common in Spain. An important finding is that casual employment is more volatile than fixed-term employment: the coefficient on exits to inactivity is significant and positive for casual workers in all countries, while for fixed-term workers this is the case only in Spain.

Part-time employment has a higher persistence than temporary employment in all countries except Spain. The above results confirm the findings from previous chapters that part-time employment plays a different role in Spain. Longer-term persistence of part-time employment is especially high in Germany and in the United Kingdom, the two countries where the extended male breadwinner model (combination of male full-time worker and female part-time worker) is especially relevant. Higher volatility of part-time employment in Denmark and, especially, Spain is probably at least in part due to the fact that in both countries part-time employment is more often combined with temporary employment than in the other two countries. As expected, downward transitions to inactivity and especially to household and care work are considerably more important among part-time workers than among full-time workers. We expected relatively similar patterns between part-time and full-time workers as regards exits to unemployment – employment protection legislation should usually hold for both, full-time and part-time employment. This is confirmed by the multivariate models except for the United Kingdom, where differences between part-time and full-time workers are evident but small.

To conclude, non-standard workers – part-time workers as well as workers with fixed-term or casual contracts – are in all countries more likely than standard workers to make downward transitions to unemployment and/or inactivity. If we look at sideward transitions to education, a more positive picture emerges. Part-time and temporary workers are both more likely to participate in education measures than full-time workers and workers with open-ended contracts. The role that education plays among non-standard workers cannot be assessed here. For example, we do not know what proportion of non-standard workers deliberately quit their job in order to participate in education to upgrade their skills, or what share voluntarily or involuntarily participate in education or training measures in order to remain employable in times of unemployment. Education among non-standard workers can thus take various forms; Chapter 3, for example, showed that especially among young people in Denmark and the United Kingdom part-time work is often combined with (university) education.

6.3 The insurance situation of non-standard workers

In their critical review of unemployment compensation and labour market transitions, Atkinson et al. (1991:1688 et seq.) state that only a fraction of the unemployed receive unemployment insurance benefits and that the extent of coverage is likely to vary with the characteristics of individual workers. Among other things, they classify part-time workers – especially marginal workers – and precarious workers with insufficient contribution records as potentially disadvantaged groups. They point out the difficulties of accurately modelling the benefit system at the individual level taking into account the relevant contribution conditions and employment record (Atkinson et al. 1991: 1708 et seq.). While they favour survey data for calculating benefit receipt over hypothetical calculations based on the characteristics of social security systems they also point out that survey data prevent modelling the full pattern of benefit receipt over an unemployment spell because benefit receipt is usually recorded only at a specific time point. Administrative data, on the other hand, have the advantage of allowing dynamic benefit calculations, but the disadvantage of lacking information on people who are not claiming benefits and often having only limited information on individual, household and job characteristics must be balanced against this.

Few empirical studies treat unemployment-related benefits among non-standard workers. Grimshaw et al. (1997) deal with unemployment insurance and part-time employment in a comparative way. As a remedy to their critique that replacement rates are in most studies treated as a homogeneous payment they calculate net replacement rates separately for women and men, taking into account threshold levels, additions for dependent spouses and, in the case of Germany, disadvantages for women due to calculation of replacement rates based on individual net earnings (household-based 'joint assessment' tax structure). Similarly, Rubery (1998a) and Klammer (2005) focus on gender differences in access to and level of unemployment benefits; they thus indirectly take into account non-standard employment, especially part-time work.

The OECD has traditionally calculated net replacement rates at unemployment on the basis of workers' profiles that are not compatible with non-standard employment because they, for example, assume long and continuous contribution records (compare OECD 2002a, 2004b). A recent conceptual OECD study assesses the scope and limits of tax–benefit indicators (see Immervoll et al. 2004). The main goal of this study is to compare estimates from alternative data sources on the number of persons participating in social programmes in different countries. The study adopts a differentiated approach by not only taking into account different concepts of benefit receipt (broad recipience, coverage and dependency), but also noting the fact that eligibility for benefits is likely to differ depending on the age and gender of the individual (lacking contributions due to short or no employment history). A cross-country comparison based on labour force survey data, for example, reveals that coverage of unemployment-related benefits among people without previous work experience is much less likely than among people with previous work experience, the situation being especially bad in Spain with close to no coverage (deficient unemployment assistance) and comparatively good in the United Kingdom (Immervoll et al. 2004: 66). Taking as the basis survey respondents that are either unemployed, inactive or employed, entitlement to unemployment benefits in 2001 was somewhat higher among women than men in Denmark, but considerably lower in Germany, the United Kingdom and, among older women (55–64), in Spain (Immervoll et al. 2004: 65).

To our knowledge, only one study uses the ECHP data to assess unemployment benefit coverage and levels in a comprehensive way, also taking account of non-standard employment (Ghysels et al. 1999). This study was intended to provide more realistic information on net replacement rates for new types of unemployment that do not satisfy the assumption of long-time contribution records. It was the basis for a section in the publication *Employment in Europe* (see European Commission 2000). Ghysels et al. (1999) examine benefit coverage, level and replacement rates and not only look at differences according to gender, age, qualification level and household type, but also try to relate benefit receipt to former working time. This exercise was only partly successful insofar as, due to sample size problems – only the first two waves of the ECHP were available at the time of the study – average unemployment benefit levels and replacement rates could not be reported for part-time workers in all 10 countries analysed. Concerning benefit coverage, based on the 1994 and 1995 waves of the ECHP data, gender differences are small in Denmark and Germany, but account for 10 to 15 percentage points in the United Kingdom and Spain.[117] Benefit coverage of former part-time workers as compared to former full-time workers hardly varies in Denmark (95% vs 91%), while entitlement of part-time workers in Germany, the United Kingdom and Spain is about 20 to 25 percentage points lower (Germany: 86% vs 60%; Spain: 55% vs 37%; United Kingdom: 58% vs 35%) (Ghysels et al. 1999: 53). Differences in average unemployment benefit levels (in ECU-PPP) and in replacement rates could be reported only for Denmark and Spain. While full-time workers in Denmark on average received 715 ECU-PPP monthly, part-time workers received about 600. In Spain the relation was about

117 For most of their calculations the authors use a very broad concept of unemployment, considering anyone who declares that they have spent at least one month in unemployment during the observation period of 24 months as eligible for the analysis of unemployment and its consequences. The above reported results refer to the age group 16 to 54 (Ghysels et al. 1999: 48).

500 ECU-PPP for full-time workers to about 390 ECU-PPP for part-time workers, the replacement rate being somewhat higher for former part-time than for full-time workers. Overall, unemployment benefit levels are highest in Denmark, closely followed by Germany; they are medium in Spain and comparatively low in the United Kingdom. The analysis of Ghysels et al. (1999) is restricted to descriptive tables, while the following analysis uses regression models in order to control for specific characteristics of non-standard workers.

A paper provided for the ECHP Working Group generated some results on the place of social transfers in the incomes and living standards of households in four countries, namely Spain, the United Kingdom, France and the Netherlands (European Commission 13–14 November 1997). An important general conclusion from this paper, which is based on ECHP data, is that countries differ sharply in terms of the concepts underlying their methods of social protection. Concerning the countries of interest here, the paper outlines the predominance of the insurance concept in the Spanish system, which is manifested in benefits paid proportionally to previous income (unemployment and invalidity benefits) as opposed to benefits aimed at families, such as family allowance, housing subsidies and social assistance. The British system, on the other hand, is characterised by the predominance of low-level flat-rate benefits that depend to a lesser extent on peoples' individual characteristics or previous jobs.

The following studies – not based on ECHP data – on unemployment benefit entitlement are noteworthy. For the German context, Klammer (2005; 2000; 2001b: 252 et seq.) deals with unemployment benefit receipt with a focus on women. The studies are based on administrative data. Access to unemployment insurance benefits (ALG) fell by 15 per cent from 1980 to 1995. In 2004, about 20 per cent of registered women in the East (10 per cent in 1998) and about 30 per cent in the West did not receive any unemployment-related benefit. The main reason, according to Klammer, was means-testing in the second-tier system (unemployment assistance). Concerning the benefit level, there are considerable gender differences in Germany. In 2004, the average monthly unemployment insurance benefit (ALG) in the West was €612 for women and €924 for men. The gender differences are smaller in the East, with women's average unemployment insurance benefit level at €605 and men's at €736 (Klammer 2005: 332). In addition, there is evidence for the late 1980s and the first half of the 1990s that the probability of returning to employment is much higher for unemployed men than for unemployed women (Klammer et al. 2001b: 259 et seq.).

Based on administrative data, Micklewright (1990) shows for the British context that in 1990 only one in five claimants received unemployment insurance benefits, while the majority received means-tested assistance. Unemployment insurance coverage had been strongly declining from the 1960s onwards, one reason being the growing incidence of long-term unemployment (exhaustion of insurance benefits). But Micklewright revealed that even among men exhaustion accounted for little more than half of the cases in which unemployment insurance benefits were not paid. Among women, too few contributions were the main reason for not having access to insurance benefits. In 2000, only about 16 per cent of all claimants received contribution-based Jobseeker's Allowance (the insurance benefit) in the United Kingdom. Insufficient contribution records were by far the most important reason for lacking entitlement (Cebulla 2001: 604 et seq.). According to Micklewright (1990) descriptive results point to a relationship between rising flexible employment and deficient unemployment insurance coverage, but more detailed analysis over longer time periods, involving flow as well as stock data, is called for.

The following section will first look at differences between non-standard and standard workers concerning coverage of unemployment benefits and then examine whether benefit level and composition varies by type of former employment contract. The analysis is exclusively based on the ECHP data. There are some downsides of household panel data in this regard. Benefit receipt, for example, is only reported at the time of the interview and in some cases benefit income is underreported (Immervoll et al. 2004: 69). A useful feature, on the other hand, is the availability of comprehensive information on the prior labour market situation of recipients, including former earnings. Furthermore, information on the household circumstances and income of a partner is provided, meaning that means-testing can be assessed.

6.3.1 Entitlement to unemployment benefits

Do the ECHP data confirm the second hypothesis that indicates that unemployment insurance systems that more strongly incorporate welfare as opposed to insurance principles are more inclusive of non-standard workers? The institutional analysis has already revealed that all unemployment insurance systems discriminate against workers with non-standard contracts to varying degrees. As a matter of fact, the ECHP does not provide separate information on unemployment insurance and unemployment assistance receipt. The term 'unemployment benefit' that is used in the following analysis will thus refer to both benefit types.[118]

118 If not stated otherwise, the following descriptive tables and regression results are valid for the age group 18 to 64.

Table 14: Registration at the employment office by former working hours*

%	1–19 hours	20–29 hours	30+ hours
Denmark	32	76	78
Germany	20	48	78
Spain	73	84	91
United Kingdom	28	28	54

Note: * The hours' category 1–14 is not shown separately because, especially in Denmark and in the United Kingdom, case numbers become critically small.
Source: Own calculations based on pooled and weighted ECHP data; basis: persons with no job who are looking for a job.

In contrast to administrative data the ECHP data distinguish between people who are registered at the employment office and those who are not. This is an advantage if we want to get a realistic picture of benefit coverage among different population groups. Focusing exclusively on the registered unemployed can be misleading because individuals who do not expect to be eligible for benefits might not register as unemployed in the first place. Micklewright (1990: 13) points out the importance of this distinction and demonstrates for the British case that more than half of all unemployed women (based on search activity) were not claimants in the administrative records. We would, for example, expect that marginal workers are less likely to register at the employment office, especially in unemployment insurance systems with high hours thresholds. Table 14 highlights this issue. Indeed, in all countries unemployed persons who have formerly worked part-time are less likely to register at the employment office. The lower the previous hours, the less likely the part-time workers are to register – this is especially evident in Denmark and Germany. Differences between part-time workers with high hours (20–29) and full-time workers are especially large in the United Kingdom and Germany, while they are non-existent in Denmark. In Spain, registration is high among both former part-time and full-time workers; there might be non-material reasons for registering as unemployed, even if benefit receipt is not expected.

A less pronounced picture emerges if former temporary and permanent workers are compared. There is no difference in Spain and only a small difference in the United Kingdom, while differences in Denmark and, especially, Germany are evident (compare Table 15).

As also suggested by Atkinson et al. (1991: 1683), one should adopt a broader definition of unemployment (going beyond the definition of registered unemployment) when assessing the difference in unemployment benefit coverage between standard and non-standard workers.

Table 15: Registration at employment office by reason for leaving last job

%	End of contract/temporary job	Obliged to leave by employer
Denmark	74	87
Germany	61	81
Spain	91	89
United Kingdom	55	62

Source: Own calculations based on pooled and weighted ECHP data; basis: persons with no job who are looking for a job.

6.3.1.1 Descriptive results

Figure 21 compares benefit coverage rates between registered full-time and part-time workers and all persons who are looking for a job (registered and not registered). Coverage rates of registered unemployed (block colours) are in all countries higher than coverage rates of all people looking for a job (stripes). Regarding only registered unemployed, differences between former part-time workers (white) and former full-time workers (black) are evident but considerably less pronounced than if all persons who are looking for a job are taken into account. In general, Denmark with its highly individualised system fares best, with the majority of former part-time workers being covered by unemployment benefits. Whereas the registered unemployed are quite well covered in Germany, the coverage rate of all unemployed looking for a job is very low, especially for former part-time workers. Different explanations for non-coverage are possible. Besides insufficient contribution records or working hours (earnings) below the hours (earnings) threshold, this group can also contain long-term unemployed who are not receiving benefits due to means-testing or people who want to return to the labour market after a child-care break, for example. These factors are controlled for in the later regression analysis. Means-testing plays an important role in the United Kingdom where, since 1996, unconditional unemployment benefits are paid only for a short period of six months. In the United Kingdom, less than 50 per cent of registered unemployed who have been full-time employed are receiving benefits, and only about one third of former part-time workers are covered. It can be expected that the low share of covered part-time workers is due at least in part to the prevalence of the extended male breadwinner model and the importance of means-testing in the British system.[119] In Spain, coverage rates in general are very low and they are even lower among former part-time workers.

119 Part-time workers in Britain are more likely to be married than the overall population (compare Tables 35 and 38, Annex).

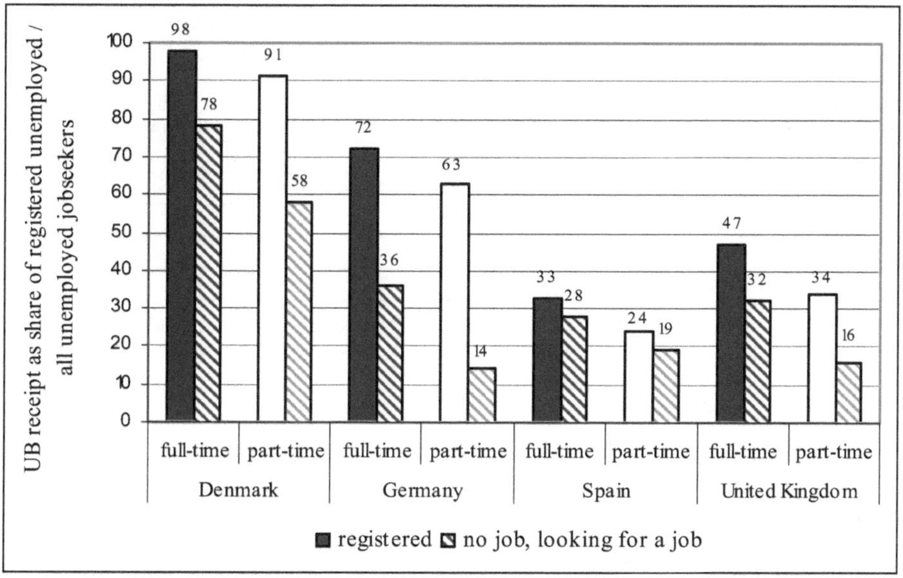

Figure 21: Unemployment benefit receipt of former full-time and part-time workers: comparison of registered unemployed and all unemployed jobseekers.
Source: Own calculations based on pooled and weighted ECHP data. The retrospective survey information on part-time employment is used.

According to the eligibility rules there should be differences in coverage rates between part-time workers with low and part-time workers with high hours. Table 16 confirms this for all countries except the United Kingdom. The relatively high coverage rate among registered British unemployed who were part-time employed in the last wave or the wave before, which is not in line with above results that are based on the more exact retrospective variable (that potentially goes further into the past), points to the fact that means-testing at an early stage of unemployment seems to play an important role in the United Kingdom.

Are former temporary workers also disadvantaged when it comes to unemployment benefit coverage? Figure 22 shows that the differences between former temporary and permanent workers are less pronounced than among former full-time and part-time workers. Among the registered unemployed, in Germany and the United Kingdom former temporary workers are even better off than former permanent workers; the opposite is true in Spain, the country with the highest share of temporary employment. If all unemployed who are looking for a job are considered, coverage rates of former temporary workers are approxi-

Table 16: Unemployment benefit receipt for low- and high-hours part-time workers: comparison of registered unemployed and all unemployed jobseekers

%	1–19 hours *		20–29 hours	
	Registered	**All looking**	**Registered**	**All looking**
Denmark	(90)**	34	92	75
Germany	49	10	75	34
Spain	12	9	31	26
UK	59	18	(48)**	15

Note: * The variable recording working time was measured at the time of the last survey before unemployment; it is therefore only a proxy of former working time;
**Unreliable, fewer than 30 cases.
Source: Own calculations based on pooled ECHP data.

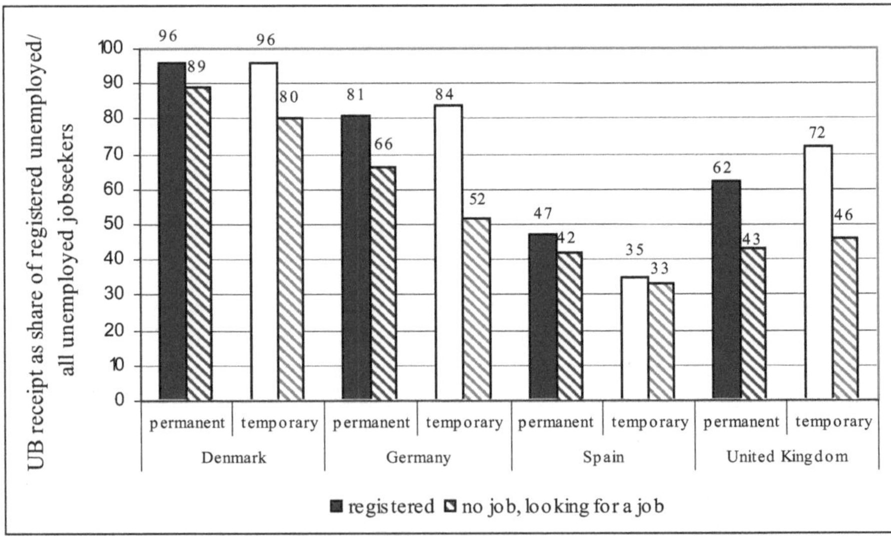

Figure 22: Unemployment benefit receipt for former permanent and temporary workers: comparison of registered unemployed and all unemployed jobseekers.
Source: Own calculations based on pooled and weighted ECHP data. A proxy is used for permanent and temporary employment.

Table 17: Duration of fixed-term contracts

%	< 6 month	6 months to <1 year	1 to <2 years	More than 2 years
Denmark	18	35	29	19
Germany	13	26	26	34
Spain	23	48	22	7
United Kingdom	26	22	25	28

Note: There is no information on this indicator in the SOEP and the BHPS data that replaced the original ECHP data for Germany and the United Kingdom after the third wave. *Source*: Own calculations based on waves 2 and 3 of the ECHP data (original ECHP data for Germany and the United Kingdom).

mately 10 percentage points below the coverage rates of former permanent workers, except for the United Kingdom where temporary workers are somewhat better off than permanent workers. The British contribution regulation that requires minimum payments instead of a certain time spent in employment (as is the case for the other countries) seems to be beneficial for temporary workers; furthermore, the second-tier system is usually open for all unemployed as long as their household income does not exceed the limit. It can be assumed that means-testing does not play an overly important role among former temporary workers who constantly change between employment and unemployment.

For temporary workers access restrictions to benefits arise mainly from insufficient contribution periods. In many schemes at least one year of continuous employment within the reference period is necessary in order to qualify for benefits; eligibility thus depends on contract length and the possibilities of changing directly between different employers without having to rely on unemployment benefits between working periods. Table 17 shows the average duration of temporary work contracts in the mid-1990s. In Denmark and, especially, Spain the majority of temporary contracts are shorter than one year; in the United Kingdom the share is almost 50 per cent and in Germany it is about 40 per cent. These numbers hide the fact that temporary contracts can usually be renewed at least once. Case numbers are large enough only in Spain to calculate access to benefits based on the contract length specified in the previous wave. Access is, as expected, strongly increasing with previously specified contract length.

In a last descriptive step it is useful to assess how far non-coverage by unemployment benefits is cushioned by subsidiary systems, such as social assistance. If we look at any social benefit receipt at unemployment, not distinguishing between different benefit types, the following picture emerges. Especially Denmark, with almost total coverage, and Germany, with coverage rates of about

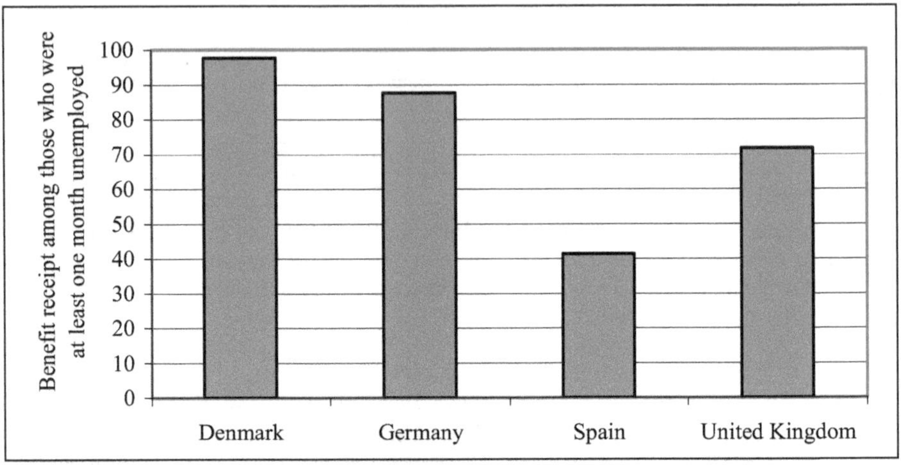

Figure 23: Any social benefit receipt at unemployment.
Source: Own calculations based on ECHP data.

90 per cent, perform well. In the United Kingdom more than two thirds of the unemployed receive some kind of benefit at unemployment, while the situation in Spain is disconcerting: only about 40 per cent of unemployed persons receive any social benefit – many unemployed thus have to rely on family income or the like (Figure 23).

The above descriptive results give a first impression of the coverage of non-standard employed persons in individual countries, but the role of the different institutional features of the benefit systems and their interaction in impeding or supporting benefit entitlement remains somewhat ambiguous. Furthermore, the above results control for neither length of unemployment nor individual or household characteristics. Differences in coverage between former temporary and permanent workers could, for example, be due merely to their different age profiles (deficient contribution records among the young). Therefore, the following section will look at the effects of part-time and temporary employment on unemployment benefit entitlement, controlling for individual, household and job characteristics. Furthermore, it will assess in more detail the influence and interaction of individual design features (hours or earnings threshold, contribution requirements and means-testing) on benefit coverage.

6.3.1.2 Multivariate analysis

A range of ECHP variables are transformed so that they reflect *regulations of the benefit systems* that potentially restrict non-standard workers' access to benefits.

There is no information on social security contribution in the data. In order nevertheless to capture *contribution time* within a specific reference period, the employment information from the calendar of events is used. There is monthly employment spell information from January 1993 to December 2000. Since we also know in which month a person was interviewed we can construct a variable that counts the number of months during which a specific person was employed before his or her last interview.[120] Every employment month within a 36-month reference period is counted; this corresponds to the Danish and the (pre-reform) German reference periods.[121]

Hours or earnings thresholds can be approached by using information on the number of hours that an unemployed person worked in his or her last job and on the wages he or she earned.[122] No retrospective information on working hours is collected in the survey. In order to compensate for this problem the information on usual working hours from the previous two survey waves is used. The information from t–2 is used only if the information on working hours is missing in t–1. Based on the lagged hours variable, four hours groups are generated: marginal part-time employment with 1 to 14 hours (the German hours threshold used to be 15 hours, the Spanish 12), intermediate part-time employment with 15 to 19 hours, high hours part-time work with 20 to 29 hours and full-time employment with more than 30 hours. The assumption is that discrimination in access to benefit systems will be stronger the lower the working hours.

Means-testing can be captured using information on the current household income or income of a partner.[123]

A random effects logit model is calculated in order to take account of the panel structure of the data (responses of the same individual at different time

120 It would have been preferable to use the month the last job ended as a reference point instead of the most recent interview. This was not possible because there are many gaps on this variable in all the countries, ranging from 25 to more than 50 per cent.

121 Since at least three years of previous calendar information are necessary to reach the maximum spell length of 36 months, only persons who were at the earliest interviewed in December 1995 will be able to reach the maximum spell length. A similar problem exists for persons interviewed in 2001 and early 2002 because the calendar of events stops in December 2000.

122 Only the annual individual net wage and salary income from the year prior to the survey is recorded in the data. In order to get a better proxy of former monthly wage income this amount is divided by the number of months a person has been employed. If the annual wage income is zero for t–1 it is replaced by the information from t–2.

123 The current net monthly wage and salary household income is used as a proxy for means-testing.

points are not independent of each other) (Rabe-Hesketh et al. 2004: 151 et seq.).[124] Since, in general, the estimated parameters from binary regression models do not provide directly useful information for understanding the relationship between the independent variables and the outcome, odds ratios, predicted probabilities and graphical display of predicted probabilities are used below for the presentation of results. Table 18 shows the odds ratios for the benefit system proxy variables. The models that are calculated separately for each country are all significant.[125] The following reference categories were chosen: full-time hours (30+) for the hours threshold indicator; a very long contribution period of 25 to 36 months for the indicator on the contribution requirement; and a former wage of more than 1000 euros-PPP for the earnings threshold indicator. The current monthly net wage and salary income of the household, as well as the unemployment duration indicator that controls for long-term unemployment, are metric variables.

Concerning the institutional features that can prevent access to benefits, Table 18 shows that the low hours threshold clearly plays a role in all countries – the odds of receiving benefits among persons with very low former hours are significantly lower than the odds of former full-time workers; the odds are increasing with the number of hours worked. Whereas hours thresholds are (were) clearly defined in the German and the Spanish unemployment system they seem to work indirectly also in the United Kingdom and in Denmark. In the United Kingdom this is probably due to the wage level threshold; the earnings threshold proxy for low earnings in the above regression table points in the right direction but is not significant for the United Kingdom. In Denmark, the strong negative influence of very low hours on access to benefits could be due either to the voluntary nature of the unemployment insurance programme – there is evidence that persons who expect low benefit levels are less likely to insure because they can expect similar benefit levels from social assistance – or to the fact that minimum contribution requirements in Denmark are achieved faster if working hours are higher.

---

124 The rho statistic displayed at the bottom of Table 18 confirms the use of a random effects model that takes into account the panel structure of the data. If rho were zero, the panel level variance component would be unimportant, and the panel estimator would not be different from the pooled estimator (StataCorp 2005a: 167). According to the likelihood ratio test, which formally compares the pooled estimator (logit) with the panel estimator, except for Denmark the panel estimator is clearly more suitable than the pooled estimator.

125 The prob>chi2 statistic, which is based on the Wald test, shows for each country that we can reject the hypothesis that all coefficients are zero at the .01 level.

Table 18: Random effects logistic regression on unemployment benefit receipt

Dependent variable: unemployment benefit receipt (no/yes)	Denmark	Germany	Spain	United Kingdom
Odds ratios				
REFERENCE: hours threshold: 30+ hours				
Hours threshold: 1–14 hours	0.17**	0.32**	0.49**	0.39**
Hours threshold: 15–19 hours	0.47+	0.35**	0.32**	0.41*
Hours threshold: 20–29 hours	0.71	0.52**	0.43**	0.54+
REFERENCE: contribution period: 25–36 months				
Contribution period: 0 months	0.15**	0.09**	0.11**	0.42*
Contribution period: 1–6 months	0.36**	0.15**	0.11**	0.58+
Contribution period: 7–12 months	0.49*	0.27**	0.20**	0.61
Contribution period: 13–18 months	0.71	0.31**	0.43**	0.85
Contribution period : 19–24 months	0.71	0.58**	0.68*	0.61+
Household wage/100 (means-testing)	0.98+	0.96**	0.95**	0.98+
REFERENCE: >1000 € PPP				
Earnings threshold proxy: 0	1.91*	0.45**	0.14**	0.34**
Earnings threshold proxy: <300 € PPP	0.44	0.40**	0.12**	0.67
Earnings threshold proxy: <600 € PPP	0.56+	1.04	0.37**	0.68
Earnings threshold proxy: <1000 € PPP	1.44	1.15	0.99	1.21
Unemployment duration proxy	1.09**	1.10**	1.01+	1.05**
Observations	925	4302	4286	1082
Number of groups	674	2761	2837	875
wald chi2 (14)	89.93	797.35	646.29	84.81
prob > chi2	0.0000	0.0000	0.0000	0.0000
rho	.03	.20	.14	.37
Likelihood ratio test of rho=0: prob>=chibar2	0.403	0.000	0.000	0.000
+ significant at 10%; * significant at 5%; ** significant at 1%				

Source: Own calculations based on ECHP data. The sample taken into account are all unemployed persons who are looking for a job.

As to *contribution period*, no contributions within the last three years clearly restricts access to benefits in all countries, though least in the United Kingdom, which is probably due to the income-based Jobseeker's Allowance that is open to all unemployed, depending on means-testing. Low contributions of less than six months significantly restrict access to benefits if compared to very long contribution periods in all countries, though least in the United Kingdom and Denmark. In Germany and Spain the odds of receiving benefits rise significantly with length of contribution time, but always stay below those of persons with very long contribution periods. For Denmark this is true only for contribution periods below 12 months. The coefficients for the United Kingdom are not significant, which could be due to the fact that the access rules for unemployment benefits are more complicated than in the other countries and might not be proxied well by the variables constructed here. Furthermore, the variable on unemployment benefit receipt in the ECHP does not distinguish between insurance and assistance benefits and the access to income-based Jobseeker's Allowance (unemployment assistance) in the United Kingdom is conditional on only means-testing and not on the length of previous contribution periods.

In order to illustrate the effects of *contribution time and hours thresholds* on access to benefits, a table of probabilities for ideal types or profiles of individuals is calculated, based on the above regression results (compare Long et al. 2006: 160 et seq.). Household income is set to its mean, and it is assumed that the individuals formerly earned between 601 and 1000 euros-PPP; earnings thresholds should thus not be a problem. Under these conditions, the average probability of all unemployed who are looking for a job receiving unemployment benefits in Denmark is 0.62, even if they worked low hours before and have short contribution times (Table 19). A combination of former full-time hours and long contribution times increases the average probability to about 0.80. The trend in the United Kingdom is similar, but at a much lower level – long contribution times and full-time hours lead to predicted probabilities of benefit receipt of only about 0.26. In Germany and Spain, low working hours and short contribution periods clearly are problematic and limit access to benefits; unemployed persons with relatively long contribution times and full-time hours have far higher predicted probabilities of receiving benefits at unemployment. In some cases, especially with low contribution times in Denmark and in the United Kingdom, the confidence intervals have large ranges.

Means-testing, introduced into the model via the household wage income, seems to play a role (compare Table 18). Higher household wages are associated

Table 19: Individual predicted probabilities of benefit receipt for ideal types (based on regression results in Table 18)

Ideal type*	**Denmark**	**Germany**	**Spain**	**United Kingdom**
Dependent variable: unemployment benefit receipt	Predicted probability (95% confidence interval in brackets)			
Contributions of 7 to 12 months and low hours (15–19)	0.62 (0.40–0.83)	0.11 (0.05–0.17)	0.03 (0.01–0.06)	0.14 (0.04–0.24)
Contributions of 13 to 18 months and low hours (15–19)	0.68 (0.46–0.90)	0.11 (0.05–0.18)	0.05 (0.02–0.09)	0.16 (0.05–0.28)
Contributions of 7 to 12 months and high part-time hours (20–29)	0.71 (0.56–0.86)	0.14 (0.10–0.20)	0.04 (0.03–0.06)	0.16 (0.06–0.25)
Contributions of 19 to 24 months and full-time hours (30+)	0.82 (0.71–0.93)	0.38 (0.30–0.45)	0.17 (0.13–0.22)	0.26 (0.16–0.37)

Note: * The above results are conditional on a mean household income and wages between 601 and 1000 euros-PPP. Basis: all unemployed who are looking for a job.
Source: Own calculations based on ECHP data.

with somewhat lower odds of receiving unemployment benefits. Figure 24 highlights the relationship between means-testing and benefit receipt for long-term unemployed by showing the predicted probabilities as a function of the household wage.[126] The idea is to draw a curve showing how the model's prediction of y (unemployment benefit receipt) changes as a function of one x variable (household income), holding all other variables at the mean. Means-testing does not play a role in the highly individualised Danish system; unemployment benefits are paid for a long period, independent of the income situation of the recipient and his family, and unemployment assistance does not exist (Figure 24). In the other three countries means-testing for long-term unemployed (in unemployment assistance systems) is evident. While it sets in very slowly with growing household income in Germany, it sets in rapidly in Spain and relatively fast in the United Kingdom. In Spain, a high household income is associated with total lack of benefit entitlement; a similar trend is observable in the United Kingdom if the confidence intervals (dashed lines) are taken into account. This is not the case in Germany, which is probably due to the fact that unemployment insurance benefits were formerly paid for long periods, depending on age and former contribution period.

126 The post-estimation commands (conditional effect plots and individual predicted probabilities) are based on pooled cross-sections (logistic regression that adjusts for repeated measurement of the same person); the post-estimation commands used here do not work after the panel models. Results of both models are quite close.

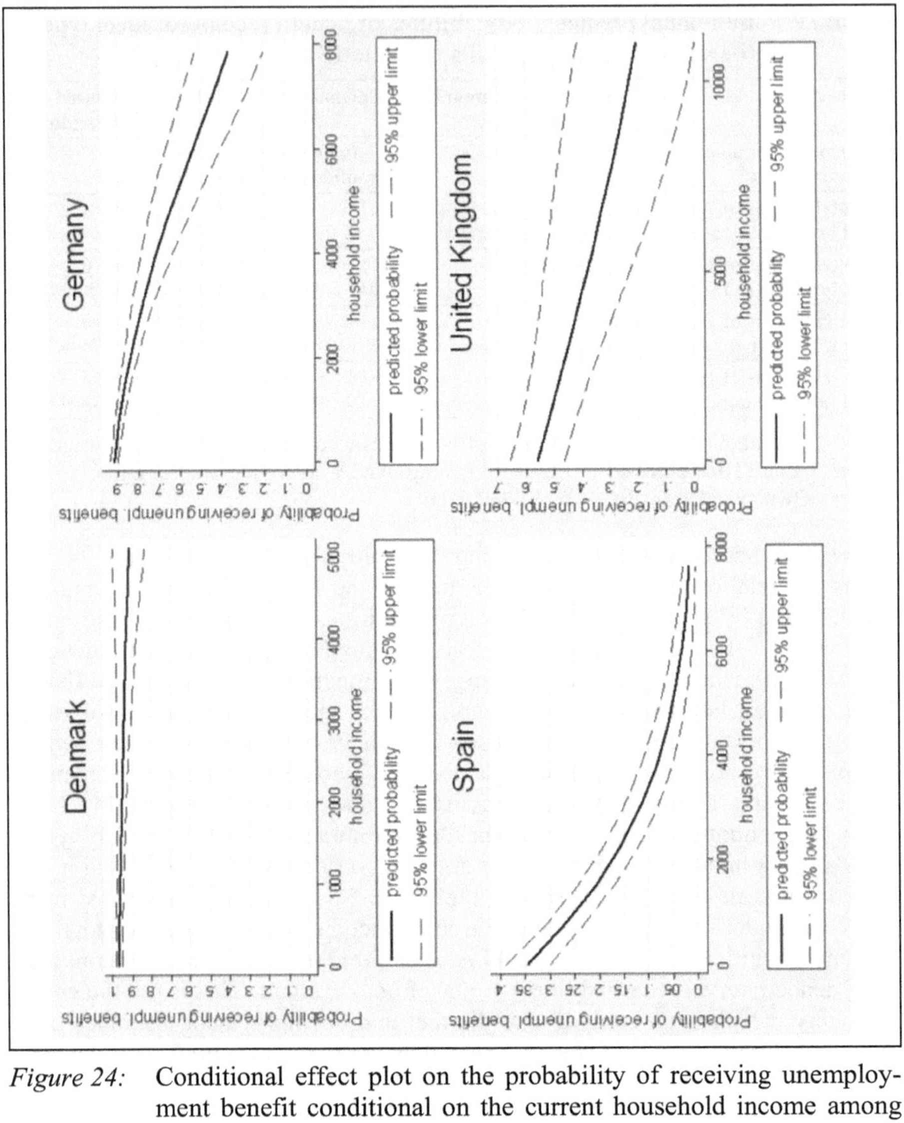

Figure 24: Conditional effect plot on the probability of receiving unemployment benefit conditional on the current household income among the long-term unemployed.

Source: Own calculations based on ECHP data. For a description of the method, see Long et al. (2006: 166–168). All other dependent variables from the regression model are set to their mean. Based on regression results in Table 18.

The wage proxy in the regression analysis captures *earnings thresholds* or alternatively, hours thresholds that should have a similar effect. Former earnings below 300 euros-PPP imply lower odds of receiving benefits than very high earnings (compare Table 18). Denmark is the only exception – the high and significant coefficient on zero earnings could be due to the very long period that benefits are granted in Denmark without being subject to means-testing. The positive coefficient on a zero wage income in the previous two years might thus point only to ongoing benefit receipt that already started some time ago. As expected, as soon as earnings pass a certain level, access restrictions are no longer in place. Plotting the predicted probabilities of benefit receipt as a function of former earnings, with all other institutional variables at their mean, is more enlightening than the above results. Former earnings do not have an influence in Denmark, while in the other countries former earnings apparently have a positive influence on the probability of receiving benefits – the higher the former earnings, the more likely the probability of receiving benefits (Figure 25).

Before moving on to benefit levels we shall look briefly at the direct effects of former part-time and temporary employment on benefit receipt, controlling for individual, household and job characteristics. Former part-time workers, if compared with their full-time employed counterparts, have significantly lower odds of receiving benefits in Denmark and in the United Kingdom (about one third), as well as in Germany (about half), even if individual factors such as age, gender and qualification level, household characteristics (composition and income) and job-related characteristics (occupation and former personal wage) are controlled for (Table 20). The part-time coefficient for Spain is not significant. None of the coefficients for temporary employment as compared to permanent employment are significant, although they point in the right direction, except for Spain. Apart from Denmark with its highly individualised system women have considerably lower odds of receiving benefits than men – the difference is especially great in the United Kingdom, which is probably due to means-testing at an early stage of benefit receipt.

To illustrate the results, predicted probabilities for part-time and full-time workers are displayed in Table 21. Since the coefficient for temporary employment is not significant we only display the results here but do not further comment on them. If women with medium qualification levels in couples without children, mean former wage income, mean current household income, and mean length of unemployment (about 10 months) are looked at, predicted probabilities for benefit receipt are in all countries lower for former part-time than for former full-time workers. Concerning Denmark, we are 95% confident that the predicted probability of receiving benefits for former part-time workers lies between 0.40

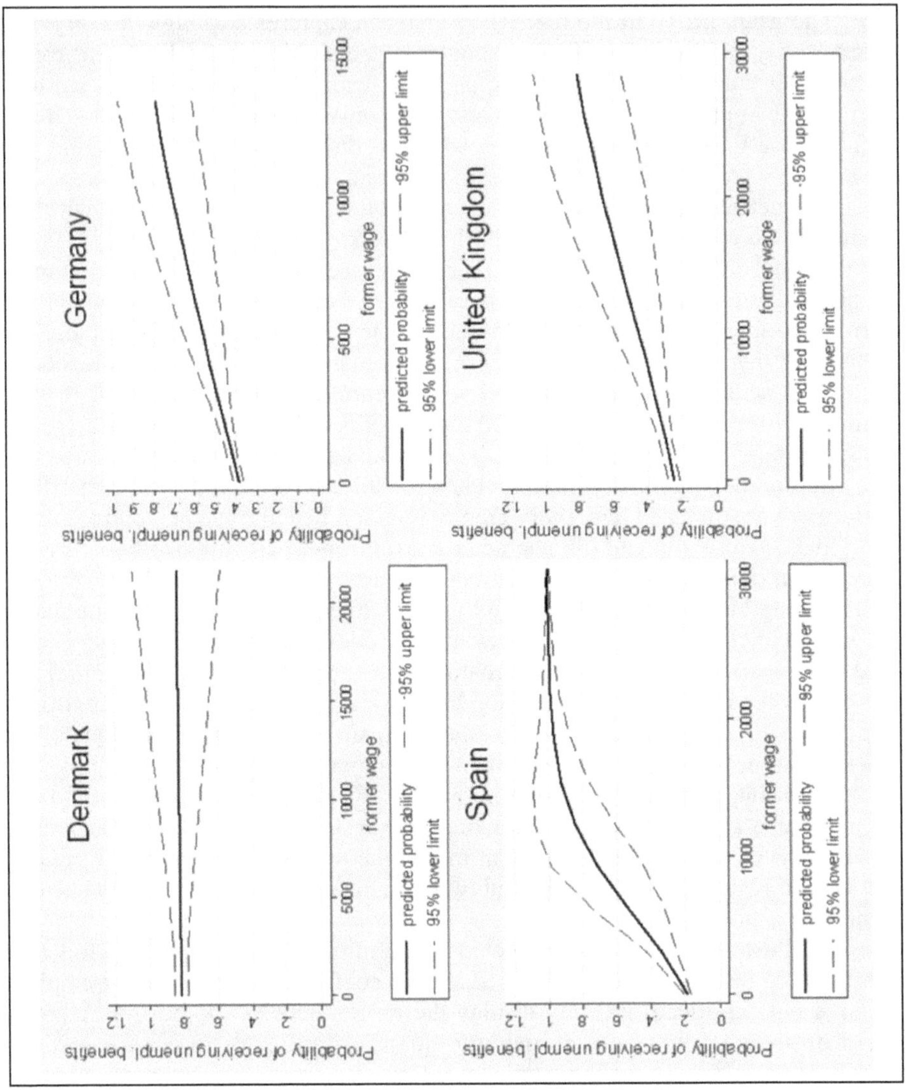

Figure 25: Conditional effects plot on the probability of receiving unemployment benefits conditional on the former wage.
Source: Own calculations based on ECHP data. All other dependent variables from the regression model are set to their mean. Based on regression results in Table 18

Table 20: Random effects logit model – access of non-standard workers to unemployment benefits

Dependent variable: unemployment benefit receipt (no/yes)	**Denmark**	**Germany**	**Spain**	**United Kingdom**
Odds ratios				
Last job part-time	0.32**	0.47**	0.80	0.29**
REFERENCE: reason for leaving last job: obliged to leave				
Reason: end of contract/temporary job	0.55	0.70	1.01	0.47
Women	1.56	0.58*	0.43**	0.36**
Observations	892	2266	4200	588
Number of groups	562	967	2280	417
Wald chi2(32) (Germany(24))	164.03	310.50	447.14	76.75
Prob > chi2	0.0000	0.0000	0.0000	0.0000
Rho	.24	.48	.45	.38
Prob >= chibar2	0.004	0.000	0.000	0.001
Further variables included in models but not shown here: age, household type, qualification level, personal wage before unemployment, current household wage, occupation last job (except for Germany), length of unemployment, and year dummies.				
+ significant at 10%; * significant at 5%; ** significant at 1%; p-values in parentheses				

Source: Own calculations based on ECHP data; all those without a job, looking for a job.

and 0.84. Probabilities of receiving benefits are very low for part-time workers in the other three countries, and also remain below 0.30 for former full-time workers with the above stated profile (all unemployed who are looking for a job form the basis).

Last but not least, some insight into interactions between temporary and part-time employment is given. It is expected that people with temporary contracts and part-time hours are especially badly off regarding unemployment benefits. The share of temporary employment exercised as part-time employment is especially large in the United Kingdom, while the majority of part-time contracts in Spain are of a temporary nature (compare Table 30, Annex 1). Significant results of interacting part-time and temporary employment can be found only for Germany and the United Kingdom (compare Table 22).[127] In these two countries

127 Interactions are included in the model by multiplying the two components of the interaction and adding this new term as a predictor to a model that includes the main effects of both variables. The main effects, in this case full-time employment and permanent employment, then show the effects for those persons for whom the interaction term is zero.

Table 21: Individual predicted probabilities of benefit receipt for typical non-standard and standard workers[128]

Ideal type*	**Denmark**	**Germany**	**Spain**	**United Kingdom**
	Predicted probability (95% confidence interval in brackets)			
Part-time women in couple without children	0.62 (0.40–0.84)	0.14 (0.07–0.20)	0.23 (0.15–0.30)	0.11 (0.03–0.19)
Full-time women in couple without children	0.83 (0.71–0.95)	0.24 (0.16–0.32)	0.27 (0.20–0.34)	0.18 (0.06–0.30)
Woman with **temporary job** in couple without children	0.91 (0.86–0.96)	0.52 (0.45–0.59)	0.34 (0.29–0.40)	0.27 (0.14–0.40)
Woman with **permanent job** in couple without children	0.93 (0.89–0.97)	0.54 (0.48–0.61)	0.51 (0.43–0.59)	0.28 (0.16–0.40)

Note: * Age, former wage, current household income and length of unemployment are set to their mean; a medium qualification level (ISCED 3) applies.
Source: Own calculations based on ECHP data, adapted from Long et al. (2006: 162).

Table 22: Interaction between working part-time and having a temporary job

Dependent variable: unemployment benefit receipt (no/yes), odds ratios	**Denmark**	**Germany**	**Spain**	**United Kingdom**
Full-time (temporary)	1.14	4.06**	1.17	8.77*
Permanent (part-time)	0.44	3.78*	1.43	18.44*
Temporary*part-time	5.22	0.33+	0.69	0.12
Observations	539	1221	3271	277
Number of groups	337	581	1764	193
Prob > chi2	0.000	0.000	0.000	0.016
Further variables included but not shown here: gender, age, household type, qualification level, personal wage before unemployment, current household wage, occupation last job (except for Germany), length of unemployment, and year dummies.				
+ significant at 10%; * significant at 5%; ** significant at 1%				

Source: Own calculations based on ECHP data. Lower observation numbers than in the models above come about because the other categories constituting reasons for leaving the last job (proxy for temporary employment) have been dropped.

128 The regression models that this table is based on have to be calculated separately for former part-time and full-time workers (no control for former contract type) and for former temporary and permanent workers (no control for working time). This is necessary due to the relatively high number of gaps on these two variables that lead to a matrix with missing values – the individual predicted probabilities cannot be calculated on the basis of this matrix with missing values.

temporary workers with full-time hours are much more likely to receive benefits in the case of unemployment than temporary workers with part-time hours. The same is true for part-time workers with permanent contracts; in the case of unemployment they are considerably more likely to receive benefits than part-time workers with temporary contracts. In countries with an extended male breadwinner model, a combination of relatively high hours or earnings thresholds (especially evident in Germany and the United Kingdom) and the high importance of means-testing[129] seems to provoke the double disadvantage. Neither the Danish nor the Spanish coefficients are significant. In the Danish unemployment insurance system means-testing does not play a role, and in Spain part-time employment takes on a different function than in Germany and the United Kingdom, the traditional breadwinner model (with a non-working mother) being much more evident.

6.3.2 Benefit levels and composition of benefits

Differences in benefit levels between former part-time and full-time workers should be especially evident in countries with benefit systems that are strongly based on insurance principles and therefore make use of pro rata rules, namely Germany and Spain. In most systems benefits are calculated based on former earnings; lower earnings due to part-time employment thus automatically lead to lower replacement income at unemployment. Low ceilings (evident in Denmark) can reduce differences between benefit levels of former full-time and part-time workers (or high and low earners). Flat-rate benefits (as in the United Kingdom) do not distinguish between former part-time and full-time workers. Nevertheless, differences in benefit levels brought about by means-testing are possible due to household composition, which may vary between part-time and full-time workers.

The contract type, permanent or temporary, should have no direct effect on the benefit level. If there are variations in benefit levels between former permanent and temporary workers this is due either to different job profiles associated with differences in wage levels or, more importantly, to schemes that require comprehensive contribution records for access to insurance benefits or that condition the duration of benefit payments on former contribution time (Germany and Spain). Such systems are likely to force an important share of former temporary workers (and also low-hours part-time workers) into means-tested unem-

129 Unemployment assistance receipt in both Germany (prior to 1999) and the United Kingdom require short or no contribution periods.

ployment or social assistance. As illustrated in Chapter 5, unemployment assistance and social assistance schemes are not only means-tested but usually provide lower replacement rates than unemployment insurance schemes.

6.3.2.1 Descriptive analysis

In order to provide a broader picture of the four countries' benefit systems the following part will not focus exclusively on unemployment benefit levels, but also look at other social benefits that may act as functional equivalents. If we look at the main source of income among individuals who have been unemployed during the preceding year for at least 10 months, clear country differences emerge (see Figure 26). In Denmark and Germany, the majority of unemployed persons state unemployment-related benefit as the main source of their individual income, while in Spain and, especially, the United Kingdom this share is much lower. While in the United Kingdom deficient unemployment benefit coverage is compensated by other social benefits – probably social assistance, hous-

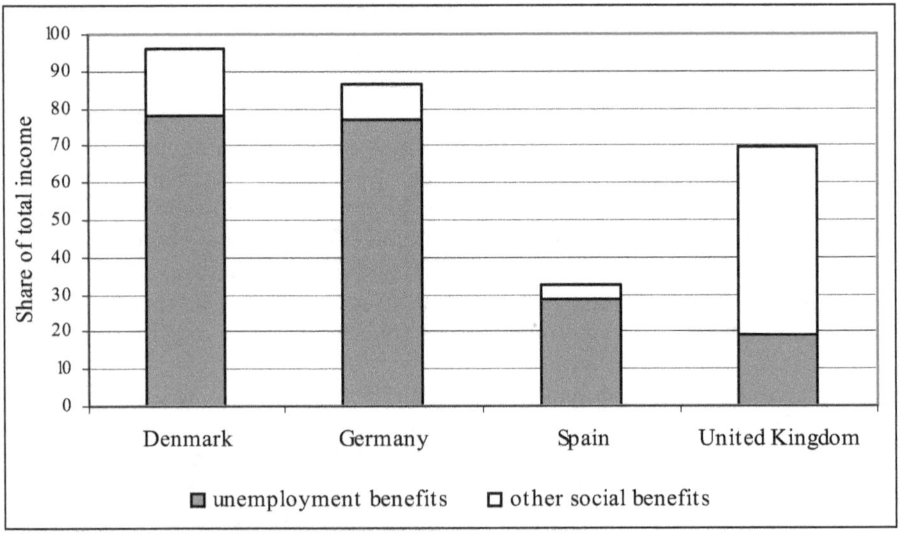

Figure 26: Social benefit receipt as main individual source of income at unemployment in per cent.
Source: Own calculations based on ECHP data. Only unemployed persons who have been unemployed at least 10 months during the last calendar year are taken into account.

ing benefits and the like – hardly any compensation is provided in Spain, where only about one third of longer-term unemployed receive unemployment or social benefits as their main source of individual income.

At the household level, in households with at least one longer-term unemployed (10 to 12 months) person, the share of unemployment and social benefits as main income still lies at around 55 per cent in Denmark, Germany and the United Kingdom, with considerably higher importance for other social benefits, while in Spain the main source of income of these households derives from wages (about 47 per cent) and a considerable share from pensions (16 per cent).

There are no big differences between former temporary and permanent workers in the extent and composition of social benefit receipt as main source of income. Among former part-time workers the share of longer-term unemployed who are receiving unemployment benefits as main source of income is about 10 per cent lower in Germany, the United Kingdom and Spain; this is fully compensated by other benefit receipt only in the United Kingdom.

Taking into account only the level of unemployment-related benefits does not do justice to the way different social insurance systems work. In some countries, social assistance or housing benefits paid in addition to unemployment benefits play an important role. Indeed, according to the ECHP data about 25 per cent of Danish unemployment benefit recipients additionally received social assistance. The respective shares were only 1 and 5 per cent in Spain and Germany – both systems incorporate a direct family component in their unemployment insurance systems. There is no information on social assistance receipt for the United Kingdom. The importance of housing benefits in the British system (compare OECD 2002a: 35) is confirmed by the ECHP data: about 40 per cent of British unemployment benefit recipients additionally received a housing allowance, while this share is only around 15 per cent in Denmark and Germany and marginal in Spain.

Figure 27 shows the average annual level and composition of social benefit receipt among unemployment benefit recipients.[130] The net average social benefit level is highest in Denmark, at around 7000 euros-PPP. Germany takes a middle position, and benefit levels in Spain and the United Kingdom are considerably lower, at around 3500 euros-PPP. The British benefit level is possibly somewhat understated because information on social assistance payments is not available. As expected from the above information, housing allowances have a consider-

130 The countries' annual average results are comparable because the distribution of unemployment duration of benefit recipients as stated in the calendar of events is relatively similar in the countries of interest (discrepancies are largest in Spain with a tendency for more longer-term unemployed).

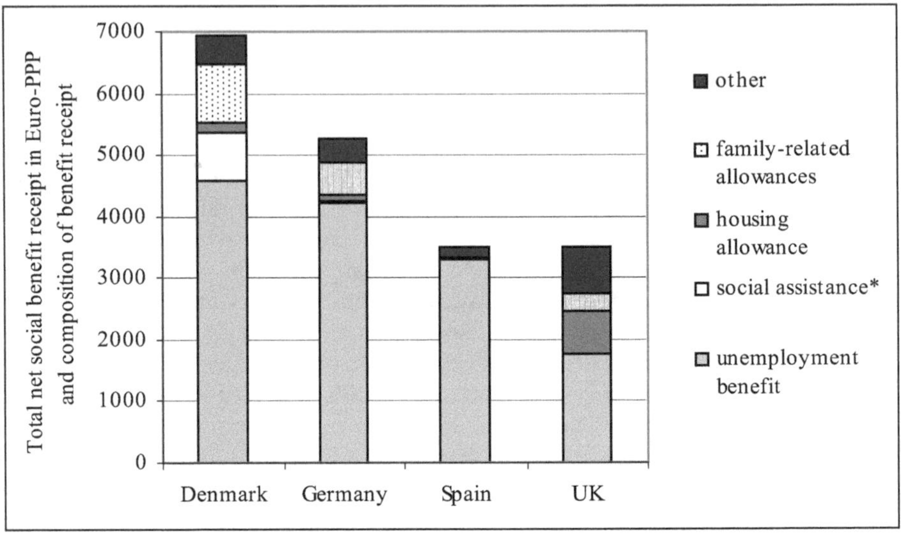

Figure 27: Average annual social benefit receipt and composition of benefit receipt.

Note: * There is no information on social assistance payments in the British data.

Source: Own calculations based on pooled ECHP data; age 18–64. Only non-zero benefit receipt is taken into account.

able influence on the overall benefit level only in the United Kingdom, while social assistance payments for unemployment benefit recipients have a discernable size only in Denmark. If we look exclusively at the average level of unemployment benefit receipt, Denmark and Germany perform best and the United Kingdom, with its flat-rate unemployment insurance system, performs worst, with annual average unemployment benefits of less than 2000 euros-PPP.

The following analysis will concentrate on monthly unemployment benefits, taking into account individuals who were unemployed between 3 and 12 months.[131] The weighted average monthly benefit level (1993–2000) for recipients of unemployment benefits lies at around 690 euros-PPP in Denmark, at

131 We do not know the number of months in which benefits were received by the sampled persons, but we can use the individual duration of unemployment from the calendar of events as a proxy. Among individuals with unemployment spells of only 1 or 2 months unusually high monthly benefit levels were recorded in some cases, which could be due to the fact that the variable 'unemployment-related benefits' includes training/education allowance and placement and resettlement benefits. For this reason it was decided to look only at benefit recipients who were unemployed for at least 3 months.

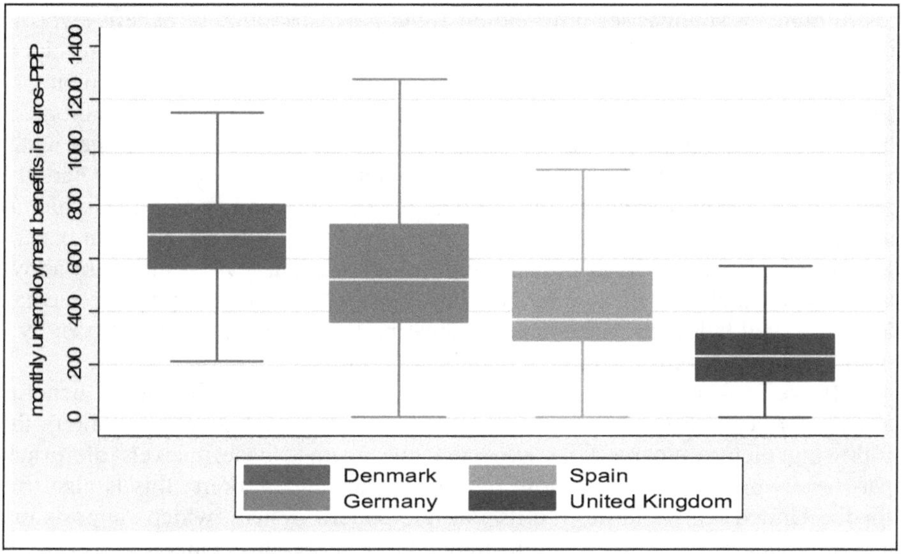

Figure 28: Comparison of distribution of monthly benefit levels.
Source: Own calculations based on pooled and weighted ECHP data (1994–2001). Outliers are not shown here. The figure refers to unemployment benefit recipients with between 3 and 12 months of unemployment.

around 615 euros-PPP in Germany, and is considerably lower in Spain, at around 440 euros-PPP. Average benefits in the United Kingdom with its flat-rate benefit system are very low, at about 270 euros-PPP. These results are close to the calculations by Ghysels et al. (1999: 12–17), which are based on the first two waves of the ECHP. The German benefit level also looks plausible if compared with results from administrative data (Klammer 2005: 332). Net replacement rates calculated on the basis of the ECHP data are about 65 per cent in Denmark and Germany, 42 per cent in Spain and a low of 26 per cent in the United Kingdom.[132]

132 The net replacement rates take into account unemployment benefit levels from all unemployed, independent of the duration of unemployment.

Figure 28 summarises information about the distribution of benefit levels in the fours countries.[133] The distribution of overall unemployment benefit receipt is symmetric and narrow in Denmark and the United Kingdom, probably owing to low ceilings in the case of Denmark and flat-rate benefits with adaptation for household situation in the United Kingdom. The distribution is somewhat wider in Spain but skewed to the right – many recipients receive relatively low benefits and few receive high benefits. In Germany the distribution is very wide, which is at least in part brought about by high earnings ceilings. While high mean benefit levels in Denmark go hand in hand with a high median level – the point above and below which half of the observations are situated – in Germany the median level lies well below the mean level, indicating that the high mean is driven by a number of observations with very high benefit levels.

If we look at the average benefit levels and the distribution of benefits among former non-standard workers compared to former standard workers the following picture emerges. As expected, the average benefit levels of former part-time workers lie below those of former full-time workers; this is also true for the United Kingdom despite its flat-rate benefit system, which supports our assumption that part-time workers rather have access to means-tested benefits than to contribution-based non-means-tested benefits (Figure 29).[134] In pro rata systems we would have expected even stronger differences between average benefit levels of former part-time and full-time workers. Specific regulations such as minimum benefits, protection of the status quo (in Germany) and low ceilings (Denmark) seem to contribute to bringing benefit levels of former part-time workers more in line with benefit levels of former full-time workers.

Comparing the distribution of benefit levels of former full-time and part-time workers between countries we get a variable picture. Median benefit levels

133 A box plot is used to illustrate the distribution of benefits. The lower border of the box is the first quartile, the upper border is the third quartile, and the line in the middle of the box represents the median. Boxes thus present benefit levels for the 50 per cent of the population situated at the middle of the distribution. One can also see the symmetry or skewness of the distribution: in symmetric distributions the distances between the median and the lower and upper bounds of the box are equal and the whiskers should be of equal length. Whiskers or boxes that are squeezed at the bottom show distributions that are skewed to the right, whiskers and boxes that are squeezed at the top show distributions that are skewed to the left (Kohler et al. 2005: 171–172).

134 The results for the United Kingdom are less reliable than the results for the other countries because, in contrast to the other countries, case numbers for former part-time workers are very low, at about 45. This is due to the fact that because the benefit level is recorded for the year before the survey, the retrospective variable on working time in the last job, which is asked only in case of non-employment, has to be lagged twice, bringing about a relatively high loss of case numbers.

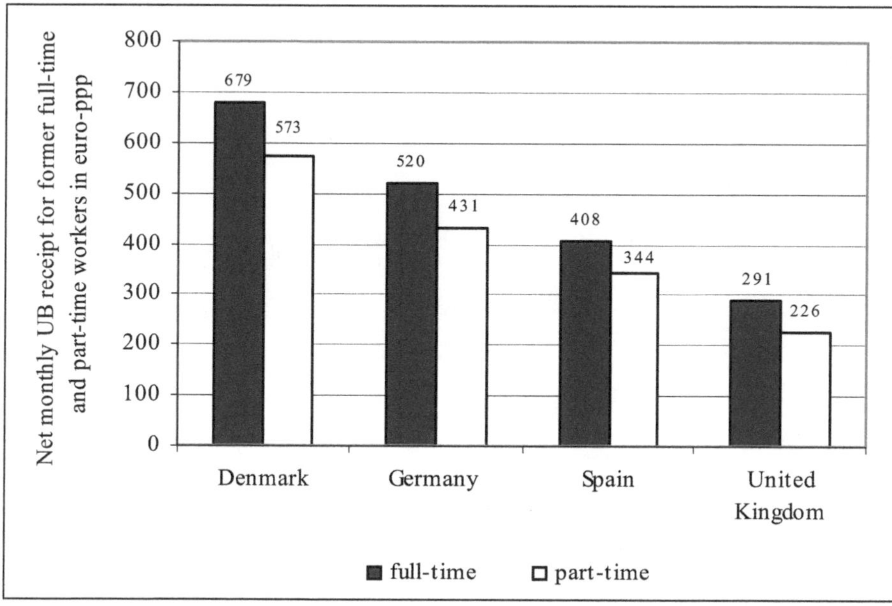

Figure 29: Average monthly unemployment benefit level by working time.
Source: Own calculations based on pooled and weighted ECHP data. The figure refers to unemployment benefit recipients with between 3 and 12 months of unemployment.

are clearly highest in Denmark and very similar for former part-time and full-time workers (Figure 30). The considerably wider distribution of unemployment benefits among former part-time workers can at least in part be explained by the fact that part-time workers can chose between being full-time or part-time insured (at two thirds of the full-time benefit level) and the minimum benefit is applicable only to individuals who have continuously worked full-time (Fink 1999a: 103). The distribution of benefit payments for former part-time workers in Germany is somewhat skewed to the right, meaning that many former part-time workers receive relatively low benefits; the very high benefit levels for some part-time workers in Germany (whisker) can be explained by the specific transitory regulation that concerns part-time workers who have formerly been full-time employed. In Spain, the distribution of the benefits of former part-time workers is much closer than the one of former full-time workers, with a distribution among part-time workers that is skewed to the left. Median benefit levels of former full-time and part-time workers in the United Kingdom are very similar, but the dispersion is wider among former full-time workers.

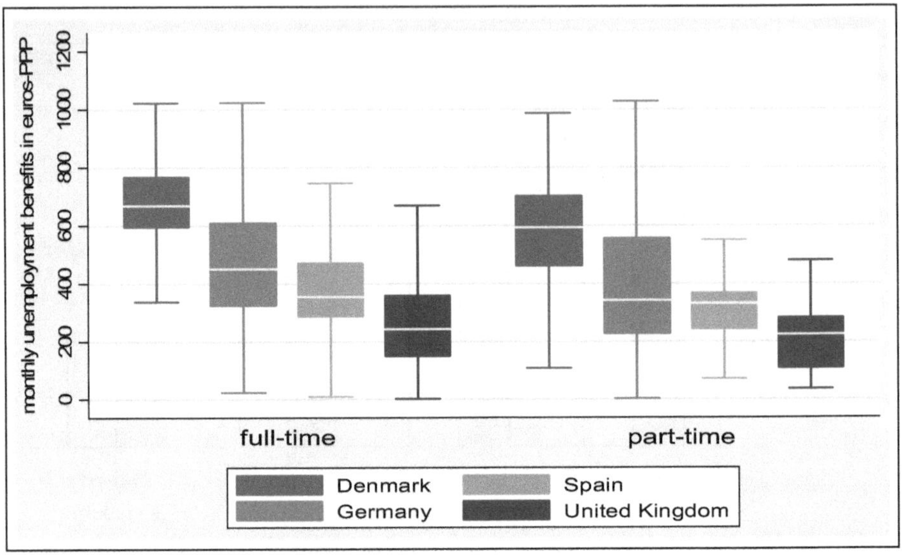

Figure 30: Distribution of monthly benefit levels for former full-time and part-time workers.
Source: Own calculations based on pooled and weighted ECHP data. The figure refers to unemployment benefit recipients with between 3 and 12 months of unemployment.

Based on rough calculations taking into account wages of part-time workers who were in paid employment for the majority of the year we get net replacement rates of around 85 per cent for part-time workers in Denmark and Germany, about 58 per cent for Spain and about 68 per cent for the United Kingdom. As the average benefit levels in Figure 29 already suggested, due to specific regulations benefiting part-time workers net replacement rates for part-time workers are considerably higher than the overall net replacement rates. Redistribution towards part-time workers thus takes place in all the countries under analysis.

We expect no great differences in benefit levels of former temporary and permanent workers. Indeed, benefit levels are very similar in Denmark, Germany and the United Kingdom (Figure 31). In Spain, on the other hand, former temporary workers have considerably lower average benefit levels than recipients who used to have a permanent contract. Although no direct discrimination should take place, insufficient contribution records could lead to a situation in which temporary workers more often have to rely on unemployment assistance that requires

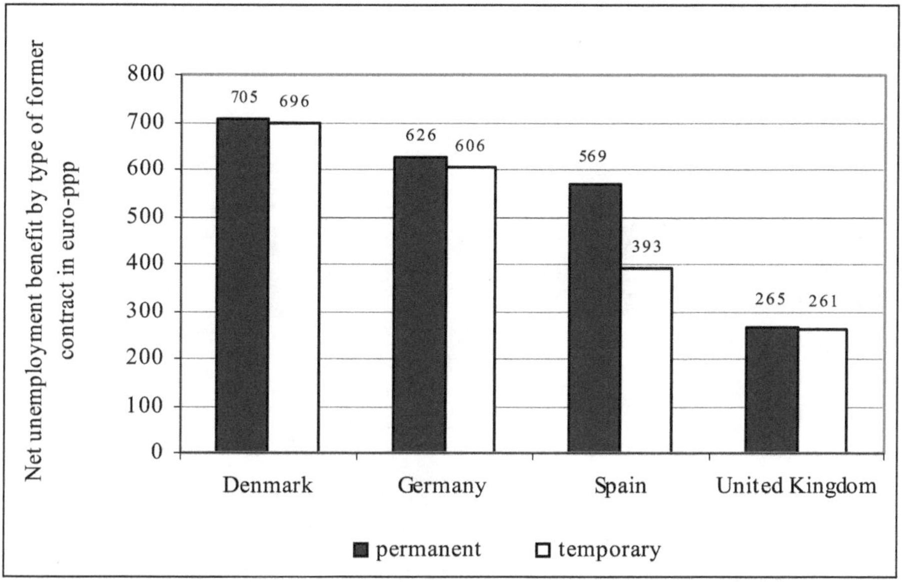

Figure 31: Average unemployment benefit level by former contract type.
Source: Own calculations based on pooled and weighted ECHP data. The figure refers to unemployment benefit recipients with between 3 and 12 months of unemployment.

shorter minimum contributions but is considerably less generous than unemployment insurance. Furthermore, temporary employment and part-time employment often go hand in hand in Spain, and there is evidence that temporary workers earn lower wages in Spain too (OECD 2003b: 80).

As to the distribution of monthly benefit levels hardly any differences between former temporary and permanent workers are evident in Denmark, Germany and the United Kingdom (see Figure 32). In Spain, the differences in average benefit levels are also visible in the distribution: former temporary workers display lower median benefit levels and a much tighter distribution. This supports the assumption that the differences in benefit levels are due at least in part to a stronger use of relatively low and flat-rate unemployment assistance benefits among former temporary workers.

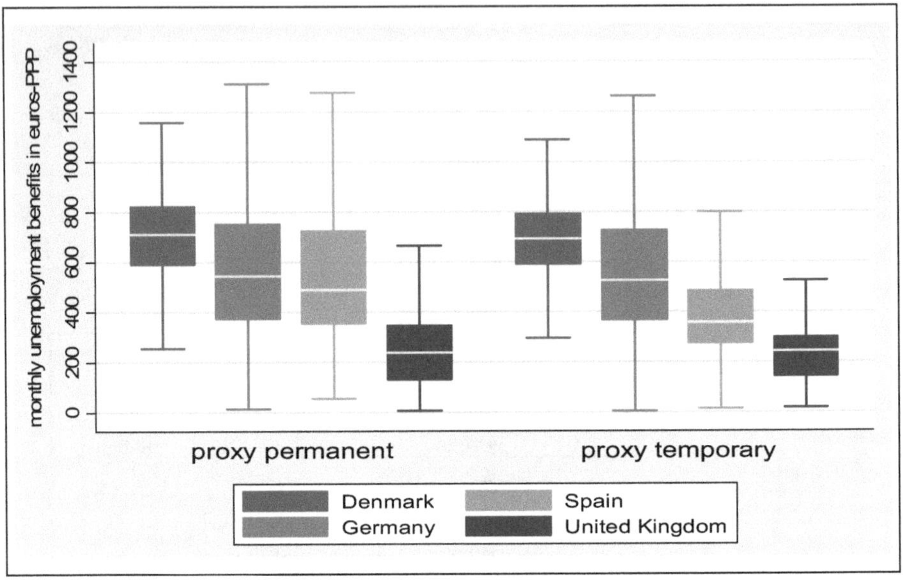

Figure 32: Distribution of monthly benefit levels for former permanent and temporary workers.
Source: Own calculations based on pooled and weighted ECHP data. The figure refers to unemployment benefit recipients with between 3 and 12 months of unemployment.

6.3.2.2 Multivariate analysis

The above results focus on non-standard employment, but do not control further for gender, job characteristics or household situation. It is a well-known fact, for example, that women tend to earn less than their male counterparts. In benefit systems that base their calculations on former wages (especially Germany and Spain and, to a lesser extent, Denmark) women should thus receive lower benefit levels. In order to isolate the influence of non-standard employment on the benefit level from other influences a random-effects model that controls for a range of variables will be run. To take account of the panel structure of the data a cross-sectional time-series regression model is fitted. A random-effects model seems to be more suitable than a fixed-effects model here because it answers questions on differences between individuals – for example, between former standard and non-standard workers. Fixed-effects models, in contrast, give answers to questions that are concerned with changes experienced by individuals.[135] In order to avoid possible selection problems the following regression model takes into account only unemployed persons who receive benefits. This strategy seems justified because access restrictions to benefit systems were discussed at length in the previous section.[136]

At the individual level, information on gender, age and qualification levels is included in the model. Benefits are expected to be lower for women than for men (wage discrimination and over-representation in low-wage sectors), and they should increase with age (seniority wages). Similarly, benefits are expected to rise with qualification level – especially in Germany and Spain. Low upper ceilings should attenuate the positive effects for the higher educated and the elderly in Denmark. The models also include a proxy for the former monthly wage level. In the United Kingdom with its flat-rate benefit system the variables are not expected to generate significant effects. On the other hand, means-testing and household composition should be important for benefit levels in the United Kingdom. Means-testing, which is a feature of unemployment assistance systems in Germany, Spain and the United Kingdom – and in the latter becomes important at a very early stage of the benefit period – is proxied by including a variable on the current household wage.[137] Household composition is included via a variable that captures whether children live in the household and whether households are made up of one or two adults. In non-individualised benefit systems households with more than one person are expected to fare better when it comes to benefit levels. In the German system households with children automatically receive higher unemployment benefits, not only in the assistance but also in the insurance system; they are similarly privileged in the Spanish system. In the United Kingdom, household composition also clearly plays a role because benefit levels depend on the family situation in the second-tier system. In Denmark, benefits are individualised to a high degree and are therefore not expected to vary significantly by family situation. Lower benefit levels due to the receipt of unemployment assistance benefits can be roughly captured by using an indicator on the length of unemployment – longer unemployment periods should be associated with lower benefit levels. Similarly, people with relatively long former

135 The strategy of opting for a random effects model because it is more in line with the question to be answered is supported by Petersen (2004: 342 et seq.), who states that the question to be addressed might be more important in choosing a specific method of analysis than focussing all attention on omitted-variable bias, which would be better served by a fixed-effects model.

136 A viable alternative to this strategy would be the application of a heckman selection two-step procedure that takes account of selection problems. Hours thresholds and the continuity criterion could be used as selection variables.

137 Alternatively, partner information can be matched to the data – the results are not significantly different.

employment periods are expected to have higher benefits because they should rather have access to insurance than to assistance benefits.

Calculating a random effects model pooling the data of all four countries leads to significant negative effects of part-time (at the 5 per cent level) and temporary employment (at the 10 per cent level). The country dummies behave as expected from the descriptive analysis: using Germany as a reference, controlling for individual and household level variables, monthly benefit levels are, on average, 110 euros-PPP higher in Denmark than in Germany, and 220 and 375 euros-PPP, respectively, lower in Spain and the United Kingdom (model and coefficients are not shown).

Table 23 shows the coefficients resulting from random effect models that are calculated separately for each country. Concerning the overall fit of the models as displayed in the tables by Prob > chi2, the models fit very well in Germany and Spain and less well in Denmark and the United Kingdom. As to the main effects of interest – former part-time employment and temporary employment – the coefficients are highly significant only in Germany for part-time employment and in Spain for temporary employment. In Germany, according to the regression model, former part-time workers receive unemployment benefits that are on average 165 euros-PPP lower than those of former full-time workers, holding all other variables constant. The seemingly important influence of wage levels on benefit levels in Germany is also evident in the case of the qualification variable. Increasing qualifications are to a significant degree associated with increasing benefit levels. The coefficient on former wages points in the expected direction, but it is significant only at the 10 per cent level. Furthermore, the increases associated with the former wage level are not as large as expected, which might be due to the impreciseness of this indicator. In Denmark and in Spain, a similarly negative association between part-time employment and benefit level was expected. While the signs of the coefficients point in the expected direction they are not significant. The effect might be taken away by the gender or wage variables that are included as controls.

Temporary employment should not generally be associated with lower benefit levels, except where temporary workers are more likely than permanent workers to receive unemployment assistance instead of insurance benefits. Another possible reason could be differences in job profiles between temporary and permanent workers that are especially evident in Spain (compare Tables 34 and 36, Annex). Consistent with the descriptive results, the regression model, controlling for additional factors, points to a highly significant negative association between temporary employment and benefit levels in Spain – temporary workers on average receive about 80 euros-PPP less than permanent workers. While the

Table 23: Random effects linear model on unemployment benefit level for unemployed benefit recipients

Dep. variable: monthly unemployment benefit level	Denmark	Germany	Spain	United Kingdom
Former part-time worker	–72.62	–165.82*	–42.06	103.56
Former temporary worker	–96.84+	25.48	–79.74**	–14.17
Female	–52.77	–125.33*	–49.56**	–51.26
Age	5.23*	3.73	3.98**	–3.05
REFERENCE: ISCED 1				
ISCED 3	–19.80	205.20**	18.41	–42.90
ISCED 5–7	84.54	408.60**	51.57+	57.58
Monthly wage before UI receipt/100	–0.59	6.21+	1.53	–0.68
REFERENCE: time employed before interview (25+ months)				
Employed 0 month	46.61	176.01	–131.46**	–175.09+
Employed 1–6 months	11.61	143.75	–128.85**	–178.47+
Employed 7–12 months	109.69	270.63	–67.63*	–204.98*
Employed 13–24 months	59.42	–11.04	–49.59+	–207.47*
REFERENCE: time unemployed before interview (1–6 months)				
Unemployed 7–12 months	–76.50	–329.40**	–102.35**	–170.53**
Unemployed 13–24 months	–165.51*	–451.90**	–170.35**	–197.19**
Unemployed 25–36 months	–240.88**	–634.27**	–204.24**	–247.55**
Unemployed 37–96 months	–224.89*	–655.82**	–220.34**	–96.65
REFERENCE: household type: 2 adults, children				
Single	–131.65+	–108.12	–65.69	–23.62
Two adults no children	–142.14*	–77.61	–10.25	–38.41
Single parent and children	119.49	75.77	10.71	–202.77+
Current monthly household wage/100	0.61	–3.68	1.70*	0.67
Constant	1174.43**	988.30**	763.92**	730.21**
Observations	911	1131	1507	306
Number of group	495	536	883	210
Wald chi2 (30)	46.85	102.05	254.79	43.53
Prob > chi2	0.0258	0.0000	0.0000	0.0526
Rho	.579	.327	.678	.666
Within	0.05	0.05	0.09	0.16
Between	0.06	0.12	0.19	0.13
Overall	0.04	0.10	0.19	0.12
Further variables included: survey year to capture changes over time.				
+ significant at 10%; * significant at 5%; ** significant at 1%				

Source: Own calculations based on ECHP data. All benefit recipients are taken into account.

length of unemployment is in all countries associated with decreasing benefit levels, short employment periods are associated with lower benefit levels to a significant degree only in Spain.

The influence of means-testing on benefit levels can apparently not be easily modelled – a significant but very small negative influence of household wage on benefit level is evident only in Spain. Means-testing often leads to total withdrawal of benefits – non-significant and small effects could thus be due to the fact that unemployed persons without benefit receipt are excluded from the analysis here. As to the influence of household composition on benefit levels, being a single person and living in a two-adult household without children is in all countries associated with lower benefit receipt than living in a two-adult household with children, though not significantly except for Denmark. The significant result for Denmark is surprising because unemployment benefits are highly individualised there – it could be due to the fact that the unemployment level variable is a mix of unemployment-related benefits including training measures and relocation benefits that might contain subsidies, depending on the family situation.

6.3.3 Summary

The above analysis has revealed that there is clear evidence of discrimination in access to benefits, depending on the hours formerly worked, and also some evidence of access restrictions based on former contribution time. The analysis also showed that it is of the utmost importance to look at all unemployed persons who are looking for a job and not only at those registered at the employment office when one is dealing with access to unemployment benefits. As regards access to unemployment benefits non-standard workers are worse off in all four countries. Differences between former part-time and full-time workers are more pronounced (especially when taking into account all job seekers) than between former temporary and permanent workers. The United Kingdom is the only country for which the descriptive analysis did not point to lower unemployment benefit coverage of temporary workers. One reason, of course, is the second-tier system that is open to all unemployed persons, but means-tested. Furthermore, unlike in the other countries the contribution requirement in the United Kingdom consists of a mix of contribution time and wage levels (persons with higher earnings gain faster access to contribution-based benefits), which seems to be more beneficial for temporary workers. Part-time workers with low hours and earnings, on the other hand, might be especially hard hit by the British contribution requirement rule. In fact, Bennett (2005) on behalf of the British Equal Opportunities Commission suggests that the contribution rules should be re-examined, including the relative speed at which higher paid as opposed to low-paid workers build up entitlement. Although differences in access to benefits for standard and non-standard workers are relatively similar between countries, the fact that overall coverage with benefits varies strongly between the four countries leads to a situation in which the average benefit coverage among part-time and temporary workers is much higher in Denmark than in the other three countries. If registered unemployment is looked at exclusively, the majority of former part-time workers and the biggest share of former temporary workers are also covered by unemployment benefits in Germany. This share drastically decreases among former part-time workers if all unemployed who are looking for a job are taken into account. In Spain, overall benefit coverage rates are low, especially for former part-time workers. Coverage rates in the United Kingdom are between the German and the Spanish ones – former part-time workers are considerably worse off than former temporary workers. The results for Spain are especially worrisome because the high unemployment rate and the extent of temporary employment lead to a situation in which many individuals repeatedly move in and out of unemployment – apparently without sufficient and reliable financial compensation. Deficient unemployment benefit coverage in the United Kingdom is in part substituted by other benefits, however, especially by housing allowances (functional equivalents); this is much less the case in Spain.

The section on benefit levels showed that once non-standard workers gain access to benefits they are not much worse off than standard workers. Compared to their former wages, part-time workers on average even receive higher net replacement rates at unemployment than full-time workers, which can be explained by regulations such as minimum benefits, upper ceilings and retention of the status quo for a transitional period. Only in Spain are average unemployment benefit levels of temporary workers (not controlled and controlled for other influencing factors) considerably lower than those of former permanent workers. This is especially problematic because temporary employment is very important in Spain.

To conclude, approaching the second hypothesis, in all countries considered here – despite very divergent underlying principles and benefit rules – unemployment insurance systems are modelled on standard employment, which leads to deficient coverage of part-time workers and, to a lesser degree, also of temporary workers (an exception being the United Kingdom for the latter). On the other hand, if non-standard workers are entitled to unemployment benefits their benefit levels will be relatively similar to those of standard workers, except for temporary workers in Spain.

6.4 Influence of institutions on benefit coverage

This section will explore whether it is possible to directly link non-standard workers' entitlement to unemployment benefits to certain aspects of the benefit systems by making use of all 15 countries covered by the ECHP data; 13 countries can be used for the subsequent validation of results and the multilevel analysis.[138] After a short literature review on country typologies, two approaches are pursued: in a first step, countries are clustered by means of their similarity concerning the design and financing of unemployment insurance (data are taken from OECD and EU sources). The expectation is that coverage for non-standard workers should be more similar between countries within the same cluster. The results are scrutinised using the ECHP data. In a second step, a more direct approach is adopted: a selection of the institutional variables that have been used to cluster countries are used in multilevel regression analysis to explain the unemployment benefit coverage of non-standard workers. This strategy should allow us to make statements about the direction and strength of the different institutional effects on benefit coverage.

6.4.1 Using institutional information to cluster countries – a literature review

Esping-Andersen's welfare regime typology (1990) has resulted in a number of critical assessments. Below, a number of studies are reviewed that modify the initial choice of variables and improve the methodological approach and thereby arrive at different compositions of welfare regimes. Bonoli (1997), pointing to the multidimensional nature of social policy, suggests the inclusion not only of the quantitative dimension of state welfare but also of the way in which welfare is delivered. Comparison only of the quantity of social expenditure is seen as useless insofar as different outcomes are often envisaged by social policy (for example, income maintenance vs poverty prevention) that cannot be captured by a single dimension. By incorporating a measure that captures the proportion of contributions as compared to tax financing, and cross-tabulating it with social expenditure, four ideal-types are created: Bismarckian high and low spenders and Beveridgean high and low spenders (see Bonoli 1997: 361). These ideal-types converge closely with Esping-Andersen's typology with an additional

138 The Swedish ECHP data are very incomplete; neither retrospective information on non-standard employment nor the benefit coverage indicator are available. For Luxembourg no retrospective information on non-standard employment is provided.

Mediterranean group; the allocation of Denmark and the United Kingdom to the high tax-financing, and of Spain and Germany to the high contribution-financing countries is consistent with our results.

In a range of studies cluster analysis is used in order to test, modify or expand Esping-Andersen's typology. Obinger et al. (1998) use the original selection of countries and data on the stratification concept and obtain five clusters: (i) a liberal cluster, (ii) a social democratic cluster, a subdivided conservative cluster incorporating (iii) the United Kingdom and Ireland (iv), as well as (v) a cluster consisting solely of the United States. Consequently, Esping-Andersen's methodological approach, as well as his overemphasis on the pension system in operationalising the stratification concept, is criticised. A broad range of variables (macroeconomic factors, extent and structure of employment and unemployment, labour market and social policy measures) is used by Rehm et al. (2001), who try to come up with a typology that can explain the variety of employment policies used in different countries. Especially noteworthy is their incorporation of an active labour market policy measure in order to take account of the current trend to enhance employability. Their Ward-cluster analysis points to four regimes: (i) neoliberal (United States and Portugal), (ii) postmodern (Denmark and Sweden), (iii) continental 'Old Labour', with France, Austria and Germany, and (iv) a less homogeneous 'postmodern' or 'New Labour', consisting of the Netherlands and the United Kingdom.[139] Spain, according to this analysis, does not fit any of the four regimes.

Powell et al. (2004) incorporate not only active labour market policy measures in their hierarchical and k-means cluster analysis in order to put a stronger focus on prevention, but also variables on the 'welfare mix' between market, state and family. They thus take account of the vital role of not only the welfare state but also the family and the market as possible sources of social risk management. The welfare mix is captured by using information on expenditure for public social security, as well as for education and active labour market policies. Furthermore, information on the proportion of private insurance premiums and household expenditure on private insurance, as well as on the strictness of employment protection legislation is included. The emerging three clusters are relatively similar to Esping-Andersen's typology. According to Powell et al. (2004), including active labour market policy measures helps to identify welfare regime clusters more clearly: the social democratic regime is ranked highest for active labour market policies, as well as for the social and education spending variables; the liberal cluster ranks highest for private insurance; and the southern

139 The authors state that the Netherlands and the United Kingdom could also be integrated into the Scandinavian postmodern group and the neoliberal group, respectively.

European members of the conservative regime rank highest for the strictness of employment protection. Only limited support is given to the often cited Mediterranean model.

In this context another paper should be mentioned that not only considerably broadens the choice of variables used in the original welfare regime typology, but also makes innovative use of the resulting clusters. On the basis of principal components analysis on a range of variables capturing welfare state policies, labour market measures and family policies, Hicks et al. (2003) identify two welfare state regime dimensions: a 'progressive liberal' one, consisting of the social democratic and the liberal regimes as two poles of one dimension, and a 'traditional conservative' dimension. These welfare state dimensions are used as independent variables in regression analysis on income redistribution, employment performance and gender equality in the labour market in order to explain welfare state outcomes. Preliminary outcomes suggest strong and highly significant positive effects on inequality and poverty reduction of the 'progressive liberal' dimension and only a weak positive effect of the 'traditional conservative' dimension. Concerning employment levels and gender equality, there are positive and, respectively, egalitarian effects for 'progressive liberalism', and solely negative effects for 'traditional conservatism'. According to the authors, their dimensions outperform the explanatory power of Esping-Andersen's welfare state regimes that were introduced in the regression analysis for comparative reasons (Hicks et al. 2003: 42–51).

In order to be able to make more general statements on the inclusiveness of unemployment insurance systems it will be most suitable to generate a new country typology that takes into account the institutional features of unemployment insurance systems. Where possible, indicators for the beginning (1994) and the end (2001) of the data time span are used to capture possible changes in the systems at least approximately.[140]

6.4.1.1 Choice of variables

Since the focus is on the security situation of non-standard workers at unemployment, the design of insurance systems has to be taken into account when constructing the typology. The hypothesis indicates that the insurance situation of non-standard workers should vary with the principles and design of unemployment insurance. Therefore, indicators capturing the access requirements for non-standard workers, net replacement rates and duration of benefits will be used for

140 Since data on some indicators are not collected every year, the closest available year is used to proxy the situation of the beginning or the end of the data time span. Since policy changes do not take place regularly, this should not distort the results very much

clustering countries. Where possible, indicators are preferred that reproduce the situation of non-standard workers as adequately as possible. One indicator is used that captures the hours threshold that is to proxy the requirements affecting the access of part-time workers to unemployment benefits.[141] Another indicator tries to capture the strictness of the minimum contribution period.[142] Due to a lack of comparative indicators from official sources, the part-time and continuity requirement indicators used here are taken from Grimshaw et al. (1997: 296). They capture the situation in the mid-1990s.

Possible influences of the voluntary nature of unemployment insurance schemes on inclusiveness were discussed in the theoretical section. A dummy variable is used to capture this design feature. The duration of unemployment insurance benefits depicts part of the generosity of the welfare system; the other part is made up of benefit levels. Benefit levels are measured via the net replacement rate. The duration not only of unemployment insurance benefits is looked at, but also that of unemployment assistance, which may act as either a follow-up or an alternative benefit. The OECD calculates net replacement rates for different household compositions, earnings levels and unemployment durations (see OECD 1998a, 2002a). Due to the comparatively low earnings of non-standard workers – this is especially true for part-time workers but often also for temporary workers (see, for example, European Commission 2004b: 169) – the net replacement rate for a person that receives earnings at two thirds of the APW level is used.[143] In order to adequately capture the insurance situation, which may vary with time spent in unemployment, net replacement rates in the first month and in the 60th month of benefit receipt are used. To account for country differences concerning derived rights for children or spouses, one cluster analysis model will be estimated based on the net replacement rates for a family with two children; another will be estimated based on the indicator for a single person.[144] Alongside unemployment benefit, the OECD net replacement rate also incorporates family and housing benefits. This is useful insofar as in some countries

141 The variable has three values: low – a minimum hours threshold of 12 hours; medium – a minimum hours threshold of more than 12 hours but less than 17; high – a minimum hours threshold of 17 hours or more; or a minimum earnings requirement or a requirement to be available for full-time work.

142 The variable has three values: low – a continuity requirement of less than six months in the past year or equivalent; medium – a continuity requirement approximately equal to six months in the past year or equivalent; high – a continuity requirement of greater than six months.

143 For a definition of the construction of OECD replacement rates, see OECD (2002a). The problems concerning the APW concept were discussed in Chapter 5.

144 The OECD reports net replacement rates for singles, married couples, couples with two children and single parents with two children (compare OECD 2002a, 2004b).

housing benefits make up a considerable part of total benefits; a broader measure therefore presents the real situation of the unemployed more adequately.

As already discussed in the theoretical part on insurance vs welfare systems, financing principles can directly or indirectly influence the distributional justice of the unemployment insurance system and therefore the insurance situation of non-standard workers. In order to uncover the structure of social protection, funding indicators are used that depict the share of social contributions made by either employers and beneficiaries or the government. General government contributions measure the degree of tax financing; we suppose that systems that rely to a considerable degree on tax financing are more redistributive towards non-standard workers than those that are heavily contribution financed.[145] As the theoretical part showed, even in the presence of high tax financing, redistributiveness can be limited if overall spending is low. Therefore indicators that capture the degree of passive and active spending are included in the analysis. Public expenditure on passive and active labour market policies is divided by the corresponding unemployment rates in order to account for different needs. A further decomposition of active labour market policies into different categories should not alter the results significantly (compare Powell et al. 2004: 97, 98). It should be kept in mind that features of the benefit system such as the level of replacement rates, duration of benefits and, most of the time, also the extent of active labour market policies are relevant to non-standard workers only if they have access to unemployment benefits in the first place. Table 24 gives an overview of the above-described variables and shows their mean levels, standard deviation and range.

---

145 These measures are taken from European Commission (2004a). The indicators are government, employers' and protected persons' contributions as a percentage of total social protection receipts. Social protection encompasses, sickness, disability, old age, survivors, family and children, unemployment, housing and social exclusion. To our knowledge, there are no comparative data on the structure of unemployment insurance financing alone.

Table 24: Cluster analysis variables as basic statistics

Variable label	Mean	St. dev.	Min.	Max.
Voluntary vs compulsory unemployment insurance			0	1
Access for non-standard workers:				
Hours threshold for unemployment benefits*	2.17	0.94	1	3
Continuity requirements for unemployment benefits	1.73	0.70	1	3
Design – benefit levels for short- and long-term unemployed:				
Net replacement rates 60th month, couple, 2 children, 66.7% of APW, 1995	0.70	0.35	0.05	1.22
Net replacement rates 60th month, couple, 2 children, 66.7% of APW, 1999	0.74	0.28	0.11	1.10
Net replacement rates 1st month, couple, 2 children, 66.7% of APW, 1995	0.78	0.14	0.46	0.95
Net replacement rates 1st month, couple, 2 children, 66.7% of APW, 1999	0.76	0.15	0.46	0.95
Design – duration of short- and long-term benefits:				
Duration of unemployment insurance, 1995	30.20	29.58	10	100**
Duration of unemployment insurance, 1999	29.80	27.56	6	100**
Duration of unemployment assistance, 1995	20.70	22.77	0	100**
Duration of unemployment assistance, 1999	25.40	22.40	0	100**
Financing – contributory vs. tax financing:				
Social protection receipt: general government contribution as % of total receipt, 1994	38.13	16.04	16.7	73
Social protection receipt: general government contribution as % of total receipt, 2001	37.60	13.30	16.3	62.6
Social protection receipt: employer/beneficiary contribution as % of total receipt, 1994	55.51	14.79	20.9	75
Social protection receipt: employer/beneficiary contribution as % of total receipt, 2001	56.80	11.95	30.4	74.4
Financing – expenditure on and distribution between active and passive benefits:				
Public expenditure on passive measures as % of GDP/unemployment rate, 1994	0.26	0.16	0.04	0.67
Public expenditure on passive measures as % of GDP/unemployment rate, 2001	0.26	0.20	0.06	0.71
Public expenditure on active measures as % of GDP/unemployment rate, 1994	0.12	0.08	0.02	0.32
Public expenditure on active measures as % of GDP/unemployment rate, 2001	0.20	0.17	0.06	0.73

Note: * no information for Greece, Italy, and Portugal; ** indefinite.
Source: Own calculations. The data are taken from OECD Employment Outlook, various years, OECD (1998a) and Grimshaw et al. (1997).

6.4.1.2 Cluster analysis

The aim of the following cluster analysis is to find country groups that are similar in terms of the characteristics of their unemployment insurance systems. A variety of cluster methods exists; we opted for hierarchical Ward cluster analysis, which is the dominant method and in comparison to other algorithms has proven to generate very good results in most cases (Aldenderfer et al. 1984: 60, 61; Backhaus et al. 2000: 366).[146] The Ward method is designed to optimise the minimum variance within clusters by making use of the error sum of squares or within-group sum of squares (Aldenderfer et al. 1984: 42, 43). Those cases that exhibit the lowest increase in the error sum of squares or, more simply, that exhibit the lowest increase of heterogeneity, are joined in a cluster. This method leads to relatively homogenous clusters. Clustering starts with the most similar group, and step by step new groups or aggregates are formed or cases are added to existing groups; therefore heterogeneity is gradually increasing.

An adequate similarity or dissimilarity measure has to be chosen. In the social sciences, correlation or distance coefficients are usually used, while other sciences also make use of association coefficients or probabilistic similarity coefficients. The default distance option, the Euclidean squared dissimilarity measure is used.[147] In order to ensure that the scaling of different variables does not influence the results by accidentally putting more weight on some variables rather than others, the variables are *z*-standardised.

Figure 33 displays the dendrogram resulting from the Ward cluster analysis of the variables described in the previous part.

The dendrogram shows the clustering of the countries; the shorter the lines, the more similar and thus homogenous are the emerging clusters. Accordingly, France and Austria, as well as Greece and Italy have very similar characteristics. Belgium and the Netherlands form a relatively heterogeneous group. At first sight, three big clusters can be discerned. Speaking in welfare regime terms, they consist of: (i) the social democratic (Scandinavian) regime, (ii) the conservative regime and (iii) a combination of the liberal and the Mediterranean regimes, excluding Spain. Since relatively homogeneous groups are probably more fruit-

146 K-means cluster analysis is advantageous insofar as, in contrast to hierarchical analysis, allocation to a cluster is reversible. Nevertheless, due to the random choice of the starting cluster, results are not stable, especially if the number of cases is small.

147 It is defined as: $dij^2 = \sum_{k=1}^{p}(xik - xjk)^2$, where dij is the distance between the cases i and j, and xik is the value of the kth variable for the ith case (Aldenderfer et al. 1984: 24 et seq.). As a result of squaring, more weight is put on big distances than on small distances.

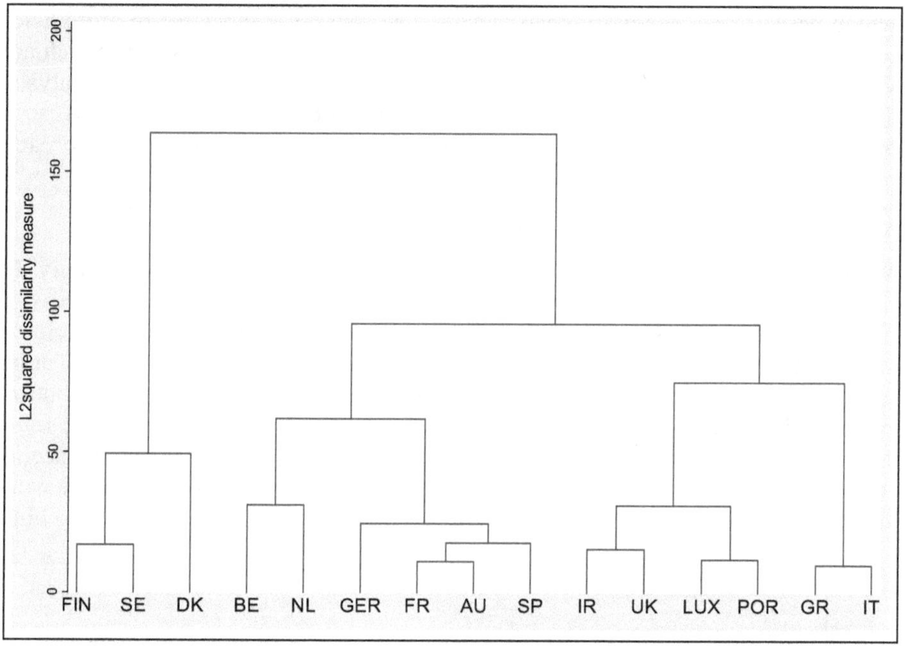

Figure 33: Ward cluster analysis of indicators on unemployment insurance systems.

Note: Net replacement rates for families have been used here, but the results are the same if net replacement rates for singles are used.

Source: Own calculations based on data from OECD Employment Outlook, various years; Grimshaw/Rubery (1997); OECD: Benefits and Wages 1998, 2002.

ful for the purpose of further analysis, a version with four clusters is preferable. Since the extended liberal regime, consisting of Ireland, the United Kingdom, Luxembourg and Portugal, and the Mediterranean regime, consisting of Greece and Italy, join at a very late stage they are subdivided into two groups.[148]

Accordingly, in the following section we shall deal with four clusters. Two of them are rather homogenous: Ireland, the United Kingdom, Luxembourg and Portugal, which we label the extended liberal cluster, as well as Greece and Italy,

148 The four-cluster solution is supported by the Duda and Hart stopping rule, which is implemented in Stata. The Calinski and Harabasz stopping rule, on the other hand, supports a six-cluster solution. The results from the stopping rules should be used sceptically; they become less informative as the number of elements in the group diminishes, which is the case here (StataCorp 2003).

which we term the Mediterranean cluster. The two other clusters are more heterogeneous. The Scandinavian cluster consists of Finland and Sweden, which are very similar when it comes to the variables used in the above cluster analysis, and Denmark. The conservative cluster is made up of Germany, France, Austria and Spain, as well as Belgium and the Netherlands, which are closer to each other than to the rest of this cluster group.

6.4.1.3 Characteristics of the resulting cluster groups

What are the characteristics of the resulting cluster groups and how strongly do they differ concerning the values of the variables of interest? As to the access of non-standard workers to unemployment insurance the country groups seem to vary considerably. This dimension was measured on relatively simple indicators capturing the working-hours requirement and the required minimum contribution period. There are no recent comparative data, so only indicators for the mid-1990s could be used. According to this rough indicator access to benefits seems to be medium for both groups in the conservative cluster and for temporary workers in the Mediterranean cluster (Figure 34). High barriers are evident for both

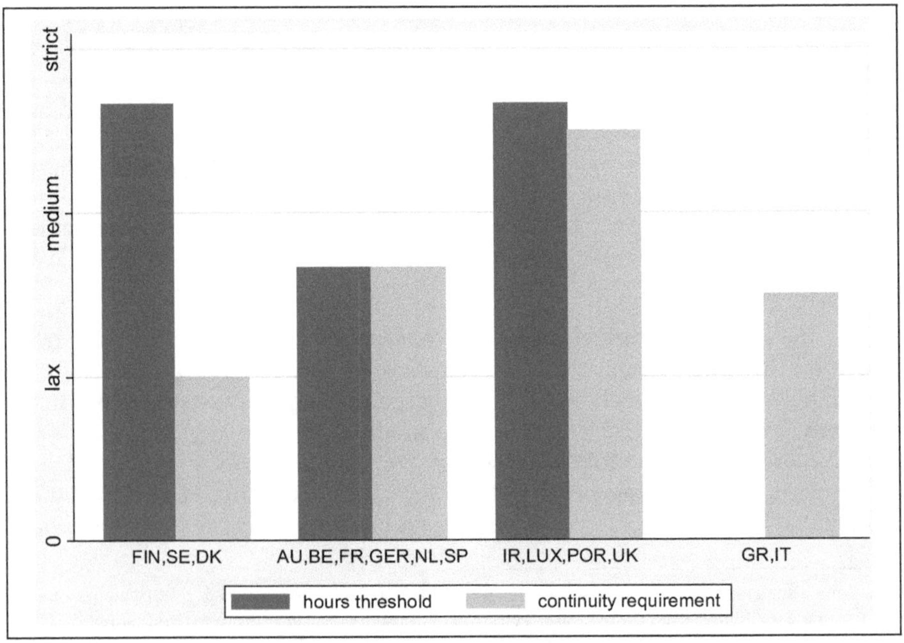

Figure 34: Access to unemployment benefits for non-standard workers.
Source: Own calculations based on data from Grimshaw/Rubery (1997).

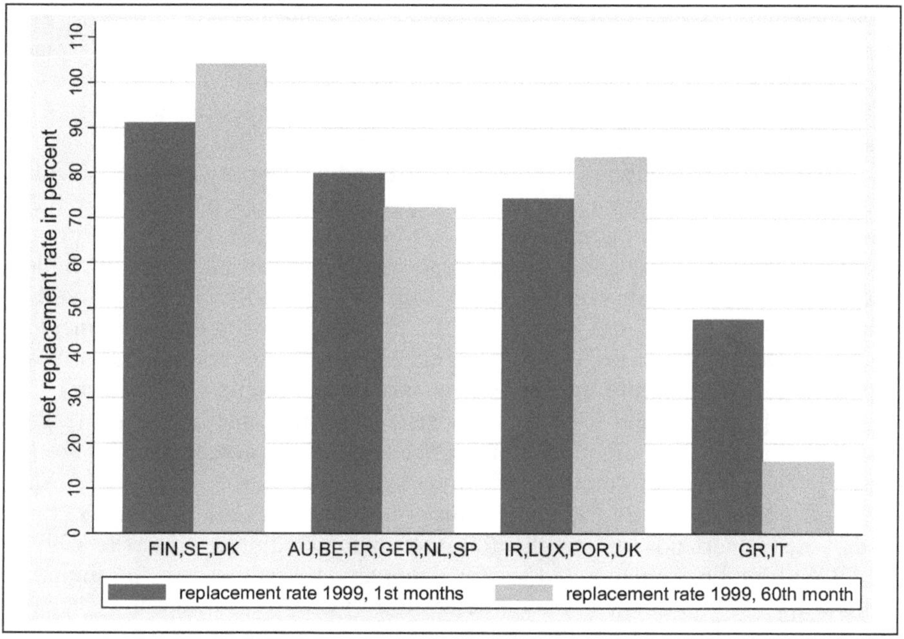

Figure 35: Net replacement rates at unemployment for couples with 2 children* and low earnings (66.7 APW) in 1999.
Note: * Family and housing benefits included.
Source: Own calculations based on OECD (2002a; 2004b).

groups in the extended liberal cluster, while for the Scandinavian cluster a low continuity requirement is coupled with a high hours threshold. The accessibility of unemployment benefits might accordingly be more difficult for part-time workers (high hours threshold) than for temporary workers (continuity requirement) in the Scandinavian cluster. We do not have any information on the hours threshold for the Mediterranean cluster.

Concerning general benefit design (replacement rates and benefit duration), both short-term and long-term indicators have been used. Net replacement rates in the first month of unemployment are considerably more generous than those in the 60th month only in the Mediterranean group (Figure 35). The reverse situation in the extended liberal and the Scandinavian clusters can be explained by the inclusion of information on family and housing benefits in this indicator that in many countries are paid together with social assistance. 1999 average net replacement rates for families in the first month of benefit receipt are highest in the

Scandinavian cluster, followed by the conservative and the liberal groups. They are considerably lower in the Mediterranean cluster. The figure on net replacement rates for singles looks similar, with net replacement rates at somewhat lower levels. A noticeable feature is that long-term net replacement rates of singles are close to zero in the Mediterranean cluster.

The duration of unemployment insurance and assistance varies considerably within the clusters (compare Tables 38–41, Annex 2); these variables are therefore not adequate for separating one cluster from another. A notable exception is the Mediterranean cluster. All in all, some countries grant indefinite unemployment assistance if certain conditions are fulfilled (United Kingdom, Ireland, Finland, Germany, France and Austria), while in other countries unemployment assistance benefits do not exist at all (Belgium, Denmark, Greece and Italy). While Belgium grants indefinite unemployment insurance benefits and Denmark very long ones, in Greece and Italy the non-existence of unemployment assistance is coupled with the short duration of insurance benefits. Insurance benefits are further of relatively short duration (<24 months) in the United Kingdom, Austria, Germany, Ireland and Sweden. Duration of insurance benefits is long in France and in the Netherlands (60 months) (all information on duration refers to 1999).

Contribution financing and tax financing are at least theoretically important criteria for redistribution. It should be easier to justify redistribution of benefits mainly financed from taxes than redistribution of benefits that are to a high degree contribution financed. How do the clusters thus perform on contribution and tax financing? Are there clear tendencies towards either tax or contribution financing within the clusters? Standard deviations within the clusters are reasonably low; the average values in Figure 36 thus represent the situation in the countries well. Government spending on social protection and contributions by employers and employees are balanced in the Scandinavian and in the extended liberal clusters. In the Scandinavian cluster tax financing of social protection has decreased since the mid-1990s. In the other two clusters contribution financing is considerably more important than tax financing.

Not only the structure of financing but also the means for financing benefits are important. In the Scandinavian cluster spending on passive benefits relative to the unemployment rate is high (Figure 37). It is medium in the conservative cluster, relatively low in the extended liberal and very low in the Mediterranean cluster. Except for the Scandinavian cluster, passive spending has increased somewhat relative to unemployment if compared to the mid-1990s, but this trend is even more pronounced for active spending, which considerably increased in the conservative and in the extended liberal clusters. The Mediterranean cluster is characterised by very low passive spending, coupled with even lower active spending.

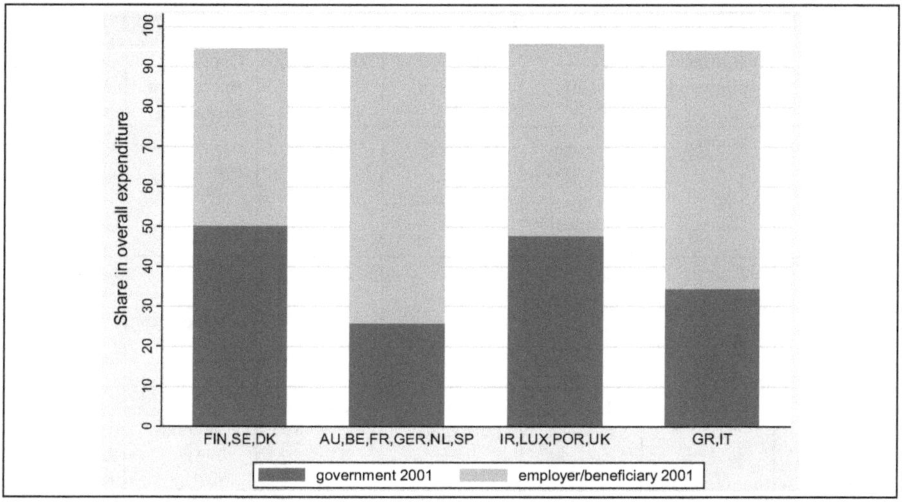

Figure 36: Social protection receipt: tax vs contribution financing, 2001.
Source: Own calculations based on data from European Commission (2004a), several years. The remaining percentage is made up of other receipts.

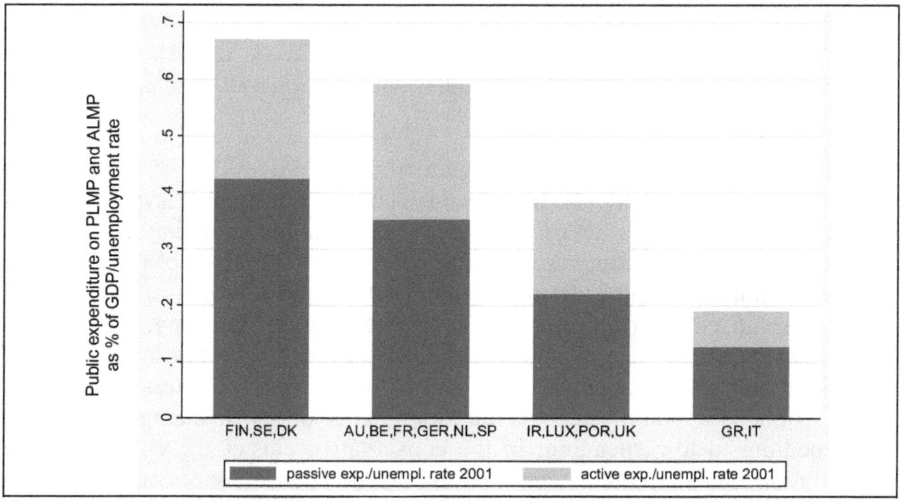

Figure 37: Expenditure on passive and active labour market policies, controlled for the unemployment rate, 2001.
Source: Own calculations based on data from OECD Employment Outlook, several years.

Table 25: How do the country cluster groups score on the different indicators?

	Voluntary/ obligatory	Strictness of access	Net replacement rates	Duration*	Social protection financing	ALMP/ PLMP spending
Scandinavian cluster	voluntary	– continuity: low – hours threshold: high	– 1st month: high – 60th month: very high	– variable	– tax higher than contribution	– passive: very high – active: medium to high
Conservative cluster	obligatory	– both medium	– both medium	– variable	– contribution much higher than tax	– passive: high – active: medium to high
Extended liberal cluster	obligatory	– both high	– both medium	– variable	– tax and contribution at about the same level	– passive: medium – active: low to medium
Mediterranean cluster	obligatory	– continuity: low to medium – hours threshold: no information	– 1st month: low – 60th month: very low	– UI: very short – UA: non existent	– contribution much higher than tax	– passive: very low – active: very low

Note: * This is not a good discriminator: high within variance in all clusters except for the Mediterranean one. *Source*: various data sources.

Table 25 gives a condensed overview of the above results. At first sight the indicators point to relatively high inclusiveness of insurance systems in the Scandinavian cluster (voluntary insurance – for example, allowing access to the self-employed – a low continuity requirement, high importance of tax financing, high expenditure and high net replacement rates), and low inclusiveness in the Mediterranean cluster (high importance of contribution financing, low replacement rates, non-existence of unemployment assistance and very low spending). The situation for the extended liberal and the conservative clusters is less clear. In the extended liberal cluster, the high importance of tax financing is combined with medium to low spending; in the conservative cluster the emphasis is on contribution financing but financial means for compensating unemployment are relatively high. Countries from both clusters should be located somewhere between the Scandinavian and the Mediterranean clusters.

6.4.1.4 Empirical validation of cluster results

To what extent do the above assumptions as to the performance of the clusters hold true if tested on the unemployment benefit coverage indicator of the ECHP data? Does it make sense to use cluster results based on institutional differences – or is too much information lost to justify this approach? We opted for a relatively simple approach. The shares of former part-time and temporary workers who receive benefits at unemployment are compared between clusters. Countries within clusters should have similar coverage rates for non-standard workers.

Figures 38 and 39 show the share of former part-time or temporary workers, respectively, who were receiving unemployment benefits at the time of the survey.[149] In order to rule out varying incentives in different countries to register at

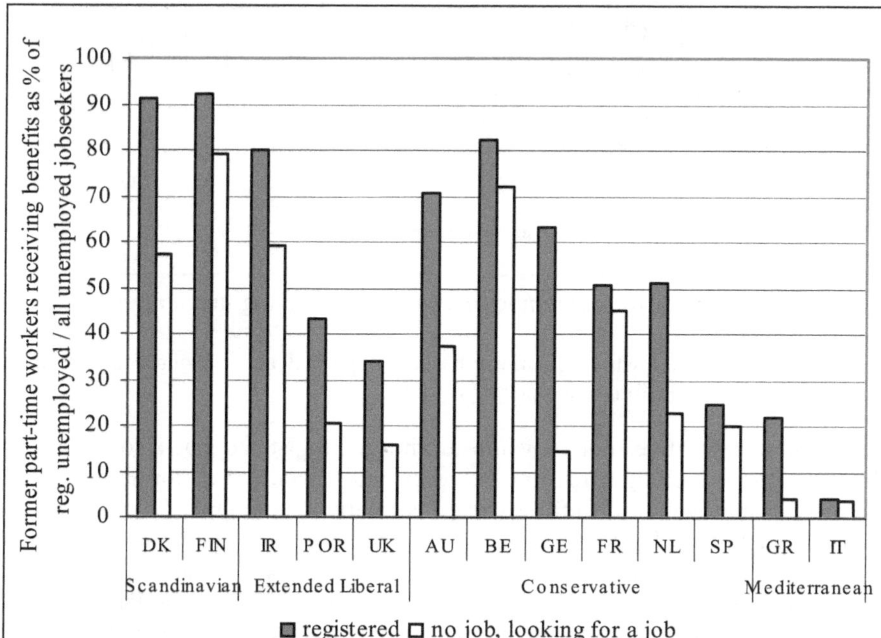

Figure 38: Share of former part-time workers receiving unemployment benefits.

Source: Own calculations based on pooled and weighted ECHP data. Basis: all former part-time workers.

149 Coverage rates in individual countries taking into account all unemployed and not only non-standard workers are shown in Figure 47, Annex 2.

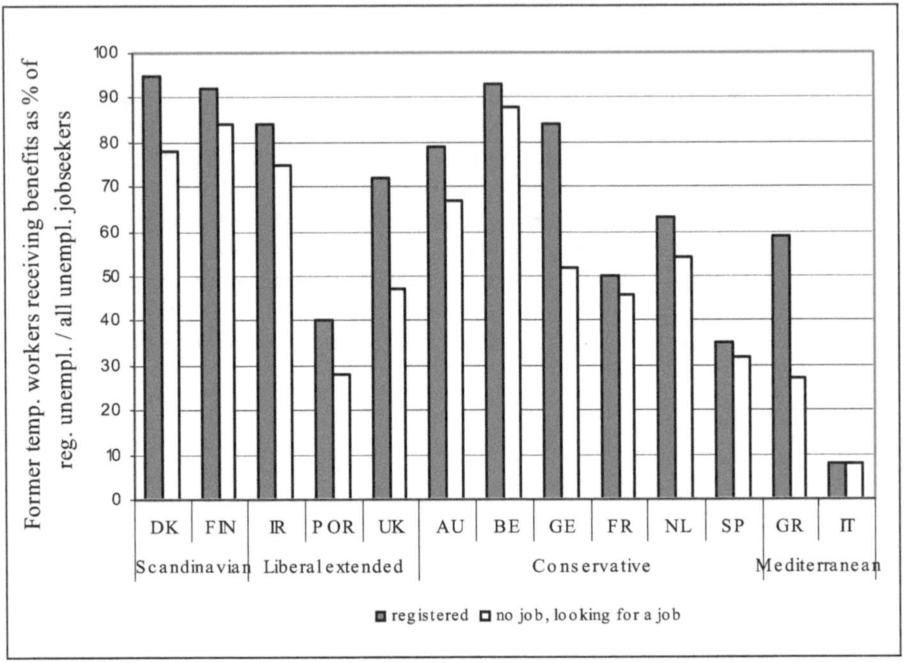

Figure 39: Share of former temporary workers receiving unemployment benefits.

Source: Own calculations based on pooled and weighted ECHP data. Basis: all former temporary workers.

the employment office, not only those who are registered but also all unemployed who are looking for a job are taken into account. For former part-time workers unemployment benefit coverage is relatively similar only in the social democratic and the Mediterranean clusters, while coverage rates strongly diverge between the countries in the liberal and in the conservative cluster (Figure 38). High benefit coverage of non-standard workers in the Scandinavian countries and very low coverage in the Mediterranean group confirms our expectations. It also proves true that the conservative and the extended liberal regimes are located somewhere between the Scandinavian and the Mediterranean clusters. The heterogeneous results concerning the degree of unemployment coverage rates within the extended liberal and the conservative clusters – Ireland and Belgium in particular have coverage rates that closely converge with those of the Scandinavian cluster – raise questions about the appropriateness of the variables used for clustering or the method of clustering in general.

A closer look at Figure 39 confirms the above concerns. While the countries making up the social democratic cluster have very similar coverage rates, there are high intra-cluster differences in the other three clusters. Once again, Ireland and Belgium, and to a lesser degree also Austria would fit better into the Scandinavian cluster. The overall picture concerning unemployment benefit coverage is more favourable among former temporary workers than among former part-time workers – a result that is in line with the outcomes of the four-country analysis.

6.4.1.5 Limitations and possible solutions

The above mentioned results affirm that clustered information should be used with care. If very general statements are sought, it might be helpful to cluster countries. It is also a solution if case numbers on some variables are low, preventing in-depth analysis on the basis of single countries. In addition, it is usually more convenient and more illustrative to talk about a small number of clusters than about a great number of single cases. There might also be topics where the use of country groups is more suitable. Generally, better results are expected if differences between the clusters' institutional characteristics are very pronounced or the countries within a cluster are very similar in their features. Clear disadvantages of cluster group analysis are a loss of variation and a stronger possibility of overlooking peculiarities in one country. If clustered information is used one should be careful to restrict the analysis to similar cases; in this example the Scandinavian and the Mediterranean clusters were acceptably close. Cross-checking the within-cluster variations on the different input variables by means of the standard deviations should take place in any case in order not to make assumptions on the basis of potentially misleading means.

It seems useful to choose variables for clustering countries that closely converge on the question of interest instead of relying on existing welfare regime classifications. Problems here are a lack of suitable data – one of the reasons that the above cluster analysis did not lead to more convincing results might be the fact that the indicators that were used are suboptimal: comparative and accurate up-to-date indicators on hours thresholds and contribution requirements do not exist, to our knowledge.

A worthwhile strategy that could contribute to generating policy-relevant evidence might be the introduction of institutional-level variables in regression models. One could thus directly test assumptions about the effects of different institutions on coverage rates instead of testing them indirectly via country clusters that are similar in terms of specific institutions. Good applied examples of this strategy that make use of the ECHP data are Uunk et al. (2005) and Russell et al. (2001), who use multilevel models in order to explain the influence of childcare on women's labour supply and, respectively, the influence of youth unemployment rates and active labour market policies on transitions from unemployment to employment.

6.4.2 *Multilevel analysis as a solution?*

If one wants to assess the effects of institutions on individual outcomes, such as benefit coverage, in a multivariate way specific methods are needed because individuals are nested within higher-level units – here, countries. Individual observations are usually not completely independent; it can be assumed that average correlation between variables measured on individuals from the same country is higher than the average correlation between variables measured on individuals from different countries. Since standard statistical tests assume independence of observation, the estimates of the standard errors of conventional statistical tests are too small and therefore tend to produce spuriously significant results (Hox 2002: 5–7). Multilevel models take account of the unexplained variability associated with each level of nesting and, as a result, correct the standard errors in an appropriate way, making the results more reliable. They differ from the usual multiple regression models in that the equation contains more than one error term – one or more for each level.

The model will be restricted to former temporary workers and will focus on benefit coverage. The question to be answered is what individual and institutional characteristics influence the benefit coverage of temporary workers. On the individual level – in line with the four country models – gender, age, qualification level, former part-time employment, former individual wage level and current household income are included. Among the institutional-level variables that were used for clustering countries, the following seem suitable for multilevel analysis on benefit coverage: concerning the design of benefits, the indicator on the strictness of minimum contribution requirements (qualifying period) provided by Grimshaw et al. (1997) will be used – results from this variable have to be treated with the utmost care, however, because it is a very crude indicator of the underlying benefit systems; furthermore, it is not up-to-date. On the financing side, the type of financing (share of tax financing in overall financing) and expenditure on unemployment as a percentage of GDP (passive benefits), which should capture the potential for redistribution, are used. Net replacement rates and duration of benefit payments are expected to influence the benefit amount rather than the access to benefits and are therefore left out of the analysis. Since there is hardly any variation on the indicator depicting voluntary unemployment insurance systems it was decided to leave it out of the analysis. Furthermore, in order to control for different needs in spending on unemployment, the country-specific unemployment rate is included as independent variable. The unemployment rate to some degree also proxies the resources that are available for redistribution.[150]

The expectations concerning the institutional-level variables are as follows: stricter qualifying conditions should lead to lower benefit coverage, tax financing is theoretically expected to be more redistributive than contribution financing – higher shares of tax-financing are thus expected to lead to more inclusive benefit systems. As to expenditure on unemployment, it is expected that providing more means for financing benefits leads to a higher inclusiveness of benefit systems – causality is somewhat unclear, here, because higher inclusiveness could also lead to greater spending. Last but not least, it is expected that countries with lower unemployment rates can allow themselves to be more generous concerning benefit coverage. This assumption is problematic insofar as unemployment rates within countries probably change faster than generosity of benefit systems.

Following Snijders et al. (1999: 43–45) a random coefficient logistic regression is applied to the data.[151] The outcome variable – unemployment benefit receipt – is specified at the individual level; it has an individual as well as a group aspect. The following model takes into account three levels: besides the individual and the country levels, longitudinal measurements within individuals – on average there are 1.7 observations per individual – are considered.

The individual-level variables expressed in odds ratios point in the expected direction (Table 26). Being a woman or having worked part-time is associated with lower access to benefits; similarly, increasing current household income on average leads to decreasing odds of benefit receipt (means-testing).

The genuine interest here lies in the influence of the institutional-level variables on the coverage of temporary workers. There is a positive and significant association between expenditure on passive benefits and the odds of receiving benefits among temporary workers. Contrary to expectations, the model does not point to a positive relationship between tax financing of benefits and access to unemployment benefits. This actually confirms findings from the theoretical section, namely that the redistributive effects of tax financing can be severely limited if it is not combined with high expenditure. The regression result that a

150 Means of the available institutional-level data have been calculated and matched to the ECHP data. In the case of expenditure on unemployment and financing type, two data points, one from the beginning of the ECHP data period and one from the end, have been taken into account. For the unemployment rate a mean has been calculated based on the eight years for which ECHP data are available (1994–2001). The indicator that captures the qualifying period refers to the mid-1990s.

151 For comprehensive information on hierarchical generalised linear models, see Snijders and Bosker (1999: Chapter 14, 207–238)).

Table 26: Multilevel analysis with individual-level and country-level variables, 3-level model

Dependent variable: unemployment benefit receipt (no/yes) **Only formerly temporary workers**	**Odds ratios**
INDIVIDUAL LEVEL VARIABLES	
Female	0.65**
Age of individual	1.08**
Last job part-time	0.73*
Former wage/100	1.02**
Current household wage/100	0.93**
COUNTRY LEVEL VARIABLES	
Expenditure on passive benefits	2.22**
General government contribution (tax financing)	1.00
REFERENCE: continuity requirement low	
Continuity requirement medium	1.59*
Continuity requirement high	1.35
Average unemployment rate 1994 - 2001	0.88**
Observations	7020
Variance and covariance of random effects (level 2: individuals)	5.72 (.68)
Variance and covariance of random effects (level 3: country)	.95 (.15)
Additional variables included: qualification level, net former earnings, net current household earnings	
+ significant at 10%; * significant at 5%; ** significant at 1%	

Source: Own calculations based on ECHP data, 1994–2001. The above model is calculated using Stata's 'gllamm'-command with a logit link function.

medium minimum contribution period is associated with on average higher access to benefits than a short minimum contribution period runs contrary to expectations. As pointed out earlier, this indicator is not very reliable because it is rather crude and furthermore only captures the situation of the mid-1990s. Last but not least, higher average unemployment rates are significantly associated with lower benefit entitlement among temporary workers, which could point to lower margins for redistribution in economies with relatively high unemployment.[152]

152 Following Rabe-Hesketh et al. (2005: 46–49) we find that at the individual level there are some extreme negative residuals, casting doubt on the normality assumptions. It might thus be better to use robust standard errors based on the sandwich estimator because they do not rely on the model being correctly specified. The estimation with robust standard errors hardly influences significance levels at the institutional level. On the individual level, the effect of former part-

To conclude, it should be stressed that the above analysis is only preliminary, but it does show that there is some potential in using multilevel analysis to explain institutional-level effects on individual outcomes. There are some important shortcomings and problems that would have to be addressed, however, in order to attain more reliable results. First, the ability to detect the effects of level-two variables depends strongly on the number of groups in the data – the fact that the above analysis is restricted to 13 countries thus raises the question of whether this is sufficient for multilevel analysis. The enlargement of the European Union to 27 countries and the collection and provision of comparative data on these countries by way of the EU-SILC will provide a better basis for multilevel models in the future.

A further important point is that multilevel analysis that seeks to assess country-level effects requires reliable and up-to-date data on the institutional configuration of the countries under consideration. This has proven rather difficult in the above example. While the basic characteristics of unemployment insurance systems are readily available, when more specific information is needed – such as hours thresholds, contribution requirements or tax financing of unemployment benefits – we find that official up-to-date sources are not readily available. Last but not least, multilevel analysis does not account for the causality problem we are facing here. Is high spending, for example, due to high inclusiveness of benefits, or is high inclusiveness of benefits due to high spending?

6.4.3 Restrictions and data problems

Kvist (1998) and Atkinson et al. (1991) stress the importance of taking account of the complex mechanisms that underlie cash benefits for unemployment. The fact that the working and non-working populations are extremely heterogeneous calls for caution when making generalisations about the effects of systems of unemployment compensation. According to Kvist (1998), only by combining institutional knowledge with panel or register data is it possible to get a proxy of benefit generosity and its effects on different segments of the population.

The above analysis tried to do exactly this but, as we have seen, the ECHP panel data, besides no longer being up-to-date, are by no means as accurate and as suitable as would be desirable for in-depth analysis of benefit-system performance for specific groups. A first problem is that, if we look at specific groups of the population – here non-standard workers that become unemployed –

time employment becomes insignificant and the effect of being a woman is now significant only at the 10 per cent level.

case numbers diminish relatively quickly, even at large initial sample sizes. The only solution is to pool the data, which deprives us of the possibility of assessing changes over time or capturing the effects of reforms in the benefit systems.

A second problem is that information on benefit receipt, although asked about in the questionnaire in great detail, is available only in an aggregated form in the User Data Base. This not only makes analysis more imprecise but prevents testing certain hypotheses in the first place. There is no separate information on unemployment insurance and unemployment assistance receipt, for example. Furthermore, the length of actual benefit receipt is not recorded. The latter is a serious shortcoming if one wants to test hypotheses on varying duration of benefit receipt among different labour market groups. Lacking separate information on unemployment assistance is equally problematic because it cannot directly be tested if non-standard workers rather have access to means-tested benefits than to insurance benefits if compared with standard workers. The data also prevent us from examining specific regulations of the kind described in the institutional part, such as the German rule that part-time workers who have formerly been full-time employed can receive benefits based on their former full-time earnings for a transitional period.

At least for Germany and the United Kingdom, recourse to the original panel data sources that were integrated in the ECHP could solve some of the above problems. The national panel data sources not only cover a longer time period but in some instances they are also more detailed than the ECHP. The British Household Panel Survey (BHPS) and the German Socio-Economic Panel (SOEP), for example, provide monthly information on part-time employment; they also provide benefit receipt information in a more detailed and precise way. The SOEP, for example, includes information on monthly receipt of unemployment insurance and unemployment assistance. The BHPS similarly offers comprehensive information on welfare benefit receipt. Besides information on the Jobseeker's Allowance, information on income support and also on the working families' tax credit is available. While comparative analysis based on household panel data covering the United Kingdom and Germany would thus be possible, for Spain and Denmark no comparable data source is readily available.

Another serious shortcoming that will not be solved with any of the existing household panel studies is that they do not provide accurate information on participation in active labour market policies. Equal access among non-standard workers to re-qualification measures could compensate or at least balance some of the shortcomings of a lack of benefit coverage. Hypotheses on links between access to unemployment insurance benefits and access to active labour market policies cannot be tested with the ECHP data. The only information that is available in the data is a general indicator on participation in training or education, which was exploited to some extent in the section on transition patterns. Activation and employability strategies, which potentially play an important role in escaping non-standard employment or in making periods out of the labour market more productive, can thus not be assessed to a satisfying degree with household panel data.

Some new data sources now provide comprehensive information not only on passive but also on active benefit receipt. A good example is the Integrated Employment Biographies sample (IEBS) (Stichprobe der Integrierten Erwerbsbiographien).153 This kind of data has other shortcomings, however. Besides not providing comparative cross-national data, only people who are in employment or in the benefit system are observed. Inactivity periods without benefit receipt, an important characteristic of non-standard employment, can therefore not be observed. As could be seen in the above analysis, looking at registered unemployment alone may seriously limit the assessment of inequalities in benefit coverage between standard and non-standard workers.

153 For further information on this data source, see Hummel et al. (2005).

7 Conclusion

The use and active promotion of fixed-term and casual contracts, temporary work agency employment and part-time employment has helped some groups to (re-)enter the labour market and has therefore contributed to increasing employment. On the other hand, these developments have enhanced labour market segmentation by increasing the risk of unemployment, inactivity, income poverty and insufficient social insurance coverage among specific labour market groups.

The analysis has shown that part-time and temporary workers are in all four countries more likely than their counterparts in standard employment to become unemployed or inactive. While temporary employment, except for Spain, also has an important bridging function to regular permanent jobs, part-time employment is persistent, especially in the countries that closely comply with the extended male breadwinner model, namely Germany and the United Kingdom.

The expectation that the unemployment insurance systems of the countries analysed here vary strongly in their potential for covering non-standard employment did not prove true. Non-standard workers in all four countries have lower access to unemployment benefits. The countries' differences in terms of coverage rates among non-standard workers are driven by differences in overall coverage levels rather than by specific principles, such as tax financing or the dominance of the welfare principle. Part-time workers are especially disadvantaged; this is most visible in the countries that operate with hours or earnings thresholds, but also in countries where means-testing takes place at an early stage. Except for the United Kingdom, entitlement to benefits is also less likely among temporary workers than among permanent workers, but the differences are not as evident as between part-time and full-time workers. Due to the high overall coverage levels, which are driven by relatively lax contribution requirements and long lasting duration of non-means-tested benefits (high individualisation of benefit receipt), coverage of non-standard workers is comparatively high in Denmark. In Spain, on the other hand, overall coverage levels are very low, which is attributable not only to the extent of non-standard employment but also to the high incidence of young unemployed who do not have access to unemployment insurance if they have never worked (see OECD 2003b: 74, 75).

Part-time and temporary workers who are entitled to benefits on average receive at least the same share of their former wages in benefits as standard workers. Due to redistributive measures such as low upper ceilings, minimum benefits and specific rules that target part-time workers, the net replacement rates of part-time workers usually surpass those of workers with regular contracts. A notable exception are temporary workers in Spain who, if they are entitled to benefits at all, on average receive considerably lower benefits than their counterparts with permanent contracts. This is due not only to on average lower wages among temporary than among permanent workers in Spain, but also to the fact that unemployed with short contribution periods have to rely on unemployment assistance benefits that are needs-based, considerably lower than insurance benefits and of short duration. The United Kingdom with its flat-rate benefits, its minimum contribution period that varies with earning levels and its second-tier system that is open to all unemployed, independent of contribution time, not only achieves equal access of temporary workers, but also generates equal results as regards benefit levels. As a downside, benefits are very low for all recipients. Part-time workers in the United Kingdom do not benefit from this system. On the contrary, due to their low earnings they have more difficulty gaining access to non-means-tested benefits, and means-testing in the second-tier system often seems to prevent benefit eligibility in the first place – unemployed persons with partners who work more than 24 hours, for instance, are excluded from benefit receipt.

In all four countries unemployment insurance reforms have been taking place during the last decade and a half, but the reforms usually have not directly tackled deficient coverage of non-standard workers. In fact, they have led to both improvements and changes for the worse. Examples of the latter – often implemented to save money – are the abolition of original unemployment assistance in the late 1990s in Germany, the shortening of reference periods in Germany, the extension of contribution requirements in Denmark and Spain and the cutting of the duration of non-means-tested unemployment benefits in the United Kingdom and Germany. On the other hand, hours thresholds have been lowered or abolished in countries such as Germany and Spain, and Germany, for example, has installed favourable but provisional benefit regulations for workers who change from full-time to part-time employment. Similarly, the Spanish government provides incentives for hiring people in permanent jobs or transforming temporary jobs into permanent ones by exempting employers from parts of their social security contributions.

If we look at the German Hartz reforms, by way of an example, we can see positive as well as negative changes for non-standard workers. The reference period for contribution payments has been shortened from three to two years, adversely affecting temporary workers. Similarly, prolonged reference periods for specific groups, namely newly self-employed and carers, and preferential contribution rules for seasonal workers have been abolished. As compensation some groups of workers are now allowed to insure against unemployment themselves voluntarily and on favourable conditions, among them founders of new businesses and people caring for relatives. A prerequisite is that they have been insured in the past. Earnings-related unemployment assistance as an exclusive follow-up benefit to unemployment insurance has been replaced by a uniform means-tested basic benefit (at the level of social assistance) that is open to all unemployed people who are able to work. It resembles the British income-based Jobseeker's Allowance. The question is, whether the basic benefit will be less stigmatising than social assistance (now limited to those who cannot work), and how far it will be more successful in actively helping people to get back to work than social assistance has been in the past. The new basic benefit also takes household income into account more strongly and thereby further erodes the individualisation of benefits. On the other hand, all unemployed (also those without benefit entitlement) can theoretically make use of active labour market policy measures, but since there is no legitimate claim the effects of this modification remain questionable. The fact that public resources made available for job training and inflows into job training have been dramatically declining over a number of years casts a damning light on this issue (compare Kühnlein et al. 2004). Under the threat of benefit sanctions, recipients of the basic benefit are required to take up any job, including marginal employment, so-called Mini-jobs with earnings below €400. Marginal employment does not qualify for unemployment insurance entitlement and furthermore only offers negligible rights to pension insurance. The newly installed Midi-jobs with earnings between €401 and €800, on the other hand, grant access to social insurance on favourable contribution conditions. As can be seen, protection of non-standard workers has not been directly on the agenda. To the contrary, forms of non-standard employment – namely marginal employment and self-employment (supported through so-called Ich-AG measures) that grant insufficient social security rights – have been actively promoted by the reforms.

How problematic deficient coverage is very much depends on the function and extent of non-standard employment. Denmark, Germany and the United Kingdom have high shares of part-time workers, especially among women. In Denmark part-time employment is prevalent among young people who combine work and education, while in Germany and in the United Kingdom, in the absence of sufficient child-care services, it is to a large degree used by mothers to combine work and care activities. Since students usually have other subsistence means, deficient benefit coverage of part-time workers should thus be more problematic in the latter two countries, even more so because part-time employment in Germany and in the United Kingdom is comparatively persistent. In Spain, part-time employment often goes hand in hand with temporary employment, further downgrading the situation of the people concerned. Temporary employment is clearly associated with being young (especially in Spain and Germany) and with low qualification levels, the United Kingdom being an exception in this regard. Deficient unemployment benefit coverage of temporary workers in Spain is especially problematic because the share of fixed-term and casual employment in overall employment has been higher than 30 per cent since the beginning of the 1990s, and temporary employment contracts in Spain are of an especially short duration. While temporary employment in Denmark and the United Kingdom – both countries with low general employment protection legislation – remained stable at relatively low levels, in Germany, in absolute numbers, it increased considerably over the 1990s. The low degree of regulation, extensive child-care provision and an ongoing positive labour market situation seem to support standard employment in Denmark; social security for non-standard workers is thus quantitatively less important than in other European countries.

The special focus on women that is evident in the literature on non-standard employment and social security benefits is justified. While for men standard employment forms have been the norm in the past and for the majority also remain the norm at present, increasing employment rates of women have gone hand in hand with increasing part-time employment, and women are in most countries also overrepresented in temporary employment. According to Sainsbury (1996) the gendered division of labour in the family and in society leads to gender stratification in entitlement as workers. This results from both differences in labour market participation and the exclusionary impact of qualifying conditions in work-related schemes. While men's maintenance usually takes place through social insurance schemes based on claims as earners, women are more likely to make their claims on the basis of domestic work and they rely more heavily on public assistance programmes. In countries that do not provide extensive public services, traditional family roles and responsibilities of women and men are reproduced in the labour market through either non-participation (Spain) or part-time employment of mothers (Germany and the United Kingdom) that is often exercised involuntarily or – due to a lack of child-care facilities – unavoidably. Although the perception of insecurity due to part-time employment very much depends on the household context, it is questionable whether the ongoing support of male breadwinner constellations through tax regulations and exemptions from contributions that favour low hours (marginal) employment is socially and financially sustainable. As the Danish example shows, extensive provision of services (especially child-care) and strong individualisation of benefits would not only allow both women and men to actively participate in the labour market but also to freely choose between full-time and part-time employment.

An important supplement to unemployment insurance entitlements is comprehensive access of all labour market groups to active labour market policy measures. Non-employment periods due to unemployment or family exigencies have to be bridged actively in order to maximise chances for re-entry. Maintenance of qualifications during non-employment periods will also contribute to alleviating possible downward movements as regards wage levels and the qualification profiles of jobs that are usually associated with longer non-employment periods. Activation measures can also be used to test willingness to work in systems that provide generous compensation for all beneficiaries or for specific labour market groups, such as low wage earners. The transition analysis showed that inactivity in most cases will not lead back to employment, which could be changed if countries further harmonised the active reintegration services they offer to unemployment insurance, unemployment assistance and social assistance recipients and make a wide variety of re-integration measures available to all unemployed, independent of their beneficiary status. In Germany, Denmark and the United Kingdom there have recently been some movements in this direction. The German situation has already been described. The United Kingdom has installed a number of target group measures (New Deal programmes), among others for young unemployed, long-term unemployed, single parents and the partners of unemployed persons. Depending on the target group, participation is either mandatory or voluntary – some of the measures are explicitly open to those who do not have access to benefits. They consist of counselling, placement, training measures, wage subsidies and child-care cost subsidies. In Denmark, the Active Social Policy Act of 1999 formulates the rights and obligations of social assistance recipients and other vulnerable groups. Its declared aim is self-sufficiency through financial independence, which is to be achieved by means of individual action plans, training, participation in subsidised 'flexjobs' and individual approaches for persons with additional problems (see Andersen et al. October 2005). All three countries have adopted a mix of strategies that, on the one hand, focus on positive activation measures open for broader groups of unemployed (placement, services, and in some instances training), but on the other hand put more pressure on the beneficiaries. The higher short-term costs associated with active labour market measures (ideally financed from taxes instead of contributions) could in the long-run (financially) be compensated and rewarded through higher employment rates and lower numbers of social assistance recipients.

Table 27: Flexibility and security: trade-offs and complementary situations

Flexibility/security	Job security (1)	Employment/ employability security (2)	Income security (social security) (3)	Combination/ option security (4)
External-numerical	t	t / c / v	t / c / v	t
Internal-numerical	c	c	t / c	t / c
Internal-functional	c	c	t / c	(t) / c
External-functional	c	t / c / v	t / c	t / c

Note: c: complementary; t: trade-off; v: vicious relationship.
Source: Leschke et al. (2006), adapted from Wilthagen et al. (2004).

Based on the country-specific institutional and empirical information discussed in the preceding chapters we can scrutinise the different security components that can support external flexibility in the form of temporary employment and internal flexibility in the form of part-time employment. Table 27 shows the complementarities, trade-offs and vicious relationships that arise between external and internal flexibility and the different forms of security.

As to external-numerical flexibility, weak employment protection legislation resulting in low job security (1) is the main feature of temporary employment. Strong country differences in this regard are evident. Especially the degree to which employment protection legislation varies between workers with permanent and workers with fixed-term or temporary work agency contracts seems to play an important role in shaping the extent of temporary employment. In Denmark and the United Kingdom job security is lower for all groups of workers, resulting in higher overall mobility, while in Germany and, especially, Spain, job security has a stronger potential for creating segmented labour markets. In this regard, systems that combine medium employment protection legislation and active support for people who make transitions might generate more equity than systems that grant very high EPL to permanent workers and thereby create a large segment of low protected temporary jobs. Concerning employability security (2), trade-offs as well as complementarities are possible. While non-employment periods among temporary agency workers are often bridged through training measures, due to the short-term nature of the relationship to the employer there is evidence that employers are less interested in providing firm-based and firm-financed further training to fixed-term contract holders. It is not clear whether temporary workers have equal access to active labour market policies – it might be suspected, however, that non-entitlement to insurance benefits will also lead to discrimination in access to the whole range of active labour market measures. Despite the recent trend of putting more emphasis on activation policies, strong country differences in the importance of active labour market policies are evident. As has been discussed at length, unemployment insurance coverage (3) can be problematic, mainly due to the required minimum contribution period; British entitlement rules seem to be preferential for temporary workers. Temporary agency workers, on the other hand, who, as in Germany for example, are employed by the agency on the basis of a permanent contract, do not face unemployment insurance problems. Vicious relationships are evident if constant cycling between temporary employment and unemployment takes place; this is most evident in Spain. Concerning combination or option security (4) clear trade-offs are evident due to insecure jobs that impede longer-term decisions or, in the case of temporary agency workers, irregular working schedules.

Part-time employment as such is usually not associated with lower job security (1); although in the United Kingdom, for example, part-time workers with low hours were until the mid-1990s worse off than full-time workers concerning employment protection legislation. In Spain, job security is very low for the majority of part-time workers because they work on the basis of temporary contracts. Employability (2) can usually be achieved through combining part-time employment and (further) education; the transition analysis showed that this is especially common in Denmark. On the other hand, part-time employment is often combined with child-care responsibilities, especially in Germany and the United Kingdom, and one can safely assume that not much time will remain for further education within or outside the firm (K. Schömann et al. 2004). Employers are also less likely to support further training among part-time workers as compared to full-time workers, either financially or organisationally (Leschke 2006). We have discussed at length the fact that the insurance situation (3) of part-time workers – and especially of marginal workers – is problematic due to hours and earnings thresholds and in some cases also minimum contribution periods. Some improvements have lately been taking place, however, in order to better include part-time workers (for example, abolition of hours thresholds). When it comes to benefit levels, redistribution towards part-time workers can be observed. Part-time employment is clearly complementary with option and combination security (4) – part-time work is engaged in (voluntarily or involuntarily) exactly in order to combine care work and paid work (Germany and the United Kingdom), or to combine education and paid work (Denmark). In order to cushion the problems associated with flexibility a coherent and reliable combination of securities should be granted to the persons concerned. The initial higher financial costs would probably be compensated by longer-term savings, thus strengthening equity (between standard and non-standard workers) and (longer-term) efficiency at the same time.

Adequate access of non-standard workers to passive and active benefits requires higher financing and different financing modes; governments, employers and employees can contribute in this regard. Several of the proposals outlined below are already used in certain countries.

What can governments do? First, although the empirical results on the advantages of tax financing were not clear a stricter separation of financing of passive and active benefits seems useful. Since at least parts of the active measures usually cater to a bigger group than the insured one, financing of active measures should take place through the tax system. The same is true for family complements that are part of insurance schemes. Decoupling of passive and active financing could also prevent cutbacks in active measures in times of rising unemployment. Secondly, stronger integration of insurance and assistance systems could not only save administrative costs that could then be used in a more active way, but it could also ensure more consistent active services for all groups of unemployed. Furthermore, an individualisation of entitlements for a sufficiently long initial period of unemployment should be high on the agenda; possible disincentive effects on taking up employment can be countered by obligatory activation measures.

Earnings and hours thresholds should be abolished, not only to increase state revenues –workers and employers would be required to pay contributions from the first working hour onwards – but also in order to set incentives to transform marginal employment into high-hours part-time employment with sufficient individual wage income. Social security revenues could also be increased by abolishing upper ceilings on contribution payments – that exist in Germany, for example – while keeping upper ceilings on benefit payments. This modification would target workers with higher earnings (mostly core workers) and could therefore strengthen the redistribution component. Another possibility, also aimed at the more affluent, would be to levy contributions or specific taxes on all income from assets. Individual private saving accounts, sometimes proposed (see, for example, Feldstein et al. 1998) as an alternative to public omnium insurance, are problematic for non-standard workers (and workers with low wages) because interpersonal redistribution usually does not take place.

While employers who use internal adaptation through training instead of hire and fire policies should be supported financially and organisationally, a risk fund would be an option to more strongly engage employers in the financing of non-employment periods. Employers who make excessive use of non-standard employment forms (especially fixed-term or casual contracts) could be obliged to pay into a special fund that is later used to, passively and actively, cushion the non-employment periods of non-standard workers. A similar solution is experience rating, which is currently extensively practiced in the United States. In this system employers' contributions depend on their hiring and firing practice. To be effective in preventing hiring on the basis of fixed-term contracts such a system would have to make sure to also take into account fixed-term contracts that are not prolonged or not transformed into permanent contracts. Situations that cannot be directly influenced by the employer (economic downturns and regional differences in the labour market situation) should be taken account of when calculating the contribution rate.

It is evident that the security situation of non-standard workers requires further investigation. Questions of financing more comprehensive social insurance schemes in an equitable and adequate way, preventing possible incentive problems, will have to take centre stage in further investigation. Furthermore, longer-term effects of non-standard employment on pension benefits (public, occupational and private) would be worthwhile topics.

References

Albarracín, D. (2004) Temporary employment examined. In: european industrial relations observatory on-line (eironline).

— (2005) Constitutional Court finds social security rules discriminatory. In: european industrial relations observatory on-line (eironline).

Alber, J. / M. Schölkopf (1996) Sozialstaat/Wohlfahrtsstaat. In: D. Nohlen (ed) Wörterbuch Staat und Politik. München: Piper. 705-715.

Aldenderfer, M. S. / R. K. Blashfield (1984) Cluster Analysis. Beverly Hills, London, New Delhi: Sage Publications.

Allison, P. D. (1982) Discrete-Time Methods for the Analysis of Event Histories. In: Sociological Methodology 13. 61-98.

Almeda, E. / S. Sarasa (1996) Spain: Growth to Diversity. In: P. Taylor-Gooby et al. (eds) European Welfare Policy. Squaring the Welfare Circle. London: MacMillan Press Ltd. 155-176.

Amuedo-Dorantes, C. (2000) Work Transitions into and out of Involuntary Temporary Employment in a Segmented Market: Evidence from Spain. In: Industrial and Labor Relations Review 53, 2. 309-325.

Andersen, J. / D. Etherington (2005) Flexicurity, workfare or inclusion? The Politics of Welfare and Activation in the UK and Denmark. Aalborg: Centre for Labour Market Research.

Anxo, D. / J. O'Reilly (2000) Working-time regimes and transitions in comparative perspective. In: J. O'Reilly et al. (2000) Working-Time Changes. Social Integration Through Transitional Labour Markets. Cheltenham: Edward Elgar. 61-90.

Arts, W. / J. Gelissen (2002) Three worlds of welfare capitalism or more? A state-of-the-art report, Journal of European Social Policy 12, 2: 137-158.

Askgaard Hyldtoft, L. (2002) Government liberalises unemployment insurance funds. In: european industrial relations observatory on-line (eironline).

Aspalter, C. (2001) Different World of Welfare Capitalism: Australia, the United States, the United Kingdom, Sweden, Germany, Italy, Hong Kong and Singapore. Discussion Paper No. 80.

Atkinson, A. (1984) Manpower strategies for flexible organisations. In: Personal Management 16, 8. 28-31.

Atkinson, A. / J. Micklewright (1991) Unemployment Compensation and Labor Market Transitions: A Critical Review. In: Journal of Economic Literature 29. 1679-1727.

Atkinson, A. / G. V. Mogensen (1993) Welfare and work incentives: A North European perspective. Oxford: Oxford University Press.

Bäcker, G. (2001) Flexibilität und soziale Sicherung in Deutschland: Bestandsaufnahmen und Reformoptionen für die Alterssicherung. In: U. Klammer et al. (eds) Flexicurity - Soziale Sicherung und Flexibilisierung der Arbeits- und Lebensverhältnisse. Ministerium für Arbeit und Soziales, Qualifikation und Technologie des Landes Nordrhein-Westfalen. 443-502.

Backhaus, K. / B. Erichson / W. Plinke / R. Weiber (2000) Multivariate Analysemethoden. Eine anwendungsorientierte Einführung. Berlin: Springer.

Ballester, R. (2005) European Employment Strategy and Spanish Labour Market Policies. Working Paper 14, Department of Economics, Universtiy of Girona.

Barbier, J.-C. (2004) Activation policies: a comparative perspective. In: A. Serrano Pascual (ed) Are activation policies converging in Europe? The European Employment Strategy for young people. Brussels: ETUI. 47-84.

Barr, N. (1992) Economic Theory and the Welfare State: A Survey and Interpretation. In: Journal of Economic Literature 30, 2. 741-803.

— (1998) The Economics of the Welfare State. Oxford: Oxford University Press.

Bauer, T. K. / S. Bender / H. Bonin (2004) Arbeitsmarkt-Reformen: Betriebe reagieren kaum auf Änderungen beim Kündigungsschutz. In: IAB Kurzbericht 15. 1-4.

Beenstock, M. / V. Brasse (1986) Insurance for Unemployment. London: Allen & Unwin.

Bennett, F. (2005) Gender and benefits, Equal Opportunities Commission. Manchester.

Bentolila, S. / J. Dolado (1994) Labour flexibility and wages: lessons from Spain. In: Economic Policy 18 (April). 55-99.

Bentolila, S. / J. Jimeno (2003) Spanish Unemployment: The End of the Wild Ride?. Documento de Trabajo.

Bertelsmann Foundation (2001) International Reform Monitor: Social Policy, Labour Market Policy, Industrial Relations. Issue 5. Gütersloh.

— (2003a) International Reform Monitor: Social Policy, Labour Market Policy, Industrial Relations. Issue 8. Gütersloh.

— (2003b) International Reform Monitor: Social Policy, Labour Market Policy, Industrial Relations. Issue 7. Gütersloh.

— (2004) International Reform Monitor: Social Policy, Labour Market Policy, Industrial Relations. Issue 9. Gütersloh.

Berthold, N. (1988) Marktversagen, Staatliche Intervention und Organisationsformen Sozialer Sicherung. In: G. Rolf et al.(eds) Sozialvertrag und Sicherung. Zur ökonomischen Theorie staatlicher Versicherungs- und Umverteilungssystem. Frankfurt/New York: Campus. 339-369.

Beveridge, W. S. (1942) Social Insurance and Allied Services. London.

Bielenski, H., et al. (1994) New Forms of Work and Activity: Survey of Experience at Establishment Level in Eight European Countries. Dublin: European Foundation for the Improvement of Living and Working Conditions.

Bishop, K. (2004) Working time patterns in the UK, France, Denmark and Sweden. In: Labour Market trends. 113-122.

Bonoli, G. (1997) Classifying Welfare States: a Two-dimension Approach. In: Journal of Social Policy 26, 3. 351-371.

Booth, A. / J. Dolado / J. Frank (2002a) Symposium on Temporary Work: Introduction. In: The Economic Journal 112 (June). 181-188.

Booth, A. / M. Francesconi / J. Frank (2002b) Temporary Jobs: Stepping Stones or Dead Ends?. In: The Economic Journal 112 (June).189-213.

Bosco, A. (1996) Unemployment benefits between protection and promotion. In: T*ransfer* 4. 660-680.

Bothfeld, S. / J. O'Reilly (2000) Moving up or moving out? Transitions through part-time employment in Britain and Germany. In: J. O'Reilly et al. (eds) Working-Time Changes. Social Integration through Transitional Labour Markets. Cheltenham: Edward Elgar. 132-172.

Bover, O. / M. Arellano / S. Bentolila (2002) Unemployment Duration, Benefit Duration and the Business Cycle, The Economic Journal 112, April: 223-265.

Box-Steffensmeier, J. / B. S. Jones (2004) Event History Modelling: A Guide for Social Scientists. Cambridge: Cambridge University Press.

Braun, T. (2001) Flexibilität und soziale Sicherung in Dänemark unter besonderer Berücksichtigung von aktiver Arbeitsmarktpolitik und Weiterbildung. In: U. Klammer et al. (2001) Flexicurity - Soziale Sicherung und Flexibilisierung der Arbeits- und Lebensverhältnisse. Ministerium für Arbeit und Soziales, Qualifikation und Technologie des Landes Nordrhein-Westfalen. 637-680.

British Household Panel Survey (BHPS), http://www.iser.essex.ac.uk/ulsc/bhps/ (access 2006).

Büchtemann, C. / U. Walwei (1996) Employment Security and Dismissal Protection. In: G. Schmid et al. (eds) International Handbook of Labour Market Policy and Evaluation. Cheltenham: Edward Elgar.

Bundesagentur für Arbeit (2004) Arbeitsmarkt in Zahlen, aktuelle Daten (Juni 2004), Nürnberg.

Bundesregierung (2005) Nationales Reformprogramm Deutschland: Innovation forcieren - Sicherheit im Wandel fördern - Deutsche Einheit vollenden. Berlin.

Card, D. (2000) Reforming the Financial Incentives of the Welfare System. Discussion Paper No. 172. Bonn: IZA.

Castellanos, M. L. (2006) New measures to reduce temporary employment. In: european industrial relations observatory on-line (eironline).

Castles, F. / D. Mitchell (1993) Worlds of Welfare and Families of Nations. In: F. Castles (ed) Families of Nations. Patterns of Public Policy in Western Democracies. Aldershot: Dartmouth Publishing Company Limited. 93-128.

Cebrián, I. / V. Gash / G. Moreno / P. J. O'Connell / L. Toharia (2000) Peripheral labour in peripheral markets? Mobility and working time within transitional labour markets among women in Ireland and Spain. In: J O'Reilly et al. (eds) Working Time Changes: Social Integration Through Transitional Labour Markets. Cheltenham: Edward Elgar.

Cebulla, A. (2001) Flexibilität und soziale Sicherung in Großbritannien unter besonderer Berücksichtigung des "New Deal". In: U. Klammer et al. (eds) Flexicurity – Soziale Sicherung und Flexibilisierung der Arbeits- und Lebensverhältnisse. Ministerium für Arbeit und Soziales, Qualifikation und Technologie des Landes Nordrhein-Westfalen. 585-636.

Chaupain-Guillot, S. / O. Guillot / E. Jankeliowitch-Laval (2004) Female part-time work in the European Union: An empirical study based on the ECHP. Conference paper presented at Second International Conference of the European Panel Users' Network. Berlin, June 2004.

Clasen, J. / W. van Oorschot (2002) Changing Principles in European Social Security. In: European Journal of Social Security 4, 2. 89-115.

Clauwaert, S. (2002) Survey on the Implementation of the Part-time Work Directive/Agreement in the EU Member States and Selected Applicant Countries. Brussels: ETUI.

Cleves, M. / W. Gould / R. Gutierrez (2002) An Introduction to Survival Analysis Using Stata. College Station: Stata Press.

Comisión de expertos para el diálogo social (2005) Más y mejor empleo en un nuevo escenario socioeconómico: por una flexibilidad y seguridad laborales efectivas. Informe de la comisión de expertos para el diálogo social.

Danish government (2005) Denmark's National Reform Programme: Contribution to EU's Growth and Employment Strategy (The Lisbon Strategy). Copenhagen.

Danish Ministry of Labour (2001) The Unemployment Insurance Scheme: http://www.ladk.dk/diverse/english/legislation/unemployment_insurance.htm (access 2004)

Davy, U. (2000) Sozialreformen unter New Labour. In: Zeitschrift für ausländisches Arbeits- und Sozialrecht 14, 2. 144-177.

Debels, A. (2004) Temporary jobs: Segmented security through the labour and welfare system. Conference paper presented at TLM.NET Conference. Amsterdam, November 2004.

— (2005) The structuring of labour market dynamics along the permanent-temporary distinction: a comparison of Denmark, France, Spain and United Kingdom. Conference paper presented at the Oslo Meeting of ISA-Research Committee on Social Stratification and Mobility. Oslo, May 2005.

Delsen, L. (1995) Atypical Employment: an International Perspective: Causes, consequences and policy. Groningen: Wolters-Noordhoff.

Department for Social Development (2005) Jobseeker's Allowance. United Kingdom, August 2005: http://www.dsdni.gov.uk/index/publications/jobseekers_allowance.htm (access 2006)

Department for Work and Pensions (2002) National Statistics: Jobseeker's Allowance. In: Quarterly Statistical Enquiry. May 2002.

— (2006) Jobseeker's Allowance: http://www.jobcentreplus.gov.uk/cms.asp?Page=/Home/Customers/WorkingAgeBenefits/497#ibjsa (access 2006)

Dickens, W. T. / K. Lang (1984) A Test of Dual Labor Market Theory. Cambridge, MA: National Bureau of Economic Research.

Dingeldey, I. (1998) Läßt sich die Zahl geringfügiger Beschäftigungsverhältnisse über Steuern und Sozialabgaben gezielt beeinflussen?, *WSI Mitteilungen* 12: 863-871.

Doeringer, P. B. / M. J. Piore (1971) Internal Labor Market and Manpower Analysis. Lexington: D.C. Heath and Company.

Dolado, J. / C. Garcia-Serrano / J. Jimeno (2002) Drawing Lessons from the Boom of Temporary Jobs in Spain. In: The Economic Journal 112 (June). 270-295.

Donnelley, C. / M. Nimmo / P. Convery (1998) The New Deal Handbook: A guide to your rights and responsibilities on the "New Deal". London: Independent Unemployment Unit & Youthaid.

Dublin European Council (1996) Presidency Conclusions, Annexes: The Jobs Challenge – Dublin Declaration on Employment.

Ehling, M. / R. Günther (2003) Europäische Erhebung über Einkommen und Lebensbedingungen. In: Statistisches Bundesamt (ed) Forum der Bundesstatistik 41. 27-36.

Eichhorst, W. / S. Profit / E. Thode (2001) Benchmarking Deuschland: Arbeitsmarkt und Beschäftigung. Berlin: Springer.

Eisen, R. (1988) "Versicherungsprinzip" und Umverteilung - Einige theoretische Überlegungen zu den Grenzen des Versicherbaren. In: G. Rolf et al. (eds) Sozialvertrag und Sicherung. Zur ökonomischen Theorie staatlicher Versicherungs- und Umverteilungssysteme. Frankfurt/New York: Campus. 117-127.

Equal Opportunities Commission (1998) Low Pay and the National Insurance System: A Statistical Picture.

Esping-Andersen, G. (1990) The Three Worlds of Welfare Capitalism. Cambridge: Polity Press.

— (1994) Welfare States and the Economy. In: N. J. Smelser et al. (eds) The Handbook of Economic Sociology. Princeton: Princeton University Press. 711-732.

— (1995) Welfare States without Work: The Impass of Labor Shedding and Familialism in Continental European Social Policy. Working Paper 71. Madrid: Instituto Juan March de Estudios e Investigaciones.

— (1996) Welfare States in Transition: National Adaptations in Global Economies. London: Sage.

— (1999) Social Foundations in Postindustrial Economies. Oxford: Oxford University Press. 47-72.

Esser, H. (2000) Soziologie. Spezielle Grundlagen. vol. 3. Frankfurt/Main: Campus.

Eurofound (2003) Flexibility and social protection: Reconciling flexible employment patterns over the active life cycle with security for individuals. Dublin: European Foundation for the Improvement of Living and Working Conditions.

— (2004) Sweden: Unemployment Insurance: http://www.eurofound.eu.int/emire/SWEDEN/ANCHOR-ARBETSL-Ouml-SHETSF-Ouml-RS-Auml-KRING-SE.html (access 2004)

Europäische Kommission (1996) Soziale Sicherheit in den Mitgliedstaaten der Europäischen Union (MISSOC). Stand am 1. Juli 1995. Luxemburg: Generaldirektion Beschäftigung, Arbeitsbeziehungen und Soziale Angelegenheiten.

European Commission (1997) The place of social transfers in the incomes and living standards of households: a comparison between Spain, France, the Netherlands and the United Kingdom. In: ECHP Working Group, Luxembourg.

— (21/01/2003) Report by the Commission's services on the implementation of Council Directive 97/81/EC of 17 December 1997 concerning the Framework Agreement on Part-time Work concluded by UNICE, CEEP and the ETUC. Luxembourg.

— (2000) Employment in Europe 2000. Luxembourg.

— (2003a) The European Union labour force survey: Methods and definitions, 2001 edition. Luxembourg.

— (2003b) Employment in Europe 2003. Luxembourg.

— (2003c) Labour market policy. Qualitative report: Germany 2001. Luxembourg.

— (2003d) Social Protection of the Self-employed: Social Protection Schemes for Self-employed Farmers, Craftsmen and Tradesmen in the Member States of the EU and the EFTA: http://europa.eu.int/comm/employment_social/missoc/2003/independents/indep_en.pdf (access 2004).
— (2004a) European Social Statistics. Labour Market Policy: Expenditure and Participation, Data 2002. Luxembourg.
— (2004b) Employment in Europe 2004. Luxembourg.
— (2004c) Organisation of social protection (MISSOC): Charts and description. Situation on 1 May 2004.
— (2005) The European Union labour force survey: Main characteristics of the national surveys, 2005 edition. Luxembourg.
— (2006) Social protection in the Member States of the European Union, of the European Economic Area and in Switzerland (MISSOC). Situation on January 2006: http://ec.europa.eu/employment_social/missoc/2006/tables_part_1_en.pdf
Eurostat (1994) ECHP - 1994, Wave 1, Variable list. DOC PAN 15/94. Luxembourg: European Commission.
— (2000a) ECHP - 2001, Wave 8, Variable list. DOC PAN 159/00. Luxembourg: European Commission.
— (2000b) ECHP: Classifications used in Questionnaires. DOC PAN 73/00. Luxembourg: European Commission.
— (2002) ECHP UDB manual. European Community Household Panel Longitudinal Users' Database. Luxembourg: European Commission.
— (2003a) ECHP UDB: Construction of variables. DOC PAN 167/2003-12. Luxembourg: European Commission.
— (2003b) ECHP UDB: Description of variables. Data Dictionnary, Codebook and Differences between Countries and Waves. DOC. PAN 166 / 2003-12. Luxembourg: European Commission.
— (2004) Income and living conditions (ECHP). Eurostat Metadata in SDDS format: Summary Methodology: http://europa.eu.int/estatref/info/sdds/en/ilc/ilc_sm01.htm (access 2006).
— (2007) Labour force survey. Online database: http://epp.eurostat.cec.eu.int/portal/ (access 2008).
Fagan, C. / J. O'Reilly / J. Rubery (1998) Teilzeitarbeit in den Niederlanden, Deutschland und Großbritannien: ein neuer Geschlechtervertrag?. In: B. Krais et al. (eds) Frauenarbeit - Männerarbeit. Neue Muster der Ungleichheit auf dem europäischen Arbeitsmarkt. Frankfurt/New York: Campus.
Falkner, G. (2000) The Council or the social partners? EC social policy between diplomacy and collective bargaining. In: Journal of European Public Policy 7, 5. 705-724.
Falkner, G. / O. Treib / M. Hartlapp / S. Leiber (2005) Complying with Europe. EU Harminisation and Soft Law in the Member States. Cambridge: Cambridge University Press.
Fassler-Ristic, M. (1999) Atypische Beschäftigung in Spanien. In: E. Tálos (ed) Atypische Beschäftigung: Internationale Trends und Sozialstaatliche Regelungen. Wien: Manzsche Verlags- und Universitätsbuchhandlung. 359-390.

Feldstein, M. / D. Altman (1998) Unemployment Insurance Savings Accounts. NBER Working Paper Series. Cambridge, MA: National Bureau of Economic Research.

Ferrera, M. (1996) The 'Southern Model' of Welfare in Social Europe, Journal of European Social Policy 6, 1: 17-37.

Fink, M. (1999a) Atypische Beschäftigung in Dänemark. In: E. Tálos (ed) Atypische Beschäftigung: Internationale Trends und Sozialstaatliche Regelungen. Wien: Manzsche Verlags- und Universitätsbuchhandlung. 82-111.

— (1999b) Atypische Beschäftigung in Großbritannien. In: E. Tálos (ed) Atypische Beschäftigung: Internationale Trends und Sozialstaatliche Regelungen. Wien: Manzsche Verlags- und Universitätsbuchhandlung. 161-190.

Frenzel, M. (2003) Sanfte Alternative zur "Agenda 2010"? Dänemarks Dritter Weg (1993-2001). In: Gewerkschaftliche Monatshefte 8, 9. 481-491.

Frey, B. S. (1992) Economics as a Science of Human Behaviour. Towards a New Social Science Paradigm. Boston/Dordrecht/London: Kluwer Academic Publishers.

Fuchs, M. (2004) Germany: part-time work - a bone of contention. In: S. Sciarra et al. (eds) Employment Policy and the Regulation of Part-time Work in the European Union: A Comparative Analysis. Cambridge: Cambridge University Press. 121-155.

Galluppi, D. (2004) Country Case Studies and Links: Spain: http://www.pitt.edu/~heinisch/ca_spai.html (access 2004).

Gash, V. (2003) Moving Up, Moving Out: The Transition of Atypical Workers to the Standard Employment Contract. Conference paper presented at 10es Journées d'études Céreq - Lasmas-IdL. Caen, Mai 2003.

Geissler, B. (1998) Normalarbeitsverhältnis und Sozialversicherungen - eine überholte Verbindung?. In: Mitteilungen aus der Arbeitsmarkt- und Berufsforschung 3. 550-557.

Ghysels, J. / A. Thirion / B. Cantillon (1999) To identify and compare social protection system benefits and replacement rates and their effect on employment participation in the light of the 1998 employment guidelines. Final report to the European Commission under project number V/031/98. Antwerp: Centre for Social Policy.

Giddens, A. (2000) Positive Welfare. In: C. Pierson et al. (eds) The Welfare State: A Reader. Cambridge: Polity Press. 369-379.

Giesecke, J. / M. Groß (2005) Arbeitsmarktreformen und Ungleichheit. In: Aus Politik und Zeitgeschichte 16. 25-31.

Ginn, J. / S. Arber (1998) How does part-time work lead to low pension income?. In: J. O'Reilly et al. (eds) Part-time prospects: An international comparison of part-time work in Europe, North America and the Pacific Rim. London/New York: Routledge.

Glismann, H. H. / K. Schrader (2001) Ein funktionstüchtiges System privater Arbeitslosenversicherung. Kiel: Institut für Weltwirtschaft.

— (2003) Zur Einführung privater Arbeitslosenversicherung in Deutschland. Kiel: Institut für Weltwirtschaft.

Golsch, K. (2004) Labour market insecurity and its impact on labour market entry and early career: a Comparison of Germany, Britain and Spain. Conference paper presented at 2nd Annual Research Conference of the European Panel Users' Network. Berlin, June 2004.

Goodin, R. E. / B. Headey / R. Muffels / H.-J. Dirven (1999) The Real Worlds of Welfare Capitalism. Cambridge: Cambridge University Press.

Gordon, D. M. (1972) Theories of Poverty and Underemployment: Orthodox, Radical, and Dual Labor Market Perspectives. Lexington, MA: D.C. Heath and Company.

Grimshaw, D. / J. Rubery (1997) Workforce Heterogeneity and Unemployment Benefits: The Need for Policy Reassessment in the European Union. In: Journal of European Social Policy 7, 4. 291-318.

— (1998) Arbeitslosenschutz bei atypischen Beschäftigungsverhältnissen: das vernachlässigte Thema. In: A. Bosco et al. (eds) Sozialer Schutz in Europa: Veränderungen und Herausforderungen. Marburg: Schüren Presseverlag. 312-336.

Grubb, D. / W. Wells (1993) Employment Regulation and Patterns of Work in EC Countries. In: OECD Economic Studies 21. 7-58.

Hansen, H. (2002) Elements of Social Security: a comparison covering: Denmark, Sweden, Finland, Austria, Germany, The Netherlands, Great Britain, Canada. Copenhagen: The Danish National Institute of Social Research.

— (2004) EUROMOD Country Report: Denmark (2001 Tax-Benefit System).

Hartlapp, M. (2005) Die Kontrolle der nationalen Rechtsdurchsetzung durch die Europäische Kommission. vol. 3. Frankfurt/New York: Campus.

Hayek, F. A. v. (1991) Die Verfassung der Freiheit. Tübingen: J.C.B. Mohr (Paul Siebeck).

Headey, B. / R. E. Goodin / R. Muffels / H.-J. Dirven (1999) The State and Economic Risk - Best Cases of 'The Tree Worlds of Welfare Capitalism': The Netherlands, United States, and West Germany. In: DIW Vierteljahresheft 2. 153-163.

Hicks, A. / L. Kenworthy (2003) Varieties of welfare capitalism. In: Socio-Economic Review 1. 27-61.

Hills, J. (2004) Heading for Retirement? National Insurance, State Pensions, and the Future of the Contributory Principle in the UK. In: Journal of Social Policy 33, 3. 347-371.

Hinrichs, K. (1996) Das Normalarbeitsverhältnis und der männliche Familienernährer als Leitbilder der Sozialpolitik. In: Sozialer Fortschritt. Unabhängige Zeitschrift für Sozialpolitik 4. 102-107.

Hoffmann, E. / U. Walwei (2003) The Change in Work Arrangements in Denmark and Germany. In: S. Houseman et al. (eds) Nonstandard Work in Developed Economies: Causes and Consequences. Kalamazoo: Upjohn Institute for Employment Research.

Holmlund, B. (1998) Unemployment Insurance in Theory and Practice. In: Scandinavian Journal of Economics 100, 1. 113-141.

Holst, E. / F. Maier (1998) Normalarbeitsverhältnis und Geschlechterordnung. In: Mitteilungen aus der Arbeitsmarkt- und Berufsforschung 31, 3. 506-518.

Holzmann, R. / S. Jørgensen (2001) Social Risk Management: a New Conceptual Framework for Social Protection, and Beyond. In: International Tax and Public Finance 8. 529-556.

Hox, J. (2002) Multilevel analysis: techniques and applications. Mahwah: Lawrence Erlbaum Associates, Inc.

Huguet Roig, A. (1999) Testing Spanish labour market segmentation: an unknown-regime approach. In: Applied Economics 31. 293-305.

Hummel, E. / P. Jacobebbinghaus et al. (2005) Stichprobe der Integrierten Erwerbsbiografien. In: FDZ Datenreport. Dokumentation zu Arbeitsmarktdaten 6. 1-135.

Hunt, J. (1995) The Effect of Unemployment Compensation on Unemployment Duration in Germany. In: Journal of Labor Economics 13, 1. 88-120.

Hutsebaut, M. (2002) Social security and atypical employment: a European trade union perspective. Conference paper presented at International Industrial Relations Associations (IIRA) 4th Regional Congress of the Americas. Toronto.

Hvinden, B. (1999) Activation: a Nordic Perspective. In: Eurofound (ed) Linking Welfare and Work. Dublin. 27-42.

Immervoll, H. / P. Marianna / M. Mira D'Ercole (2004) Benefit Coverage Rates and Household Typologies: Scope and Limitations of Tax-Benefit Indicators. OECD Social, Employment and Migration Working Papers, No. 20. Paris: OECD.

Inland Revenue (2005) National Insurance contributions, tables A and J.

Jahn, E. / U. Walwei (2003) Reform in Trippelschritten oder besser mit großem Sprung?. In: IAB Kurzbericht 21. 1-6.

Jenkins, S. (18 July 2005) Survival Analysis, manuscript.

Jensen, P. H. (1999) Activation of the Unemployed in Denmark since the early 1990s. Welfare or Workfare?. Aalborg: Aalborg University.

Jepsen, M. / D. Meulders (1997) Ungleichbehandlung der Geschlechter in der europäischen Arbeitslosenversicherung. In: Internationale Revue für Soziale Sicherheit 50, 4. 45-66.

— (2002) The Individualization of Rights in Social Protection Systems. In: H. Sarfati (ed) Labour Market and Social Protection Reforms in International Perspective: Parallel or Coverging Tracks?. Burlington: Ashgate.

Jimeno, J. / L. Toharia (1993) The effects of fixed-term employment on wages: theory and evidence from Spain. In: Investigaciones Económicas 17, 3. 475-494.

Jørgensen, C. (2001) EU part-time work Directive implemented through new dual method. In: european industrial relations observatory on-line (eironline).

Kaiser, L. C. (2002) Job Satisfaction: A Comparison of Standard, Non-Standard, and Self-Employment Patterns across Europe with a Special Note to the Gender/Job Satisfaction Paradox. Colchester: University of Essex.

Keller, B. / H. Seifert (2002) Flexicurity - Wie lassen sich Flexibilität und soziale Sicherheit vereinbaren?. In: Mitteilungen aus der Arbeitsmarkt- und Berufsforschung 35, 1. 90-106.

— (2004) Flexicurity - the German trajectory. In: Transfer 10, 2. 226-247.

Kilpatrick, C. / M. Freedland (2004) The United Kingdom: how is EU governance transformative?. In: S. Sciarra et al. (eds) Employment Policy and the Regulation of Part-time Work in the European Union: A Comparative Analysis. Cambridge: Cambridge University Press.

Klammer, U. (2000) Soziale Sicherung. In: Klammer et al. (eds) WSI-FrauenDatenReport. Düsseldorf: Hans-Böckler-Stiftung. 267-345.

— (2001) Flexibilität und soziale Sicherung: Grundsätzliche Überlegungen zu einem komplexen Forschungsfeld in: I. Becker et al. (eds) Soziale Sicherung in einer dynamischen Gesellschaft. Festschrift für Richard Hauser zum 65. Geburtstag. Frankfurt/ Main: Campus. 130-159.

— (2004) Flexicurity in a life-course perspective. In: Transfer 10, 2. 282-299.

— (2005) Soziale Sicherung. In: Bothfeld et al. (eds) WSI-FrauenDatenReport 2005: Handbuch zur wirtschaftlichen und sozialen Situation von Frauen. Düsseldorf: Hans-Böckler-Stiftung.

Klammer, U. / K. Tillmann (2001a) Flexicurity: Soziale Sicherung und Flexibilisierung der Arbeits- und Lebensverhältnisse. Düsseldorf: Ministerium für Arbeit und Soziales, Qualifikation und Technologie des Landes Nordrhein-Westfalen.

— (2001b) Unerwünschte Diskontinuitäten - Längsschnittergebnisse zur Veränderung des Arbeitslosigkeitsrisikos in der Erwerbsbiographie. In: U. Klammer et al. (2001) Flexicurity – Soziale Sicherung und Flexibilisierung der Arbeits- und Lebensverhältnisse. Ministerium für Arbeit und Soziales, Qualifikation und Technologie des Landes Nordrhein-Westfalen. 225-269.

Kohler, U. / F. Kreuter (2001) Datenanalyse mit STATA. Allgemeine Konzepte der Datenanalyse und ihre praktische Anwendung. München/Wien: R. Oldenbourg Verlag.

— (2005) Data Analysis Using Stata. College Station: Stata Press.

Kolberg, J. E. / G. Esping-Andersen (1992) Welfare States and Employment Regimes. In: J. E. Kolberg (ed) The Study of Welfare State Regimes. Armonk, NY: Sharpe.

Korpi, W. / J. Palme (1998) The Paradox of Redistribution and Strategies of Equality: Welfare State Institutions, Inequality, and Poverty in the Western Countries. In: American Sociological Review 63. 661-687.

Kosonen, P. (1999) Activation, incitations au travail et workfare dans quatre pays scandinaves. In: Travail et Emploi 79. 1-16.

Krimsky, S. (1992) The Role of Theory in Risk Studies. In Krimsky et al. (eds) Social Theories of Risk. Westport, Connecticut/London: Praeger Publishers. 3-22.

Krupp, H.-J. (1988) Zur Begründung und zur Praxis des Wohlfahrtsstaats. In: G. Rolf et al. (eds) Sozialvertrag und Sicherung. Zur ökonomischen Theorie staatlicher Versicherung- und Umverteilungssysteme. Frankfurt/New York: Campus. 491-511.

Kühnlein, G. / B. Klein (2004) Bildungsgutscheine - mehr Eigenverantwortung, mehr Markt, mehr Effizienz? - Erfahrungen bei der Neuausrichtung der beruflichen Weiterbildung. Arbeitspapier. Düsseldorf: Hans-Böckler-Stiftung.

Kvist, J. (1998) Complexities in assessing unemployment benefits and policies. In: International Social Security Review 61, 4. 33-55.

— (2000) Activating Welfare States: Scandinavian Experiences in the 1990s. Copenhagen: The Danish National Institute of Social Research.

Langan, M. / I. Ostner (1991) Gender and Welfare: Towards a comparative framework. In: G. Room (ed) Towards a European Welfare State?. Bristol: SAUS. 127-150.

Larsen, F (2004) The importance of institutional regimes for active labour market policies. The case of Denmark. Aalborg: Danish National Centre for Labour Market Research.

Lauterbach, W. (1994) Teilzeitarbeit - Nur Brücke zum Wiedereinstieg oder Möglichkeit zur langfristigen Erwerbsbeteiligung?. in: W. Lauterbach (ed) Berufsverläufe von Frauen. Erwerbstätigkeit, Unterbrechung und Wiedereintritt. Frankfurt/New York: Campus. 174-218.

Leiber, S. (2005) Europäische Sozialpolitik und nationale Sozialpartnerschaft. vol. 2. Frankfurt/New York: Campus.

Leibfried, S. / I. Ostner (1991) The Particularism of West German Welfare Capitalism: The Case of Women's Social Security. In: M. Adler et al. (eds) The Sociology of Social Security. Edinburgh: Edinburgh University Press.

Lemaître, G. / P. Marianna / A. van Bastelaer (1997) The Definition of Part-Time Work for the Purpose of International Comparisons. OECD Labour Market and Social Policy Occasional Papers. No. 22. Paris: OECD.

Leschke, J. / G. Schmid / D. Griga (2006) On the Marriage of Flexibility and Security: Lessons from the Hartz-reforms in Germany. Discussion Paper No. SP I 2006-108. Berlin: Wissenschaftszentrum Berlin für Sozialforschung.

Leschke, J. (2007) To what extent are temporary work and part-time work cushioned by different forms of security?. In: H. Jørgensen et al. (eds) Flexicurity and Beyond: Finding a new agenda for the European Social Model. Copenhagen: DJØF Publishing. 561-601.

Lessenich, S. / I. Ostner (1998) Welten des Wohlfahrtskapitalismus: der Sozialstaat in vergleichender Perspektive. Frankfurt/M.: Campus.

Levy, H. / M. Mercader-Prats (2003) EUROMOD Country Report: Spain (2001 Tax-Benefit System).

Lind, J. (1999) Labour market flexibility and regulation. In: J. Lind et al. (eds) Inclusion and Exclusion: Unemployment and Non-standard Employment in Europe. Aldershot: Ashgate. 187-215.

Lind, J. / I. Hornemann Møller (1999) European convergence or national specificities?. In: J. Lind et al. (eds) Inclusion and Exclusion: Unemployment and Non-standard Employment in Europe. Aldershot: Ashgate. 219-230.

Lister, R. (2002) Citizenship and changing welfare states. In: J.G. Andersen (ed) Changing labour markets, welfare policies and citizenship. Bristol: Policy Press. 39-58.

Long, S. / J. Freese (2006) Regression Models for Categorical Dependent Variables Using Stata. 2nd edition,.College Station: StataCorp.

Luckhaus, L. (2000) Equal treatment, social protection and income security for women. In: International Labour Review 139, 2. 149-178.

Madsen, P. K. (2002a) "Flexicurity" through labour market policies and institutions in Denmark. In: P. Auer et al. (eds) Employment stability in an age of flexibility. Geneva: ILO. 59-105.

— (2002b) Security and Flexibility: Friends or Foes? Some Observations from the case of Denmark. In: P. Auer et al (eds) The Future of Work, Employment and Social Protection: The dynamics of change and the protection of workers. Proceedings of the France/ILO symposium. Lyon.

Maier, F. (1992) The Regulations of Part-Time Work: A Comparative Study of Six EC Countries. Discussion Paper No. FS I 91-9. Berlin: Wissenschaftszentrum Berlin für Sozialforschung.

McGinnity, F. (2004) Welfare for the Unemployed in Britain and Germany. Who benefits?. Cheltenham: Edward Elgar.

McGinnity, F. / A. Mertens / S. Gundert (2004) A bad start? Fixed-term contracts and the transition from education to work in West Germany. In: European Sociological Review, 21, 4. 359-374.

Michon, F. (1999) Temporary agency work in Europe. In: European industrial relations observatory on-line (eironline).
Micklewright, J. (1990) Why do less than a quarter of the unemployed in Britain receive unemployment insurance?. Working Paper. No. 90/17. Florence: European University Institute.
Miguélez, F. (1998) Agreement between government and unions on part-time contracts. In: european industrial relations observatory on-line (eironline).
Ministerio de la Presidencia. Secretaría General Técnica (2005) Convergencia y Empleo. Programa Nacional de Reformas de España. Madrid.
Ministerio de Trabajo y Asuntos Sociales (2005) Seguridad Social: http://www.seg-social.es/inicio/?MIval=cw_usr_view_Folder&LANG=6&ID=30124#documentoPDF (access 2006).
— (2006) Protección por desempleo de los trabajadores eventuales agrarios en Andalucía y Extremadura: http://www.inem.es/ciudadano/desempleo/pdf/GuiaTrabajadoresEventualesREASS.pdf (access 2006)
— (2006a) Prestación por desempleo de nivel contributivo: http://www.inem.es/ciudadano/desempleo/pdf/GuiaPrestacionContributiva.pdf (access 2006)
— (2006b) Subsidio de desempleo por agotamiento de la prestación contributiva: http://www.inem.es/ciudadano/desempleo/pdf/GuiaSubsidioAgotamientoPrestacion.pdf (access 2006)
— (2006c) Subsidio de desempleo por pérdida del empleo: http://www.inem.es/ciudadano/desempleo/pdf/GuiaSubsidioPerdidaEmpleo.pdf (access 2006)
Mohr, K. (2004) Pfadabhängige Restrukturierung oder Konvergenz? Reformen in der Arbeitslosensicherung und der Sozialhilfe in Großbritannien und Deutschland. In: Zeitschrift für Sozialreform 50, 3. 283-311.
Muffels, R. / R. Luijkx (2005) Job Mobility and Employment Patterns across European Welfare States. Is there a "Trade-off" or a "Double Bind" between Flexibility and Security?. TLM.NET Working Paper 2005-12.
Muffels, R. / T. Wilthagen / N. van den Heuvel (2002) Labour Market Transitions and Employment Regimes: Evidence on the Flexibility-Security Nexus in Transitional Labour Markets. Discussion Paper No. FS I 02-204. Berlin: Wissenschaftszentrum Berlin für Sozialforschung.
Neuhold, C. (1999) Atypische Beschäftigung in Deutschland. In: E. Tálos (ed) Atypische Beschäftigung: Internationale Trends und Sozialstaatliche Regelungen. Wien: Manzsche Verlags- und Universitätsbuchhandlung. 36-81.
North, D. C. (1990) Institutions, Institutional Change and Economic Performance. Cambridge: Cambridge University Press.
Obinger, H. / U. Wagschal (1998) Drei Welten des Wohlfahrtsstaates? Das Stratifizierungskonzept in der clusteranalytischen Überprüfung. In: S. Lessenich et al. (eds) Welten des Wohlfahrtskapitalismus. Der Sozialstaat in vergleichender Perspektive. 109-135.
O'Connell, P. J. / V. Gash (2003) The Effects of Working Time, Segmentation and Labour Market Mobility on Wages and Pensions in Ireland. In: British Journal of Industrial Relations 41, 1. 71-95.

OECD (1992) Unemployment Benefit Rules and Labour Market Policy. In: OECD Employment Outlook. Paris. 199-262.

— (1998a) Benefit Systems and Work Incentives. Paris.

— (1998b) OECD Economic Surveys: United Kingdom 1997-1998. Paris.

— (1999a) Employment Protection and Labour Market Performance. In: OECD Employment Outlook. Paris. 50-132.

— (1999b) The Tax/Benefit Position of Employees 1997. Paris.

— (2001a) Balancing Work and Family Life: Helping Parents into Paid Employment. In: OECD Employment Outlook. Paris. 129-166.

— (2001b) Innovations in Labour Market Policies: The Australian Way. Paris.

— (2002a) Benefits and Wages - OECD Indicators 2002. Paris.

— (2002b) The ins and outs of long-term unemployment. In: OECD Employment Outlook 2002. Paris. 187-239.

— (2002c) Taking the measure of temporary employment. In: OECD Employment Outlook 2002. Paris. 127-185.

— (2002d) Women at work: who are they and how are they faring?. In: OECD Employment Outlook 2002. Paris. 61-125.

— (2003a) Making Work Pay - Making Work Possible. In: OECD Employment Outlook. Paris. 113-170.

— (2003b) OECD Economic Surveys: Spain. vol. 7. Paris.

— (2004a) Benefits and Wages Country Chapter: Denmark. Paris.

— (2004b) Benefits and Wages: OECD Indicators. Paris.

— (2004c) A Detailed Description of Employment Protection Regulation in Force in 2003: Background Material for the 2004 edition of the OECD Employment Outlook. Paris.

— (2004d) Employment Protection Regulation and Labour Market Performance. In: OECD Employment Outlook 2004. Paris. 61-125.

— (2005) Statistical Annex. In: OECD Employment Outlook 2005. Paris.

— (2007) Babies and Bosses - Reconciling Work and Family Life (Vol. 5): A Synthesis of Findings for OECD Countries. Paris.

— (2008) OECD family database: www.oecd.org/els/social/family/database (access 2008).

Okun, A. (1975) Equality and efficiency. The big tradeoff. Washington, D.C.: Brookings Inst.

O'Reilly, J. / S. Bothfeld (2002) What happens after working part time? Integration, maintenance or exclusionary transitions in Britain and western Germany. In: Cambridge Journal of Economics 26. 409-439.

Oschmiansky, F. (2004) Bekämpfung von Schwarzarbeit (Ich-AG, Mini-Jobs). In: W. Jann et al. (eds) Eins zu Eins? Eine Zwischenbilanz der Hartz-Reformen am Arbeitsmarkt. Berlin: Sigma.

Ostner, I. (1998) Quadraturen im Wohlfahrtsdreieck. Die USA, Schweden und die Bundesrepublik im Vergleich. In: Lessenich et al. (eds) Welten des Wohlfahrtskapitalismus. Der Sozialstaat in vergleichender Perspektive. Frankfurt/M.: Campus. 225-252.

Parsons, D. O. / T. Tranaes / H. Bie Lilleør (2003) Voluntary Public Unemployment Insurance. Copenhagen: The Danish National Institute of Social Research.

Pearson, M. / S. Scarpetta (2000) An overview: What do we know about policies to make work pay?. In: OECD Economic Studies 31, 2. 11-24.

Peck, J. (1996) Work-Place: The Social Regulation of Labor Markets. New York/London: Guilford Press.

Peijpe, T., van (1998) Employment Protection under Strain: Sweden, Denmark, the Netherlands. The Hague/London/Boston: Kluwer Law International.

Pennings, F. (1990) Benefits of Doubt: a Comparative Study of the Legal Aspects of Employment and Unemployemnt Schemes in Great Britain, Germany, France, and the Netherlands. Deventer/Boston: Kluwer Law and Taxation Publishers.

Petersen, H.-G. (1989) Sozialökonomik. Stuttgart/Berlin/Köln: Kohlhammer GmbH.

Petersen, T. (2004) Analysing Panel Data: Fixed- and Random-Effects Models. In: M. Hardy et al. (eds) Handbook of Data Analysis. London: Sage Publications. 331-345.

Polavieja, J. G. (2003) Temporary Contracts and Labour Market Segmentation in Spain: An Employment-Rent Approach. In: European Sociological Review 19, 5. 501-517.

Powell, M. / A. Barrientos (2004) Welfare regimes and the welfare mix. In: European Journal of Political Research 43. 83-105.

Rabe, B. (2001) Flexibilität und soziale Sicherung in Deutschland: Bestandsaufnahme und Reformoptionen für die aktive Arbeitsmarktpolitik. In: Klammer et al. (ed) Flexicurity: Soziale Sicherung und Flexibilisierung der Arbeits- und Lebensverhältnisse. Düsselsdorf: Ministerium für Arbeit und Soziales, Qualifikation und Technologie des Landes Nordrhein-Westfalen.

Rabe-Hesketh, S. / B. Everitt (2004) A Handbook of Statistical Analyses using Stata. Boca Raton: Chapman & Hall/CRC.

Rabe-Hesketh, S. / A. Skrondal (2005) Multilevel and Longitudinal Modeling Using Stata. College Station: StataCorp.

Rehm, P. / J. Schmid (2001) Die vier Welten der Beschäftigung: Eine explorative Analyse der arbeitsmarktpolitischen Performanz und politisch-ökonomischen Korrelate in 10 Industrieländern 1980-2000. Occasional Paper Series. Tübingen: Institut für Politikwissenschaft.

Renn, O. (1992) Concepts of Risk: A Classification. In: S. Krimsky et al. (eds) Social Theories of Risk. Westport, Connecticut/London: Praeger Publishers. 53-79.

Riggs, L. (2000) Introduction to Contestability in the Delivery of Employment Services in Australia. In: OECD (ed) Labour Market Policies and the Public Employment Services. Paris: OECD. 365-390.

Røed, K. / P. Jensen / A. Thoursie (2002) Unemployment Duration, Incentives and Institutions: A Micro-Econometric Analysis Based on Scandinavian Data. Discussion Paper No. 9/2002. Oslo: University of Oslo.

Rogowski, R. / K. Schömann (1996) Legal Regulation and Flexibility of Employment Contracts. In: Schmid et al. (eds) International Handbook of Labour Market Policy and Evaluation. Cheltenham: Edward Elgar. 623-651.

Rolf, G. (1988) Kontroversen über Begründung und Ausgestaltung staatlicher Versicherungs- und Umverteilungspolitik. In: G. Rolf et al. (eds) Sozialvertrag und Sicherung. Zur ökonomischen Theorie staatlicher Versicherungs- und Umverteilungssysteme. Frankfurt/New York: Campus. 515-541.

Rolf, G. / P. B. Spahn / G. Wagner (1988) Sozialvertrag und Sicherung. Zur ökonomischen Theorie staatlicher Versicherungs- und Umverteilungssysteme. Frankfurt/New York: Campus.

Romans, F. / Ó. S. Hardarson (2005) Main results from the EU Labour Force Survey. Labour Market Latest Trends: 4th quarter 2004 data. In: Statistics in focus: population and social conditions 6. 1-12.

Rowe, W. D. (1977) An Anatomy of Risk. New York: John Wiley & Sons.

Rubery, J. / M. Smith / C. Fagan / D. Grimshaw (1998a) State Policies and Women's Employment and Unemployment Rates. In: J. Rubery et al. (eds) Women and European Employment. London/New York: Routledge. 151-193.

— (1998b) Women and European Employment. London/New York: Routledge.

Rudolph, H. (2003) Mini- und Midi-Jobs: Geringfügige Beschäftigung im neuen Outfit. In: IAB Kurzbericht 6. 1-5.

Russell, H. / P. J. O'Connell (2001) Getting a Job in Europe: The Transition from Unemployment to Work among Young People in Nine European Countries. In: Work, Employment and Society 15, 1. 1-24.

Sainsbury, D. (1996) Gender, equality, and welfare states. Cambridge: Cambridge University Press.

Schmid, G. (2002) Transitional labour markets and the European social model: towards a new employment compact. In: G. Schmid et al. (eds) The Dynamics of Full Employment. Social Integration through Transitional Labour Markets. Cheltenham: Edward Elgar.

— (2003) Gleichheit und Effizienz auf dem Arbeitsmarkt. Überlegungen zum Wandel und zur Gestaltung des "Geschlechtervertrags". Discussion Paper No. SP I 2003-102. Berlin: Wissenschaftszentrum Berlin für Sozialforschung.

— (2006) Social risk management through transitional labour markets. In: Socio-Economic Review 4. 1-33.

Schmid, G. / B. Gazier (2002) The Dynamics of Full Employment. Social Integration through Transitional Labour Markets. Cheltenham: Edward Elgar.

Schmid, G. / B. Reissert (1996) Unemployment Compensation and Labour Market Transitions. In: G. Schmid et al. (eds) International Handbook of Labour Market Policy and Evaluation. Cambridge: University Press. 235-276.

Schömann, I. / S. Clauwaert / W. Düvel (2003) Legal Analysis of the Implementation of the Fixed-term Work Directive. Brussels: ETUI.

Schömann, K. / J. Leschke (2004) Lebenslanges Lernen und Soziale Inklusion - Der Markt alleine wird's nicht richten. In: R. Becker et al. (eds) Bildung als Privileg? Erklärungen und Befunde zu den Ursachen der Bildungsungleichheit. Wiesbaden: Verlag für Sozialwissenschaften.

Schömann, K. / R. Rogowski / T. Kruppe (1998) Labour Market Efficiency in the European Union: Employment Protection and Fixed-Term Contracts. London/New York: Routledge.

Schönbäck, W. (1988) Subjektive Unsicherheit als Gegenstand Staatlicher Intervention. In: G. Rolf et al. (eds) Sozialvertrag und Sicherung. Zur ökonomischen Theorie

staatlicher Versicherungs- und Umverteilungssysteme. Frankfurt/New York: Campus. 45-63.
Schönig, W. (2001) Gibt es einen Reformtrend der Sozialordnungen in der EU? Skizze einer Typologie zur Diskussion um einen neuen dritten Weg. In: Jahrbücher für Nationalökonomie und Statistik 221, 4. 404-417.
Schreyer, P. / F. Koechlin (2002) Purchasing power parities - measurement and uses. Statistics Brief No. 3. Paris: OECD.
Schulte, B. (1998) Wohlfahrtsregime im Prozeß der europäischen Integration. In: S. Lessenich et al. (eds) Welten des Wohlfahrtskapitalismus. Der Sozialstaat in vergleichender Perspektive. Frankfurt/M.: Campus. 255-271.
Schulze Buschoff, K. (2004) Neue Selbständigkeit und wachsender Grenzbereich zwischen selbständiger und abhängiger Erwerbsarbeit: Europäische Trends vor dem Hintergrund sozialpolitischer und arbeitsrechtlicher Entwicklungen. Discussion Paper No. SP I 2004-108. Berlin: Wissenschaftszentrum Berlin für Sozialforschung.
— (2006) Die soziale Sicherung von selbständig Erwerbstätigen in Deutschland. Discussion Paper No. SP I 2006-107. Berlin: Wissenschaftszentrum Berlin für Sozialforschung.
Seifert, H. (2005) Was bringen die Hartz-Gesetze?. In: Aus Politik und Zeitgeschichte 16. 17-24.
Selenkewitsch, I. (2004) Teilzeit- und Befristungsrecht in Spanien. In: Zeitschrift für ausländisches und internationales Arbeits- und Sozialrecht 18, 2. 160-178.
Shanahan, S. E. / N. B. Tuma (1994) The Sociology of Distribution and Redistribution. In: N.J. Smelser et al. (eds) The Handbook of Economic Sociology. Princeton: Princeton University Press.
Singer, J. D. / J. B. Willett (2003) Applied Longitudinal Data Analysis. Modelling Change and Event Occurrence. Oxford: Oxford University Press.
Sinn, H.-W. (1997) A Theory of the Welfare State. In: Scandinavian Journal of Economics 97, 4. 495-526.
Slater, G. (2003) Temporary Work in the UK: Evolution and Regulation. Occasional Paper Series. Nottingham: The Nottinghamshire Research Observatory.
Smith, M. (2003) Re-regulating transitions? Continuity and change in the UK. In: J. O'Reilly (ed) Regulating Working-Time Transitions in Europe. Cheltenham: Edward Elgar. 280-317.
Smith, M. / I. Cebrián / M. Davia / V. Hernanz / M. Malo (2000) Transitions through part-time work in Spain and the United Kingdom: a route into secure employment?. In: J. O'Reilly et al. (eds) Working Time Changes: Social Integration Through Transitional Labour Markets. Cheltenham: Edward Elgar. 173-204.
Snijders, T. / R. Bosker (1999) Multilevel analysis: an introduction to basic and advanced multilevel modelling. London: Sage Publications.
Snower, D. J. (1995) Unemployment benefits: An assessment of proposals for reforms. In: International Labour Review 134, 4-5. 625-647.
Social Welfare Statistics & Consultancy Branch (2005) Jobseeker's Allowance: http://www.dsdni.gov.uk/jsa_background_information.pdf (access 2006)
Spahn, B. / H. Kaiser (1988) Soziale Sicherheit als Öffentliches Gut? - Zur Problematik der Steuerfinanzierung sozialer Sicherung. In: G. Rolf et al. (eds) Sozialvertrag und

Sicherung. Zur ökonomische Theorie staatlicher Versicherungs- und Umverteilungssysteme. Frankfurt/New York: Campus. 195-218.
Stascheit, U. / E. Turk (2004) Leitfaden für Arbeitslose. Der Rechtsratgeber zum SGB III. Stand 1.1. 2004. 21. Auflage. Leck: Fachhochschulverlag.
StataCorp (2003) Cluster Analysis. release 8. College Station: Stata Press.
— (2005a) Longitudinal/Panel Data. release 9. College Station: Stata Press.
— (2005b) Survival Analysis and Epidemiological Tables. release 9. College Station: Stata Press.
Storrie, D. (2002) Temporary Agency Work in the European Union. Dublin: European Foundation for the Improvement of Living and Working Conditions.
Sutherland, H. (2004) EUROMOD Country Report: United Kingdom (2001 Tax-Benefit System).
Tálos, E. (1999) Atypische Beschäftigung. Internationale Trends und sozialstaatliche Regelungen. Wien: Manzsche Verlags- und Universitätsbuchhandlung.
Tangian, A. (2004) Defining the flexicurity index in application to European countries. Discussion Paper No. 121. Düsseldorf: WSI.
Taskforce, E. (November 2003) Jobs, Jobs, Jobs. Creating more employment in Europe, Luxembourg.
The Council of the European Union (6.8.2005) Council decision of 12 July 2005 on Guidelines for the employment policies of the Member States. In: Official Journal of the European Union, L205/21. 1-7.
— (1997) Council Directive 97/81/EC of 15 December 1997 concerning the framework agreement on part-time work concluded by UNICE, CEEP and the ETUC. In: Official Journal of the European Communities, L14. 9-14.
— (1999) Council Directive 1999/70/EC of 28 June 1999 concerning the framework agreement on fixed-term work concluded by ETUC, UNICE and CEEP. In Official Journal of the European Communities, L175/43. 43-48.
The National Directorate of Labour (2006) Being insured against unemployment in Denmark. Copenhagen.
The Social Protection Committee (June 2003) Key Issues on Social Protection and Employment. Brussels.
Titmuss, R. (1974) Social Policy: An Introduction. In: B. Abel-Smith et al. (eds) Social Policy. London: George Allen & Unwin Ltd.
Toharia, L. (1999) The emergence of fixed-term contracts in Spain and their incidence on the evolution of employment. Paper presented at the Conference organised by the Fondazione Rodolfo Debenedetti. Rome, May 1999.
Toharia, L. / M. A. Malo (2000) The Spanish Experiment: Pros and Cons of Flexibility at the Margin. In: G. Esping-Andersen et al. (eds) Why Deregulate Labour Markets?. Oxford: Oxford University Press. 307-335.
Treib, O. (2004) Die Bedeutung der nationalen Parteipolitik für die Umsetzung europäischer Sozialrichtlinien. vol. 1. Frankfurt/New York: Campus.
Trifiletti, R. (1999) Southern European Welfare Regimes and the Worsening Position of Women. In: Journal of European Social Policy 9, 1. 49-64.
Trube, A. (2002) Entwicklungslinien in der Arbeitsmarkt- und Sozialhilfepolitik: Trends und Gegenvorschläge. In: Arbeit und Sozialpolitik 56, 1/2. 18-25.

UK government (2005) Lisbon Strategy for Jobs and Growth: UK National Reform Programme. London.

United Nations Economic Commission for Europe (UNECE) (2003) Trends in Europe and North America: the Statistical Yearbook of the Economic Commission for Europe 2003: http://www.unece.org/stats/trend/glossary.htm (access 2005).

Uunk, W. / M. Kalmijn / R. Muffels (2005) Impact of Young Children on Women's Labour Supply: A Reassessment of Institutional Effects in Europe. In: Acta Sociologica 48, 1. 41-62.

Valdés dal-Ré, F. (2004) Spain: the difficulty of marrying flexibility with security. In: S. Sciarra et al. (eds) Employment Policy and the Regulation of Part-time Work in the European Union: A Comparative Analysis. Cambridge: Cambridge University Press. 224-257.

Wagner, T. / E. Jahn (1997) Neue Arbeitsmarkttheorien. Düsseldorf: Werner Verlag.

Westergaard-Nielsen, N. (2001) Danish Labour Market Policy: Is it worth it?. Working Paper No. 01-10. Aarhus: Centre for Labour Market and Social Research.

Wilthagen, T. (1998) Flexicurity: A New Paradigm for Labour Market Policy Reform. Discussion Paper No. FS I 98-202. Berlin: Wissenschaftszentrum Berlin für Sozialforschung.

Wilthagen, T. / F. Tros (2004) The concept of 'flexicurity': a new approach to regulating employment and labour markets. In: Transfer 10, 2. 166-186.

Wirtz, C. / L. Mejer (2002) The European Community Household Panel (ECHP). In: Schmollers Jahrbuch 122. 143-154.

Wissing, G. (1996) Die Arbeitszeit, Begriff und Funktion in der Arbeitslosenversicherung. In: Die Sozialgerichtsbarkeit 43. 1-7.

Zachert, U. (2004) Kündigungsschutz, Befristung und Leiharbeit in Europa. In: WSI Mitteilungen - Schwerpunktheft Deregulierung am Arbeitsmarkt? Wege aus der Denkfalle 57, 3. 132-137.

Ziegelmayer, V. (2001) Sozialstaat in Deutschland: Ein Systemwechsel?. In: K. Krausen et al. (eds) Sozialstaat in Europa: Geschichte, Entwicklung, Perspektiven. Wiesbaden: Westdeutscher Verlag. 63-88.

Legislation

Bundesgesetzblatt (30. Dezember 2002) Zweites Gesetz für moderne Dienstleistungen am Arbeitsmarkt, Bundesgesetzblatt 2002, Teil I Nr. 87.

Gesetz über Teilzeitarbeit und befristete Arbeitsverträge (Teilzeit- und Befristungsgesetz – TzBfG).

ILO (1994a) Part-Time Work Convention, C175.

ILO (1994b) Part-Time Work Recommendation, R182.

Notification (No. 874 of 2005) of the Unemployment Insurance Act.

Royal Decree No. 15/1998. 27 November 1998.

Royal Decree No. 489/1998. 27 March 1998.

Sozialgesetzbuch (SGB), Drittes Buch (III), Arbeitsförderung.

The Social Security (Credits and Contributions) (Jobseeker's Allowance Consequential and Miscellaneous Amendments) Regulations. 1996 No 2367.

Annex

Annex 1: Construction of ECHP variables and descriptive statistics

The *part-time employment* variable in the ECHP data is derived from the question 'How many hours per week do you work in your main job, including paid overtime, if any?' (pe005a).[154] Respondents working 30 hours or more are categorised as full-time workers; those working less than 30 hours as part-time workers. Compared to Labour Force Survey data this variable generates reasonable results for all countries, except for the United Kingdom.[155] To remedy this problem, the part-time variable is recalculated based on the variable that captures hours worked in the main job (pe005a) and the variable that captures the ILO main activity status at the time of the interview (pe003). The information on the main activity status is needed in order to include information on persons working fewer than 15 hours a week because the question on working hours in the main job is only asked to persons working more than 15 hours a week. The new variable captures part-time employment as defined by the OECD: those reporting fewer than 30 working hours a week are characterised as part-time workers; those working 30 hours or more as full-time workers. The results of the new part-time variable (see Table 28) are fairly close to the Labour Force Survey statistics.[156]

---

154 The following information is based on Eurostat (1994; 2000a; 2002; 2003a; 2003b); if not otherwise stated, the tables refer to people between 18 and 64 years.

155 From the first to the second wave the share of part-time workers drops from 23.7 per cent (which closely matches the Labour Force Survey results) to 10.5 per cent and remains at this low level until wave 8. This is probably due to an error that occurred when data were transferred from the BHPS to the ECHP format. The average part-time employment in the original BHPS data lies at around 23 per cent during the years 1995 to 2001 (compare http://www.iser.essex.ac.uk/ulsc/bhps/).

156 Results for Denmark vary most strongly as compared to the Labour Force Survey (LFS) results. The difference can in part be explained by the fact that the LFS data, in contrast to the ECHP data, capture self-assessed part-time employment.

Table 28: Part-time employment by year and country as share of working population in dependent employment

%	Denmark	Germany	Spain	United Kingdom
1994	15.0	16.5	12.6	22.2
1995	14.3	18.7	12.4	22.4
1996	14.7	19.3	9.9	22.7
1997	14.1	19.8	10.4	21.3
1998	14.3	20.7	10.0	22.3
1999	13.3	21.2	10.3	22.2
2000	13.9	19.3	9.2	21.2
2001	13.7	19.1	11.0	22.2

Source: Own calculations based on weighted ECHP data.

In the pooled ECHP data, *marginal part-time employment* (<15 hours) as a share of total part-time employment amounts to about 12 per cent in Denmark, about 11 per cent in Germany and about 14 per cent in Spain and the United Kingdom. In Denmark and Germany, men are overproportionally affected by marginal part-time employment. The calculation of separate models for regular and marginal part-time workers is restricted due to the fact that not all job-related information in the survey has been collected for persons regularly working fewer than 15 hours.

The variable that captures *temporary employment* (pe024) is based on the following question: 'What type of employment contract do you have in your main job? Please indicate which of the following best describes your situation.' The possible answer categories are 'permanent employment', 'fixed- or short-term contract', 'casual work with no contract' and 'other working arrangement'. Due to uncertainties about the content of 'other working arrangement', and missing information for Germany and the United Kingdom, this category is not used in the analysis.[157] Information on the contract type is not available for the first survey year. Table 29 shows the share of fixed-term and casual workers in the working population of the four countries. The ECHP results are fairly close to the Labour Force Survey results: the rank order between the countries, as well as the differences between the shares in 1995 and 2001, are captured in the ECHP data.

157 The shares of all contract forms in this category are below 1 per cent in Denmark and between 1.9 and 3.6 per cent in Spain.

Table 29: Employment contract by type in 1995 and 2001 as share of working population in dependent employment

%	Denmark		Germany		Spain		United Kingdom	
	fixed-term	casual work	fixed-term	casual	fixed-term	casual work	fixed-term	casual work
1995	6.8	6.4	7.3	0.6	31.3	4.7	3.6	3.2
1996	6.4	7.7	7.1	0.4	30.0	4.0	3.3	3.4
1997	5.1	6.5	8.1	0.6	29.3	4.2	3.4	3.6
1998	5.6	4.8	6.9	0.1	29.6	3.6	3.5	3.4
1999	4.3	4.3	8.2	0.6	28.5	3.6	5.4	0
2000	5.2	5.0	7.3	6.9	28.4	2.5	5.1	0
2001	4.3	3.4	7.5	6.9	26.7	3.6	5.3	0

Source: Own calculations based on weighted ECHP data.

Where possible, the analysis distinguishes between casual work with no contract and fixed-term employment. For the United Kingdom as well as for Germany the 'casual work' category is somewhat problematic, as can be seen in Table 30. The sudden increase in the proportion in this category in Germany from 2000 onwards, and the reporting of zeros in the United Kingdom from 1999 onwards, are probably artefacts due to changes in the SOEP and BHPS questionnaires. This shows the problems and shortcomings of output-harmonising country-specific survey data. The problem can be remedied by pooling the variables over the years. In most cases this has to be done anyway because case numbers, especially on the casual category, are rather small.

How large is the incidence of *simultaneous part-time and temporary employment*, and are there marked differences between the countries? If the seven-year reference period is considered, the share of temporary contracts engaged in as part-time employment ranges from 12 per cent in Spain to more than 30 per cent in the United Kingdom (Table 30). On the other hand, the majority of part-time employment in Spain is of a temporary nature, which is also confirmed by Fassler-Ristic (1999: 371) and Cebrián (2000: 213). The share of part-time employment that is of a temporary nature is lowest in the United Kingdom, at about 12 per cent.

The self-defined main activity status (*unemployment, employment, inactivity, and so on*) is especially important for the transition analysis. It is asked at the time of the interview (pe001), but also recorded for every month of the preceding year (pc001–pc012). The employment status variables include several exclusive

Table 30: Share of persons that simultaneously work part-time and on a temporary contract

%	Denmark	Germany	Spain	United Kingdom
Share of temporary contracts which are part-time as compared to full-time	20.3	18.0	12.2	32.4
Share of part-time contracts which are of a temporary nature as compared to permanent	23.3	14.3	55.7	11.7

Source: Own calculations based on pooled and weighted ECHP data.

categories.[158] The self-defined main activity status at the time of the interview explicitly asks for employment activities comprising more than 15 hours a week; this is due to the so-called main-activity concept that is used throughout the ECHP. Originally, one list of questions was asked of people who normally work 15 hours and more; another list was asked of people working fewer than 15 hours. In the User Data Base this information was then combined into single variables. There are some variables, however, that display information separately for both groups and some variables that apply only to people working more than 15 hours.

All participants in the survey who have no job or a job with fewer than 15 hours, and who are looking for a new or an additional job (ps001), are asked whether they at present receive any *unemployment benefit or assistance* (ps009). Since the question is aimed not only at people registered at the employment office, different reference groups can be compared. In a second step, all survey people who have no job but who are looking for a job, or who are marginally employed and are looking for a new or an additional job, are asked whether they are registered as unemployed at the employment office. There is no information in the data on why unemployed people decide to register or refrain from registering at the public employment office.

The following question is asked in relation to the *unemployment benefit level* (pi131): 'Did you receive in *t*–1 (year prior to the survey) any benefit related to unemployment, job creation or training?' Possible answer categories are

158 The categories are (1) paid employment (15+ hours a week), (2) special employment-related training scheme, (3) paid apprenticeship/training (15+ hours a week), (4) self-employment (15+ hours a week), (5) unpaid family work (15+ hours a week), (6) education or training, (7) unemployed, (8) retired, (9) housework/carer, (10) community/military service, (11) other economically inactive, (12) working fewer than 15 hours. Categories 2 and 12 do not apply to the calendar of event variables (pc001–pc012). Category 12 exists only for waves 3 to 8; in waves 1 and 2 people working fewer than 15 hours a week were automatically classified in categories 6 to 11.

'unemployment insurance benefit', 'unemployment assistance', 'training/education allowance', 'placement', 'resettlement', 'rehabilitation benefit' and 'other'. For the User Data Base the components were aggregated and the monthly information was annualised. Therefore only one variable is provided that captures the annual level of unemployment-related benefits. Even though the participants were asked how many months they received benefits this information is not available in the User Data Base. The only valuable information that can be used as a proxy is the number of unemployment months from the calendar of events and the main source of personal income in the year prior to the survey (pi001). After comparing benefit levels declared in the survey and possible maximum benefits under the national unemployment benefit schemes a few observations with unrealistically high benefit levels were dropped from the survey so as not to disturb the results.[159]

In some parts of the analysis *retrospective information on part-time and temporary employment*, but also on the other employment characteristics such as occupational group or sector of activity, has to be used. There are two possibilities: the use of retrospective information that survey participants have been asked about directly or the use of lagged information (information taken from preceding waves of the survey). An advantage of lagged information is that it is probably more accurate than retrospective information generated at a later time period. A serious drawback is the fact that the information of interest (part-time and temporary employment before the present unemployment spell) is available only for the time of the survey and not for every calendar month. Accurate matching of present unemployment spells with information on former part-time or temporary employment is thus not possible. The retrospective variables, on the other hand, directly refer to the last job. All survey participants who at the time of the survey worked fewer than 15 hours a week, are inactive, discouraged or unemployed persons are asked a variety of questions on their last job, for example, whether they had worked full-time or part-time (pj012) and for what reason they left their previous job (pj004). Here, the answer option 'end of contract/temporary job' captures temporary employment.[160] Table 31 compares the retrospective information with the lagged variables.

159 Some of the Spanish observations in particular were unrealistically high. Therefore, in Spain 23 observations were dropped on the individual as well as on the household level. No observation was dropped in Germany, and only two and one, respectively, in Denmark and the United Kingdom (individual benefit).

160 Those who finished their last job before 1980 (1986 from the second wave onwards) are treated as missings in the data.

Table 31: Comparison of retrospective and lagged information, wave 8

%	Denmark	Germany	Spain	United Kingdom
Temporary employment				
Retrospective (pj004)	12.1	18.0	39.8	6.9
Lagged (based on pe024)	8.9	14.3	32.7	5.1
Part-time employment				
Retrospective (pj012)	25.1	35.1	14.8	32.3
Lagged (based on pe005c)	14.2	19.9	9.4	22.5

Source: Own calculations based on weighted ECHP data.

Retrospective and lagged information vary considerably. Retrospective indicators show shares of temporary employment and part-time employment that are significantly higher than those evident in the lagged and in the annual information. As described above, retrospective information potentially reaches further into the past than lagged information; furthermore, the lagged information relates only to the time of the interview.

Tables 32, 33 and 34 show the distribution of individual and job-related variables among part-time and temporary workers. Characteristics of the overall sample population can be found in Annex 2, Tables 36 and 37. Part-time workers are more likely to be *married* in Germany and the United Kingdom than in the other two countries (Table 32). In these two countries the share is also higher than in the overall population, while it is lower in Spain and Denmark. The share of temporary workers never married is considerably higher than among the total population, especially in the United Kingdom and Spain. This is at least in part due to the *age profile* of temporary workers; in all countries they are on average younger than the overall population, ranging from a difference of four years in Germany and Denmark to seven years in the United Kingdom. The age profile of part-time workers is similar to the overall population. The ECHP data confirm that part-time employment is mainly exercised by women, while gender differences are not very pronounced when it comes to temporary employment.

Tables 33 and 34 display job-related characteristics of part-time and temporary workers. The ECHP classifies individuals into different qualification groups by using the International Standard Classification of Education (ISCED). Only aggregated *qualification levels* are provided: less than first stage of secondary level education (ISCED 0–2), first stage of secondary level education (ISCED 3),

Table 32: Individual characteristics of part-time and temporary workers

Part-time	DK	DE	SP	UK
Marital status %				
Married	53.8	66.1	50.6	68.5
Separated/ divorced	3.8	6.9	4.0	9.7
Widowed	1.2	2.4	2.3	2.4
Never married	41.2	24.6	43.1	19.4
Age (mean)				
Age	38.0	40.4	35.8	41.3
Share %				
Female	73.4	77.1	69.5	83.2

Temporary	DK	DE	SP	UK
Marital status %				
Married	45.8	50.5	42.0	40.5
Separated/ divorced	6.7	8.1	2.9	6.8
Widowed	0.5	1.3	0.8	0.4
Never mar-ried	47.1	40.2	54.4	52.3
Age (mean)				
Age	35.8	37.7	32.3	34.3
Share %				
Female	46.2	47.9	39.1	54.0

Source: Own calculations based on pooled and weighted ECHP data.

and recognised third level education (ISCED 5–7).[161] The national data units were requested to use country-specific categories according to the Labour Force Survey (Eurostat 2000b: 8–14). There are high country-specific differences in the distribution of the three qualification levels. In Spain almost 60 per cent of the sample population has a qualification level that corresponds to the lowest ISCED category, while the lowest ISCED category accounts for only about 20 to 25 per cent in Germany and Denmark. In these two countries, especially in Germany, a large share of the sample population has intermediary qualification levels, while in the United Kingdom 40 per cent of the sample persons have the highest education level. As to part-time workers, in the United Kingdom and Denmark the share of low qualified among part-time workers is somewhat higher than in the overall population, while in Spain it is somewhat lower; there are hardly any differences in Germany. Temporary workers are more likely to hold highest level qualifications in Germany and, especially, the United Kingdom. In the latter country the share of the lowest qualified among temporary workers is only about 32 per cent, while it is 46 per cent in the overall population. There are hardly any differences in Spain and somewhat lower shares of temporary workers in the highest qualification category in Denmark.

161 Less than upper secondary education is composed of ISCED 0: pre-primary education; ISCED 1: primary education; and ISCED 2: lower secondary education. Upper secondary education consists of ISCED 3: upper secondary education (for example, 'A' level, *Abitur* or equivalent). Recognised third level education consists of ISCED 5: education leading to an award not equivalent to a first university degree; ISCED 6: education leading to a first university degree or equivalent; and ISCED 7: education leading to a postgraduate university degree or equivalent (compare Eurostat 2004; United Nations Economic Commission for Europe (UNECE) 2003).

Occupations in the ECHP are based on the International Standard Classification of Occupation (ISCO-88); the 1-digit level with nine different categories is used. Germany and Denmark display high shares of technicians and associate professionals; the United Kingdom, on the other hand, has a comparatively high share in the category of legislators, senior officials and managers. Spain takes the lead in skilled agricultural and fishery workers, as well as in elementary occupations and, together with Germany, shows relatively large shares in craft and related trade occupations. As to the groups of interest here, only in Denmark is the share of professionals as well as technicians and associate professionals among part-time workers considerably lower than in the overall population. The share of service, shop and market sales workers is higher among part-time workers in all countries, but especially in the United Kingdom and Denmark. The same is true for elementary occupations; Spain and Denmark show the largest differences with more than twice the share of part-time workers compared to all employees in elementary occupations. In contrast, part-time workers have very low shares in the group of legislators, senior officials and managers; the difference is especially high in the United Kingdom. In Spain, about a quarter of temporary workers are employed in elementary occupations, while the overall share is only about 15 per cent. Spain in this regard performs considerably worse than the other three countries, where the overall share of elementary occupations is clearly lower, although somewhat higher among temporary workers than among the overall working population. The United Kingdom and, especially, Germany stand out with overproportionally high shares of professionals among temporary workers. In Spain, on the other hand, the share of professionals among temporary workers is lower than in the reference group; this is also true for technicians and associate professionals in Denmark. All countries display considerably lower shares of temporary workers in the group of legislators, senior officials and managers, the difference being especially pronounced in Spain and the United Kingdom.

Concerning the allocation of jobs to different *industries*, the United Kingdom and Denmark show similar patterns with almost three-quarters of jobs in the service sector, Germany still has more than one third of jobs in the industry sector, while Spain shows comparatively high shares in agriculture. Part-time employment is in all countries most likely to take place in services; shares of part-time workers in services are everywhere considerably higher than shares of the overall working population; the difference is especially great in Germany and Spain. No clear trend emerges for temporary employment: shares in the industry sector are higher than overall shares in Germany and the United Kingdom, but lower in Spain and Denmark.

Table 33: Employment characteristics of part-time workers

	DK	DE	SP	UK
Qualification level %				
ISCED 0–2	28.8	23.2	53.1	49.5
ISCED 3	48.1	60.0	21.5	14.0
ISCED 5–7	23.1	16.8	25.4	36.5
Current occupation %				
Legislators, senior officials and managers	1.8	1.9	2.6	5.7
Professionals	6.7	12.5	13.4	10.4
Technicians and associate professionals	15.6	21.5	7.9	10.7
Clerks	15.1	17.3	8.5	21.1
Service, shop and market sales workers	29.4	20.5	20.6	32.7
Skilled agricultural and fishery workers	3.2	1.2	5.7	0.6
Craft and related trades workers	2.1	3.4	6.1	1.8
Plant and machine operators and assemblers	2.2	3.1	2.4	2.9
Elementary occupations	23.8	18.7	32.8	14.1
Current industry %				
Agriculture	3.9	2.4	9.1	0.7
Industry	9.5	14.7	11.1	9.2
Services	86.7	82.9	79.8	90.1
Sector of employment %				
Private sector	48.2	66.6	86.9	70.3
Public sector	51.8	33.4	13.2	29.7
Additional characteristics (mean)				
Person was unemployed after 1989	39.7	51.7	62.0	24.9

Source: Own calculations based on pooled and weighted ECHP data; age: 18–64.

Public sector employment is comparatively most important in Denmark, and weakest in Spain with a share of around 19 per cent in the 2001 ECHP data. Pronounced differences between part-time workers and all employees are evident only in Denmark with noticeably higher shares of part-time workers in the public sector; in Germany the share is somewhat higher. Sectoral differences between temporary and overall employment are very pronounced in Germany, where the share of temporary workers in public sector employment is considerably higher.

Unemployment history is recorded by a variable that captures whether a person was unemployed after 1989. In the whole sample, it displays shares of around 45 to 50 per cent in Denmark, Germany and Spain, and 30 per cent in the United Kingdom. The unemployment incidence was about one quarter higher

Table 34: Employment characteristics of temporary workers

	DK	DE	SP	UK
Qualification level %				
ISCED 0–2	25.0	16.8	57.3	31.7
ISCED 3	51.2	58.5	20.1	17.6
ISCED 5–7	23.8	24.7	22.6	50.7
Current occupation %				
Legislators, senior officials and managers	1.9	1.9	0.6	3.8
Professionals	14.9	20.5	8.4	16.8
Technicians and associate professionals	11.6	20.8	6.6	12.2
Clerks	9.2	8.8	8.5	20.5
Service, shop and market sales workers	19.9	12.4	15.5	21.0
Skilled agricultural and fishery workers	2.9	2.3	2.1	1.3
Craft and related trades workers	14.3	14.4	22.3	6.5
Plant and machine operators and assemblers	10.3	8.2	8.9	6.6
Elementary occupations	15.0	10.8	27.1	11.3
Current industry %				
Agriculture	4.1	2.7	6.5	0.9
Industry	31.5	25.0	38.5	19.3
Services	64.4	72.3	55.0	79.7
Sector of employment %				
Private sector	58.9	59.2	86.3	70.8
Public sector	41.1	40.8	13.7	29.3
Additional characteristics (mean)				
Person was unemployed after 1989	68.4	65.5	83.7	46.0

Source: Own calculations based on pooled and weighted ECHP data.

among part-time workers than among the overall population in Spain, while it was lower in the United Kingdom and somewhat lower in Denmark. As expected, temporary workers are in all countries more likely than the overall sample to have previously been unemployed – the difference is most pronounced in Spain and least pronounced in Germany.

Annex 2

Table 35: Individual characteristics of the total sample

	DK	DE	SP	UK
Marital status %				
Married	57.9	59.8	58.7	60.8
Separated/divorced	7.6	8.2	2.3	10.0
Widowed	1.3	2.5	2.0	2.0
Never married	33.2	29.5	37.0	27.2
Age (mean)				
Age	40.1	41.4	38.6	41.0

Source: Own calculations based on pooled and weighted ECHP data.

Table 36: Employment characteristics of the total sample

	DK	DE	SP	UK
Qualification level %				
ISCED 0–2	24.9	21.9	58.0	45.8
ISCED 3	46.2	58.4	21.8	13.9
ISCED 5–7	28.9	19.7	20.2	40.3
Current occupation %				
Legislators, senior officials and managers	6.8	5.4	8.2	15.7
Professionals	15.2	13.4	12.4	13.0
Technicians and associate professionals	19.3	22.3	10.4	12.4
Clerks	12.5	12.2	8.9	16.4
Service, shop and market sales workers	14.1	11.2	13.6	15.6
Skilled agricultural and fishery workers	2.3	1.5	6.0	1.0
Craft and related trades workers	11.8	18.7	17.7	10.9
Plant and machine operators and assemblers	8.3	7.5	8.6	7.9
Elementary occupations	9.8	7.8	14.4	7.2
Current industry %				
Agriculture	4.0	2.1	8.2	0.9
Industry	25.3	36.7	29.9	26.0
Services	70.7	61.2	61.9	73.1
Sector of employment %				
Private sector	61.5	73.5	81.3	76.4
Public sector	38.5	26.5	18.7	23.6
Additional characteristics (mean)				
Person was unemployed after 1989	43.8	50.3	45.7	30.3

Source: Own calculations based on pooled and weighted ECHP data.

Table 37: Multinomial logit models for single countries (reference category: remaining in employment)

beta coefficients	DK	DE	SP	UK
EXIT UNEMPLOYMENT				
Part-time	–0.098	0.069	–0.147+	0.286**
Reference: permanent workers				
Fixed-term	1.290**	1.304**	1.399**	0.979**
Casual	1.180**	0.346	1.344**	1.209**
Female	0.113	–0.302**	0.099+	–0.153*
Reference: ISCED 0–2				
ISCED 3	–0.096	0.128	–0.097	–0.128
ISCED 5–7	–0.236	0.077	–0.171**	–0.017
Unemployed before	3.762**	4.577**	3.143**	3.902**
Reference: children, no child-care				
No children	0.223	–0.069	–0.054	–0.171+
CHILDREN + child-care	0.107	–0.081	–0.065	–0.537**
log(time in employment)	–0.442**	–0.208**	–0.467**	–0.437**
EXIT INACTIVITY				
Part-time	0.771**	–0.792	0.772**	0.024
Reference: permanent workers				
Fixed-term	0.568	–0.007	0.638**	0.277
Casual	1.139**	1.559**	1.028**	0.831*
Female	0.671*	–0.009	0.561**	0.350*
Reference: ISCED 0–2				
ISCED 3	0.557+	–0.119	0.040	0.193
ISCED 5–7	0.146	–0.475	–0.201	0.226
Unemployed before	0.314	0.204	–0.137	0.564**
Reference: children, no child-care				
No children	–0.554+	0.512	–0.180	–0.068
Children + child-care	–0.661+	–0.047	0.099	–1.012**
log(time in employment)	–0.154	–0.314**	–0.252**	–0.274**
EXIT HOUSEHOLD/CARER				
Part-time	1.029*	0.890*	0.044	0.249*
Reference: permanent workers				
Fixed-term	–0.591	1.046**	1.309**	0.236
Casual	0.544	1.029	2.247**	0.231
Female	2.449**	0.491	5.392**	3.357**

beta coefficients	DK	DE	SP	UK
Reference: ISCED 0–2				
ISCED 3	2.094*	–0.314	–0.354	0.248
ISCED 5–7	1.520	–0.185	–0.572⁺	0.297*
Unemployed before	–0.598	0.733*	0.433*	0.127
Reference: children, no child-care				
No children	–1.277**	–0.767*	–0.539**	–2.511**
Children + child-care	–0.547	–0.353	0.038	–0.086
log(time in employment)	–0.465*	–0.398**	–0.416**	–0.296**
EXIT EDUCATION				
Part-time	0.708**	0.777*	1.162**	1.277**
Reference: permanent workers				
Fixed-term	1.393**	1.256**	0.975**	1.315**
Casual	1.218**	1.327*	0.920*	1.695**
Female	–0.263	–0.889**	–0.229	0.013
Reference: ISCED 0–2				
ISCED 3	0.359⁺	0.289	0.925**	0.467*
ISCED 5–7	0.092	0.040	1.351**	0.462*
Unemployed before	–0.384*	–0.282	–0.814**	–0.471*
Reference: children, no child-care				
No children	0.728*	0.962*	0.131	0.227
Children + child-care	0.197	0.111	–1.238	–0.350
log(time in employment)	–0.335**	–0.434**	–0.719**	–0.465**
Pseudo R2	0.1734	0.1402	0.2046	0.1928
Number of observations (person month periods)	141870	248871	261884	303574

Note: *Additionally in the model but not displayed here: age, marital status, occupation (9 categories). Coefficients for the exit category ‘other’ are not shown.
Source: Own calculations based on ECHP data; single country models are calculated.

Table 38: Cluster Analysis: summary statistics for cluster 1

Finland, Sweden, Denmark				
	Mean	**Std. Dev.**	**Min.**	**Max.**
Requirement	2.67	.58	2	3
Continuity	1	0	1	1
Voluntary	1	0	1	1
Replacement rate, 60th month 1999	1.04	.05	1	1.1
Replacement rate, first month, 1999	.91	.04	.88	.95
Unemployment insurance duration 1999	33.33	23.63	15	60
Unemployment assistance duration 1999	38.33	53.93	0	100
Government social protection spending 2001	50.17	10.83	42.8	62.6
Employers/beneficiaries social protection spending 2001	44.43	12.20	30.4	52.5
Passive expenditure/unemployment rate, 2001	.38	.28	.21	.71
Active expenditure/unemployment rate, 2001	.25	.13	.10	.37

Source: Own calculations based on ECHP data.

Table 39: Cluster Analysis: summary statistics for cluster 2

Austria, Belgium, France, Germany, Netherlands, Spain				
	Mean	**Std. Dev.**	**Min.**	**Max.**
Requirement	1.67	1.03	1	3
Continuity	1.67	.52	1	2
Voluntary	0	0	0	0
Replacement rate, 60th month 1999	.72	.12	.57	.85
Replacement rate, first month, 1999	.80	.04	.75	.85
Unemployment insurance duration 1999	44.33	35.29	10	100
Unemployment assistance duration 1999	57	47.76	0	100
Government social protection spending 2001	25.68	6.22	16.3	34.1
Employers/beneficiaries social protection spending 2001	67.85	3.57	64.7	74.4
Passive expenditure/unemployment rate, 2001	.31	.20	.10	.69
Active expenditure/unemployment rate, 2001	.24	.24	.07	.72

Source: Own calculations based on ECHP data.

Table 40: Cluster Analysis: summary statistics for cluster 3

Luxembourg, Ireland, Portugal,* United Kingdom				
	Mean	**Std. Dev.**	**Min.**	**Max.**
Requirement	2.7	.58	2	3
Continuity	2.5	.58	2	3
Voluntary	0	0	0	0
Replacement rate, 60th month 1999	.84	.12	.66	.93
Replacement rate, first month, 1999	.74	.17	.54	.88
Unemployment insurance duration 1999	15.75	10.21	6	30
Unemployment assistance duration 1999	56	51.74	0	100
Government social protection spending 2001	47.63	8.42	37.8	58.3
Employers/beneficiaries social protection spending 2001	48.15	6.36	39.3	54.4
Passive expenditure/unemployment rate, 2001	.19	.08	.08	.28
Active expenditure/unemployment rate, 2001	.16	.10	.072	.3

Note: * There is no information on requirement for Portugal.
Source: Own calculations based on ECHP data.

Table 41: Cluster Analysis: summary statistics for cluster 4

Italy, Greece				
	Mean	**Std. Dev.**	**Min.**	**Max.**
Requirement	–	–	–	–
Continuity	1.5	.71	1	2
Voluntary	0	0	0	0
Replacement rate, 60th month 1999	.16	.07	.11	.21
Replacement rate, first month, 1999	.48	.02	.46	.49
Unemployment insurance duration 1999	9	4.24	6	12
Unemployment assistance duration 1999	0	0	0	0
Government social protection spending 2001	59.5	3.54	57	62
Employers/beneficiaries social protection spending 2001	34.45	9.4	27.8	41.1
Passive expenditure/unemployment rate, 2001	.06	.00	.06	.06

Source: Own calculations based on ECHP data.

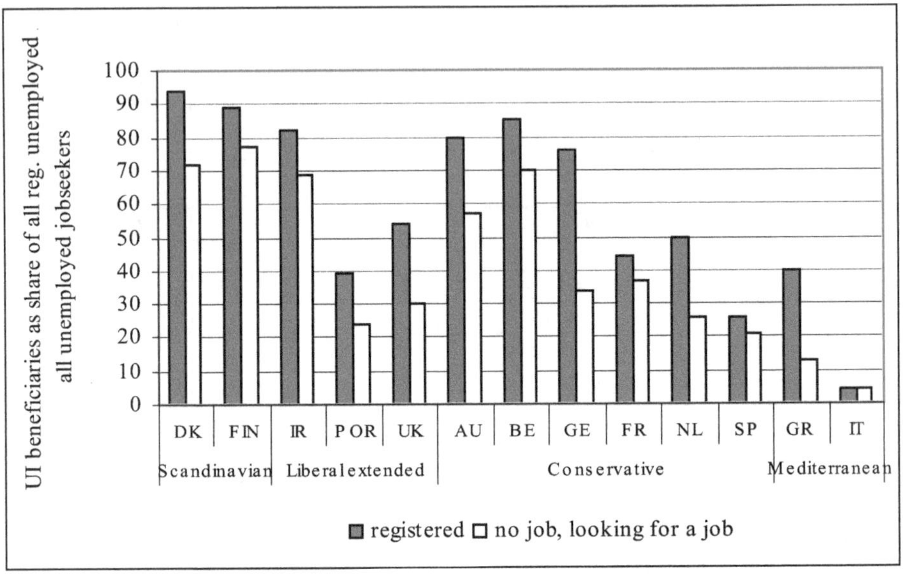

Figure 40: Share of unemployed (registered and all unemployed jobseekers) receiving unemployment benefits.
Source: Own calculations based on weighted ECHP data.

FSC
www.fsc.org
MIX
Papier | Fördert
gute Waldnutzung
FSC® C083411

Kolibri 360 GmbH
Ferdinand-Jühlke-Straße 7
99095 Erfurt, Deutschland
produktsicherheit@kolibri360.de